THE GOOD
THE BAD
& THE
DIFFERENCE

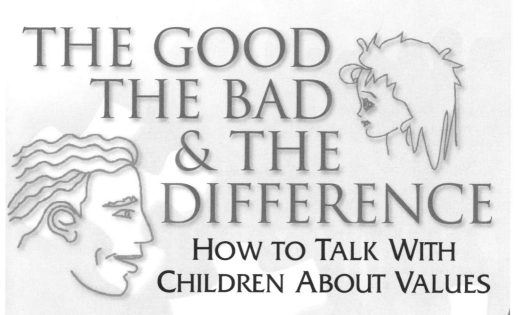

HOW TO TALK WITH
CHILDREN ABOUT VALUES

Courage • Integrity • Wisdom
Justice • Compassion • Reason

MICHAEL SABBETH

TEVYE PUBLISHING • DENVER, COLORADO

Tevye Publishing LLC publishes this book in a variety of electronic formats. Some content that appears in print may not be available in electronic books.

LIBRARY OF CONGRESS CATALOGING IN PUBLICATION DATA
Sabbeth, Michael
The Good, The Bad and The Difference: How to Talk with Children About Values
ISBN 978-0-615-36245-8 (paperback)
1. Moral Reasoning. 2. Ethics—Teaching and Study. 3. Moral Development of Children. 4. Ethics and Rhetoric.
Library of Congress Control Number: 2010926104
ISBN 978-0-615-36245-8

COVER DESIGN: Lorna Bosnos, New York, New York
BOOK DESIGN: Robert Schram, Bookends Design, *bookendsdesign@earthlink.net*

WHAT PEOPLE HAVE SAID

"The Good, The Bad and The Difference is an intelligent and well written book by an experienced parent. This is how a parent should think, at a high level. Stories are the best teacher—they allow children to think for themselves. This book has hundreds of stories. I love the quotations—readable and humorous. I'm not aware of any other books in this niche even though this is my line of work. I think it's unique. I'd buy it and recommend it."

—MICHAEL GERMER, M.D.

"I had the pleasure of meeting Michael Sabbeth last year and I have been extremely impressed by his passion and commitment towards children ever since. When he talks about his class at the Ebert Polaris Elementary school and his experiences with them, one can't help but understand why he has written this wonderful book. The teachings and examples he presents for communicating with our children are extremely valuable and make this book a great tool for parents and educators. I also found that the life situations seen through these children's eyes are very insightful and make you wonder as an adult how much we need a child's perspective in life. This book is not only educational but inspirational as well!"

—MADELAINE ROHAN, Hispanic Political Consultant

"This book is more than a system to teach ethics and reasoning to young children. It is a personal and passionate statement by Michael Sabbeth, a deeply felt expression of who he is and what he wants to achieve. Read this book and you have the sense that you have read something important, something that will change you."

—ROGER FRANSCECKY, CEO and Founder, The Apogee Group

"This book is absolutely filled with wonderful and inspiring dialogue. These children will amaze you with their curiosity, their moral core which Michael elicits and ultimately illustrates their profound wisdom about the moral dilemmas in everyday life—and not just children's dilemmas, but the big stuff—moral issues which many adults fail to grasp—let along seriously consider and debate.

Most inspiring however, is Michael's guidance to parents. Michael observes from his discussions with children that the people children look up to most are their parents. Being a child's parent trumps all other roles—teachers, ministers, peers, siblings—the whole works. He lowers the bar—he tells parents in a clear, no nonsense manner that they are the persons their child most wants to talk to. Just do it and don't worry about being eloquent—just be real and honest.

I strongly urge any educator to first read this book carefully and then consider giving it as a gift to the parents of each and every one of your students. Mobilizing the front-line moral educators—parents—is perhaps one of the most important things you can do. The moral voice of parents is a tremendously under-leveraged resource in our culture. I'm convinced that this is quality work! And a much needed book for parents."

–FRED KIEL, Author, with Doug Lennick, *Moral Intelligence: Enhancing Business Performance and Leadership Success*, Wharton School Publishing Paperbacks

"This book is fabulous! We could hardly wait to get to the next chapter. *The Good, The Bad and The Difference* should be handed out to every parent in the delivery room. It's like a recipe book for a chef. It gave us the skills, the tools and the confidence to talk with our children. It helps give a voice to what we've been trying to say. It gave us the confidence that what we thought was right was right and it gave us the skills to express what we thought was right and why."

–DONNA AND PAUL NEWMYER, Mom and Dad

"This is a creative and original work that presents moral reasoning and ethics in ways that are challenging to and comprehensible for young children. The principles won't define an answer but they do more; they give guidance that can be used in different and varied circumstances. Think of the principles as a corral and not as a chute. If you stay within the corral, you're likely to move in the right direction. The best parts are the wonderful metaphors and similes, which are especially effective for teaching young children."

–FRED ABRAMS, M.D.

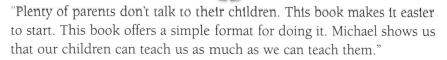

"The chapter on the Super Bowl and John Elway alone is worth the price of the book. Even more, delicious sentences like this one abound in the book:

> "In the movie *Love Story*, Ryan O'Neal muttered the signature line: 'Love means never having to say you're sorry.' Few phrases propel the hand to the airline sickness bag more quickly."

Clever, witty and profound, Michael's affection for the children warms the pages. The book is a joy to read, but more significantly, it will make any person a better teacher and role model for children."

–DON SCHOMER, M.D.

"Plenty of parents don't talk to their children. This book makes it easier to start. This book offers a simple format for doing it. Michael shows us that our children can teach us as much as we can teach them."

–MELODY, a Denver Mom

"This book is not a luxury. It is an imperative."

–IRWIN GREENSTEIN, Internet Entrepreneur and Writer

"It's not a question of whether your children will learn ethics. They will. The questions are: what sort of ethics will they learn and from whom? If you don't want to abdicate such a critical parental responsibility to television, the web, the school system and to your children's peers, then read this book."

–ERNIE MOSTELLER, Independent Commercial Director/Interactive Marketing and Advertising Consultant

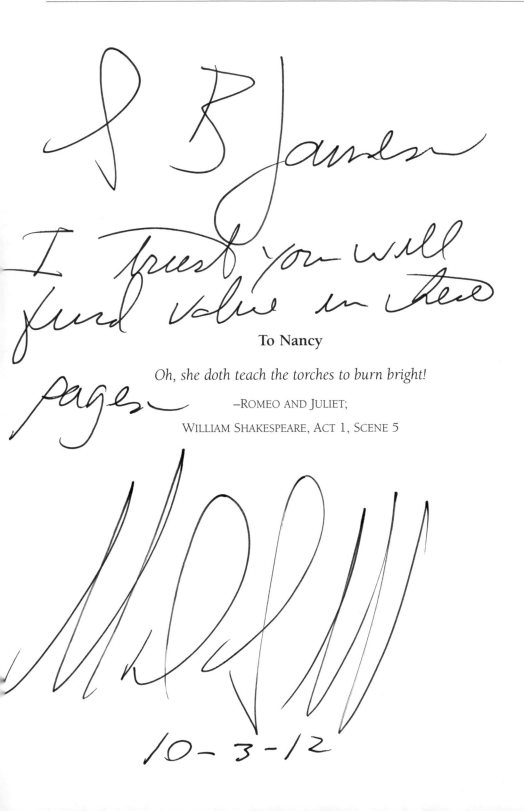

To Nancy

Oh, she doth teach the torches to burn bright!

—ROMEO AND JULIET;

WILLIAM SHAKESPEARE, ACT 1, SCENE 5

CONTENTS

THE GREATEST POEM

The greatest poem ever known
Is the one all poets have outgrown:
The poetry, innate, untold
Of being only four years old.

Still young enough to be a part
Of Nature's great impulsive heart.
Born comrade of bird, beast and tree,
And unselfconscious as the bee.

And yet with lovely reason skilled
Each day new paradise to build
Elate explorer of each sense,
Without dismay, without pretense!

In your unstained transparent eyes
There is no conscience, no surprise.
Life's queer conundrums you accept.
Your strange Divinity still kept.

And life that sets all things in rhyme,
May make you poet, too, in time.
But there were days, O tender elf,
When you were poetry yourself.

–CHRISTOPHER MORLEY

ACKNOWLEDGMENTS

Writing a book is a major task, and the more the writer tries to say, the more major the task seems to become, growing like kudzu in an unattended field. As with any major task in one's life, the writer becomes indebted to those who have provided innumerable acts of kindness, thoughtfulness and assistance during the process.

The Good, The Bad and The Difference: How to Talk with Children About Values was forged on the anvil of a bit of a medical miracle, a surgical procedure which removed my infected aortic heart valve and replaced it with a mechanical artificial one. I felt more than a hint of relief when I regained consciousness after the anesthesia wore off. I wiggled my toes and fingers and concluded with subdued joy that no scalpel had accidentally sliced my spinal cord or punctured anything else important.

Shortly thereafter the endotracheal tube down my throat—to keep it open so oxygen could be pumped into my lungs while under general anesthesia—and the two drain tubes sticking out of my chest—to draw off the plasma leaking from the damaged tissue in my chest so it wouldn't place pressure on my lungs and heart—were ripped out of me as if by a gardener angrily pulling dandelions from the strawberry patch.

Within days of the surgery, I felt a sense of what I called a cosmic debt, a sense of gratitude to the many unknown and known people whose labor and vision and dedication made possible the Saint Jude aortic valve and my successful surgical procedure. I felt indebted to the economic and political systems that encouraged and rewarded such medical innovation. The hundreds of hours volunteered in classrooms throughout Denver and, in a few instances, in other cities, and this book, are my self-imposed efforts to repay my debt.

I express my thanks and appreciation to Dr. Ira Kowal, my cardiologist, for his friendship and his consummate expertise. I thank Dr. Daniel Smith and his flawless surgical team at Porter Memorial

Hospital in Denver, the folks who have literally touched my heart. As I think back about the operation, I imagine someone on the surgical team saying something like "As long as we're putting a new valve in this 1947 lawyer, we might as well get a new muffler also!"

Sir Isaac Newton, of the falling apple fame, attributed his success to standing on the shoulders of giants that preceded him in his field. I confide I've stood on the shoulders of so many giants that I get dizzy when I look down. I acknowledge the epic works of those people in the fields of ethics and moral reasoning cited in this book, all the way back to Plato and Aristotle, with particular appreciation for those who have been giants in the field of raising moral children.

I acknowledge those giants who have sharpened my thinking over the decades. Of the many that could be named, I specifically mention Dennis Prager, the gentlemen at POWERLINE Blog and Denver talk radio commentator, Mike Rosen, the best cross-examiner in the business. I mention these people not for their political views but for their clarity of thought and reasoning.

I am grateful to the encouragement given to me at the start of this project by literary agent Damaris Rowland of New York City. She had faith that if done well, my book would be a meaningful contribution to moms and dads trying to raise moral children.

Friends and other helpful people seemed to arise from the ethers when I needed them. I am grateful to Debra Moser, who helped organize the initial massive amount of material and ideas and who provided valuable guidance identifying and clarifying the book's themes. I thank my dear neighbor, Dr. Fred Abrams, and Roger Fransecky of The Apogee Group and consultant Fred Kiel, co-author, with Doug Lennick, of *Moral Intelligence: Enhancing Business Performance and Leadership Success*, for their encouragement and selfless and patient review of my manuscript as it trundled along toward completion.

I am grateful my friends John Coombe and Peter McLaughlin allowed me to whine and complain to them at all times of the day and night about the difficulty of the project, and I note Peter's repeated admonition, "You have to get mentally tough." I express my appreciation for the warmth and encouragement bestowed upon me by my neighbors, Donna and Paul Newmyer, who read several complete versions of the manuscript, affirmed that my book had value to parents and urged me to see it through.

My gratitude goes to Michael Daniels, a friend and colleague, who spent hours reading my material and talking with me on the phone, motivating me to "just get it done" by expressing his faith that my book was needed and had value. I met Michael through the Colorado Independent Publishers Association, one of the most marvelous and inspiring organizations for writers and for all those folks that work in the many related fields necessary for publishing a book.

I thank my friend, the Honorable John L. Kane, for hours of conversations about Aristotle's Ethics and Rhetoric, the role of aesthetics in the law and his views on the theory and practice of justice. Judge Kane's words always caused me to reach for pen and paper to write a note or two and then get it into my manuscript no matter the state of completion. It is a blessing to have such a friend with an intergalactic IQ who is morally grounded and practical.

I thank Lorna Bosnos of New York City for her patient design and seemingly endless re-designs of the book cover. I acknowledge the vital assistance of Thubten Comerford, social media consultant, for patiently guiding me toward reasonable competence with Twitter and Facebook social media formats. I also thank Robert Schram, owner of Bookendsdesign, *bookendsdesign@earthlink.net*, for his alchemy-like work transforming my words into a real page-turning book.

I thank my children, Erik, Alexandra and Elise, for reading chapter sections and versions of the manuscript over the years in order to share their 'young person's' point of view. Their comments have been illuminating and they found lots of spelling and grammatical mistakes. I pointedly acknowledge Elise scolding me for not having more confidence as a writer. She works with many successful writers and, thus, her words were both poignant and uplifting.

This book would not be possible, of course, without the faith and trust placed in me by many school principals and teachers. My entry into the classrooms began at Cherry Hills Village Elementary School a few weeks after being released from Porter Memorial Hospital. It is therefore appropriate to first acknowledge Sandy Pratt, Elise's first grade teacher, one of the most dedicated teachers and one of the finest people I've been honored to meet. I could not have had access to the classrooms at CHVE without the consent and trust of principal, Jerry Kraal. His sole admonition to me was, "Don't embarrass me." I said I wouldn't and I trust I never did.

During the past four years or so I have been teaching at the Ebert Polaris Elementary School, a sparkling jewel of a school in downtown Denver. I thank principals Diana Howard and Karin Johnson for trusting me with their students. I warmly and enthusiastically acknowledge fifth grade teacher Mrs. Maria Abeyta, who combines intellectual rigor with humor and affection and who gives me a sense of optimism every time I leave her classroom.

Finally, I thank the little children. For twenty years I have been awed by their decency, their compassion, their exuberance and their wisdom. I have been honored that they have shared their words and given me their trust. I have learned never to take young children for granted or to expect that they will be only childish and whimsical. These children consistently demonstrated their commitment to thinking seriously about things that matter and a desire to seek fairness and justice when given guidance and support.

I have faithfully captured their words and, hopefully, their glitter and profundity. I took notes carefully during each class and transmitted them to my computer shortly thereafter. Changes from exact quotations or reconstructions were primarily grammatical or were made to shorten comments that were similar or repetitious. In rare instances, I combined comments from more than one child if one child had dominated a particular discussion and if combining comments would help the flow of the idea. I have not added my words to enhance theirs.

To all of you who have helped make this joyous and anguishing and sometimes tearful project a reality, thank you.

FOREWORD

An article in the New York Times a few years ago cataloged the efforts of our Congress to address the most recent rash of ethical transgressions committed by our elected leaders. The list of the accused is bipartisan and diverse. The misconduct ranges from plain old kick backs to "VIP" loans to bribing senators for votes. Incidents of sexual dalliance, the politicians' nemesis, were detailed in abundance.

With the nation in economic tailspin, much blame is being leveled at the banking and the securities industries and the lobbyists for special interests. Of course, many conflicts of interest allegations arise in this context, as reformers ask hard questions about how our financial system could have become so engulfed by deceit and rampant speculation. The picture thus painted is a Washington rife with partisanship, greed, dishonesty, and pandering brinksmanship on anything of grave importance. So what else is new?

In my lifetime, born 1946, I have witnessed half a dozen or so of these political / business scandals that triggered cries for reform or regulation. Remember the shale oil boom of the '80's, the penny stock boom of the early 1990's, and the dot com boom less than a decade ago? It seems that the forces of greed and deceit can always find traction. I read recently of a theory that such a surge of speculation can be tracked every seven years in the world economy going back a couple hundred years. I believe the author of the theory was serving a jail term for defrauding many investors.

Please don't mistake me for a fatalist. While I recognize the inevitability of history relentlessly producing rascals and villains, I nevertheless believe that society as a whole can and should behave in a moral and ethical manner. In fact I think that we need nothing short of an ethical revolution in America to purge ourselves of the past several decades of decay in our collective devotion to the public good.

The spiritual low points have been excessively low in recent times, leading to the absence of much in the way of residual optimism now when we so sorely need it. I think we as a people yearn to feel virtuous again; to have faith in our political institutions and that the good guys will win in the end. Above all else, we need to make sure that our children do not emerge from this era with a cynical outlook and absence of a moral compass.

We should work to restore the ethical underpinnings of the lessons learned in childhood. We should ask who our children view as heroes. More importantly, we should ask how our children will learn right from wrong, good from evil, respect from disrespect and that most complex of human traits, empathy.

Paddling upstream in this river of doubt, questions and challenges comes Michael Sabbeth, lawyer, teacher, father and concerned citizen. As his friend, for years I have observed Michael's struggle to conceptualize and write this ambitious book. It flows from two decades of teaching the difficult subject of ethics to grade school and middle school students. Michael has also presented this subject to graduate business and law school students, but he knows that he makes the most impact on young children.

As you will discover in the pages that follow, the young often hunger for guidance on basic ethical questions. Pounded by peer pressure, buffeted by a video game culture and often lacking in parental oversight, all too often our kids pick up ethical principles or the lack thereof, by serendipitous osmosis. As Michael points out, this is no way to run a family or school system or the most virtuous country in the world.

Using his countless teaching moments, which include children teaching him, Michael proves the thesis that youth are receptive to and curious about ethical reasoning. They want to be good and virtuous. Yet, our youth need support and guidance, first and foremost from their parents. The conclusion is inescapable that if we wish our children to have a sense of civic responsibility and optimism about the role they are to play in the future of America, we should do several things, including helping parents raise moral children and infusing ethics and moral reasoning into school curricula at every level. Michael's book, *The Good, The Bad and The Difference: How to Talk with Children About Values* is a valuable contribution toward achieving those goals.

–JOHN COOMBE, retired Vice Chancellor of
the University of Denver, attorney and friend

INTRODUCTION

I HAVE TALKED WITH YOUNG CHILDREN in Denver-area schools for twenty years —mostly first graders through fifth graders— about grown-up themes: right and wrong, honor, virtue, personal responsibility, character and merit. In hundreds of conversations I listened with what my clarinet teacher called a "musical ear," hearing their tone and pace and enthusiasm, giving voice to their struggles and the melodies that carried their beliefs and dreams.

The discussions gave me insights into children's values, aspirations and expectations. Children are curious. They are educable. They want to understand the flow of an argument and expand the scope of their thinking. They are not weak. They are resilient, tough and don't mind getting scraped or bloodied, physically or metaphorically, if the cause is just and if it will make them moral and decent. I always leave the classroom with a rejuvenated optimism because these little folks were serious about serious issues. They wanted to become better people.

I learned children want many things from their parents. They want ice cream, candy, iPhones and over-priced running shoes. They want food and shelter, and, of course, they want to be loved. But as much as anything, children want parents to make them stronger, physically and morally. They want to be taught to behave so they will be respected and to rightly feel proud; more 'show me the virtue' than 'show me the money.'

To become stronger, to be respected by people worthy of respect, to feel proud, children want parents to teach right from wrong. They want parents to teach them to be good. They want this from parents because children consider parents the primary architects of their moral structure and the educators that teach them to liberate virtue from vice.

Morality is not a matter of opinion or whim or wishing or convenience but is deeply rooted in the truth of life itself. Morality is based on and measured by truth, that is, an accurate assessment of relevant facts in their proper context coupled with understanding the consequences of decisions, policies and behaviors. Therefore, to make children stronger, to teach them to be decent and good, parents owe children the truth.

We owe our children the truth about the world—that doing good is hard work, that goodness is not always rewarded, that right and wrong are not determined by popular vote but by unwavering ethical standards, that self-esteem must be earned, that knowledge does not necessarily lead to wisdom, that bad people do bad things and that good people sometimes do bad things even when they intend to do something good.

We owe our children the truth that morality cannot defend itself and that ethical values will wither if they are not defended. We owe our children the lesson that truth is not an end in itself but a springboard to moral action in pursuit of virtue.

To convey these truths, parents must be credible. Parents are up against the world to establish and maintain their moral standing with their children. To do so, to be competitive, parents must be informed, authoritative and present. The parent who fails to influence its child's morality can be sure someone else will do so. Trust and credibility are constantly being challenged. They can quickly be undermined and transferred. Parents must continuously earn the trust of their children for it can no longer be commanded or taken as a given. Your children judge your credibility and integrity.

Yet, parenting is more difficult now than at any time in history. Parenting is trying, tedious, expensive and humbling. It is painful, full of anxiety and fear and sometimes seems thankless. Parenting requires backbone. Someone will always disagree; tell us we could have done better or that we were wrong.

Parents cannot be like pandering politicians who run everything through focus groups before deciding what to say or do. We cannot stick fingers up to see which way the winds of public opinion are blowing before deciding how to raise our children. Parents must see the big picture and be accountable, duties that do not burden children. Parents can have no exit strategy and cannot be voted off the island. Parents *are* the island. Parents are, as the poker expression goes, "all in."

In my early school years, the greatest sins were talking in line, running in the hallways and the occasional fist fight. Now schools are infested with knives, guns, drugs, unchecked bullies and perverse sex education classes. Our youngsters have high rates of sexually transmitted diseases, teen pregnancies, suicides and homicides and watch thousands of hours of TV featuring unending violence. Edgy entrepreneurs offer pimp and 'ho' costumes in pre-school sizes.

In addition to these grim societal distortions, children's access to the Internet and other easy communication resources can place parents at a competitive disadvantage in influencing their children. Today's plugged-in, media immersed and savvy children get data, ideas, philosophies and direction from a multitude of sources. There are free markets of delivery systems and free markets of information. Parents have no monopoly. Parents must now compete for what Hugh Hewitt, in his book, Blog, calls "mindspace," in this case, the conscious attention and awareness of their children.

Parents must talk to their children or they are likely to lose them. I don't mean your children will stop asking for pizza or to use your credit cards or to pay for their lawyers. Rather, parents risk loss of influence. Parents that do not speak credibly and authoritatively with their children will be defined by other forces. To a significant extent, your children will know you based on what you talk about—what you find worthwhile and value and what you don't; what you take seriously and what you don't; whether you value moral reasoning and truth or whether you don't. A single phrase spoken by a parent that praises or demeans a person will have a greater moral impact on a child than a dozen weighty books or sermons.

In advertising terms, your words and actions are your 'brand.' As advertising guru Ernie Mosteller describes it, parents must be consistent across all the platforms, expressing a consistent morality for themselves, their children, in-laws, sports coaches and colleagues, whether on vacation, at work and so forth. A Velcro-type morality that can be ripped off or slapped on when it suits a momentary convenient purpose will subvert the parent's 'brand' as well as the parent's character and integrity.

Ironically, in our communications-enriched world parents often have difficulty talking with their children. Many parents have told me they feel left out of the conversations in their children's lives. The little munchkins come home from school and you ask, "How was your day?" and you get a shrug as they trek to the phone or the Internet or homework or sports or the TV. Parents confided in me that they feel uncomfortable talking to their children. They fear they won't be interesting or won't know what to say about some subjects.

Some parents fear their minds are not fast enough to successfully deal with their children's challenges and rebuffs. Some topics make parents anxious and defensive. Who of us has not felt discomfort from the risk of criticism or rejection or unfavorable judgment when our thoughts, emotions and values are placed in the open? I have. Consequently, interaction diminishes.

The Good, The Bad and The Difference: How to Talk with Children About Values provides techniques and a format for talking with your children about moral issues. The book is divided into four sections. Part I presents skills for having conversations, for moral reasoning and the Moral Measures, a structure to evaluate the moral content of an action or belief or consequence. Part II discusses four moral principles. Part III presents seven virtues which I call the Seven C's. Part IV contains in-depth discussions on three topics and a concluding chapter about parents' moral stature in the home.

Ethics is not an exact science that can deliver certainty in all moral questions. Ethics is based on principles that guide reasoning and draw upon virtuous qualities. Moral reasoning is the process that uses ethics to figure out how to act virtuously. Through moral reasoning a person can develop the ability to do the right thing in a wide variety of different circumstances. This capability or competence is the result of employing several distinct virtues and skills; moral, intellectual and behavioral.

By the way, I am fully aware that any subject can be taught unethically, including ethics. Therefore, I determined to be the children's fiduciary, a term in law that means I owed them the highest standard of care, the highest duty of protection. I never lost sight of the trust bestowed upon me when invited into the classrooms. I kept my personal opinions to myself. My thoughts on wars, presidents, fiscal policy, oil spills and terrorists were irrelevant. I did not advise children *what* to think. I tried to teach them *how* to think.

If the reader finds a sentence or two in this book that seem to hint at some grand political ideology, the reader has misconstrued my intentions and has given me undeserved credit. I am neither that clever nor that ambitious.

I distinguish moral reasoning from ordinary logical reasoning since, in the words of Dennis Prager, reasoning itself does not create moral values. Reasoning itself does not teach good from bad and right from wrong. Only virtuous reasoning has morality and ethics woven through the mental process of individuation, that is, where a situation's unique facts and context are evaluated using moral standards. Virtuous reasoning is the blossom, not the original root, of reasoning.

This book shows parents how to teach moral reasoning by having conversations that incorporate moral themes and principles. Parents will see how current and historical events and all the little day-to-day dilemmas and challenges that saturate our lives can be logically and fluidly looped into morally-oriented discussions. Parents can give moral direction to their dialogues with purpose, passion and love. Conversations will be illuminating, challenging, joyous and welcome. Such dialogues not only develop the moral character of children but also enhance the parents' credibility and integrity.

However, *The Good, The Bad and The Difference* is not a book about absolute moral truths or about moral absolutism. It is not a simplified statement of right and wrong. It is about reasoning and about skills to find to the truth. A person doesn't acquire values and reasoning skills as if they were sunlight flooding into the living room after pulling the curtains open. One struggles through the reasoning process. Humility and hard work are required. Through this book I try to go beyond moral reasoning and encourage those habits and attitudes that nurture it.

Hundreds of conversations serve as templates that parents can duplicate, modify or enhance. Just add a parent, sprinkle with enthusiasm and success is assured. The book's structure and process make it easy to understand the content's lessons. The moral issues in each conversation topic are analyzed, argued and learned just as an airline pilot can be taught to fly using a simulator.

The conversations are the marketing research for the parents; the stories have been proven to engage children, exercise their minds and stir their souls. The ideas and analyses are accessible and the topics progress in a dynamic learning sequence that builds upon skills and principles toward reasoning of greater complexity.

Each chapter can stand alone regarding the specific issue, virtue or principle addressed, although the book is intended to be read as a unified statement on moral reasoning. Direct quotes from the children show how they grapple with serious issues. I hope the reader can also 'hear' the children's melodic voices— sometimes poetic and majestic, often humorous, sometimes despairing and sometimes downright exasperating, but always respectful of the conversation's importance.

As in a musical ensemble, the children play off each other in a jam session of words and arguments, adding their riffs and tunes, but also listening and responding to their classmates with dazzling attentiveness.

Their comments may cause a chuckle to bubble out like a little trout stream. Some may bring a tear to the eye. Through their words the eloquence and wisdom and compassion inherent in young children are illuminated, and I honor these children by sharing their words.

I've been asked by inquisitive folks, "What's your market for the book?" I confess I was taken aback because the answer seemed self-evident: anyone that wants to raise or influence a child to be moral.

No special skills are required, other than, perhaps, the willingness to admit you don't know everything or that you might have changed your mind about something.

Nothing more presumptuous or grandiose is required than a parent putting an arm around its child and asking, "What do you think?" Then you prospect and inquire, knowing you will leave a little gold dust in your child's soul.

The classroom is one of many venues where moral learning takes place, but it is not the best or most effective. Families are the most efficient and successful institution for conveying moral values and for creating good people. Borrowing from the movie ratings system, I hope this book inspires parents to get a little more P in the PG realm. Children want their parents to be moral leaders; they want their parents to be adults, that is, something honorable, noble and steadfast; not a sullied adjective slapped in front of words like 'bookstore' or 'videos' or 'entertainment.'

Parents who have read this book as it evolved told me it has given them support and strength to stand up for what they know is right. One mom said the skills in the book helped her do things that made her proud. "We're all in this together," another mom said, "so this helps us all. The more skilled we get, the more we will be inclined to speak with our children."

These words are affirming of course, for many reasons. But high on the list is that those words support the overarching theme of this book: my faith that if given even the slightest encouragement and guidance to do so, most parents will be more likely act to advance honor, beauty and virtue. They will seek the truth that will enhance purpose, meaning and self-awareness with those they love. Parents are the best source for creating good people and I have faith that they will try to do so. Most likely none of us will finish the task but we should begin.

The Good, The Bad and The Difference offers a collection of dialogues that get children involved in their heads and in their hearts. They will give children the voice to tell their stories to you. I am confident this book will help you create your own magic, your own poetry, your own memorable phrases and turn otherwise unre-markable moments into something remarkable. The memories and words will linger.

As for your children, they may forget many things—the new pair of shoes once upon a time, a vacation, a soccer victory or a gift certificate, but they will never forget your words. Even more, they will never forget that you took the time to speak them. Those will be your finest hours.

Success

To laugh often and much;
to win the respect of intelligent people
and the affection of children;
to earn the appreciation of honest critics
and endure the betrayal of false friends;
to appreciate beauty; to find the best in others;
to leave the world a bit better,
whether by a healthy child,
a garden patch
or a redeemed social condition;
to know even one life has breathed easier
because you have lived.
This is to have succeeded.

–RALPH WALDO EMERSON

A CULTURE OF CONVERSATION REASONING SKILLS

CHAPTER 1

*"The genius of the artist is to
free the angel locked in the marble."*

—MICHELANGELO

THE CALL OF THE CHILD

I F THERE'S ONE FACT THAT'S BEEN POUNDED into my aging brain more than any other, it's that children want to talk to their parents. They want to, they need to, they expect to and they are resentful when they can't. They want to talk for two main reasons: as a general rule, children respect their parents more than any other people; and children—certainly most of them—want to become capable and honorable human beings. They know parents offer the best prospect for achieving those goals.

Eyebrows may raise and skeptical chuckles may escape like gas from a shaken soda pop can, but my statements are drawn from hundreds of conversations with school children as young as first graders.

Children have told me who their heroes are and who they most respect. Initially they name people of fame and wealth and public achievement; athletes, celebrities, rock stars and some corporate mogul in the news. After 9/11, many named firefighters and police. One impressive child chose Abraham Lincoln because he unified our country. One youngster respected her wheelchair-bound neighbor born with spinal bifida because "he never complained and always seemed happy."

No child named the chairman of the Federal Reserve Board for lowering interest rates.

As they further ponder the values that underlie their selections, children say they respect people that impacted them directly, such a doctor that saved their life or the life of a friend or family member. As the minutes in class tick by, children increasingly acknowledge that the people they respect the most and view as heroes are the people that help them every day, their parents.

Parents are the folks that sacrifice for them, devote so much of their lives and resources caring for them, feeding them, clothing them, taking them to soccer practice and music lessons and generally instructing them to be responsible participants in society. "I know they could have more stuff if they didn't have to raise me," many a child has said.

But of all the reasons they respect their parents, the most honored is that parents help them become stronger better people. "They have more experience," Tulley explained. "They may have made mistakes so they can give advice to help us avoid them." But it was Samantha, a second grader, who described parents' highest virtue. "Parents teach us how to live right"

IT'S ONLY A SAY AWAY

Teaching right from wrong is the foundation for teaching children to live virtuously. I've learned that children are hungry for this guidance. They value it. They want to talk about it. They respect the good that their parents do; helping fix a stranger's flat tire, saving a drowning child, volunteering at a battered women's shelter, and they want to be like them.

Parents teach right from wrong by their actions, of course, and that is probably the most powerful and effective method of teaching. But they also teach by their words. For example, Sarah, a first grader in my first class in 1990, said, with pride piggy-backing on every word, "You sit down for dinner with your mom and dad and they teach you what is right."

Max, a fifth grader, eloquently echoed Sarah's words when he told me that he loved "learning how to help humanity." I asked where his love came from? "It comes from my parents," he replied, his unscheming eyes glittering. "My parents talk to me if I've done something wrong or if I've made a mistake and they tell me what is right."

I've never met a parent who didn't want to talk with their children about right and wrong. One mom's comment is typical: "It's my job to raise moral children. It's a matter of pride. It gives me satisfaction to know I am doing a good job. My children reflect upon me."

Speaking to our children about right and wrong should be easy. We parents are more experienced, more educated and, generally, more verbal than our children. Wise words should flow to angelic children like warmed honey from a jar. Yet, as Gershwin wrote in 'Porgy and Bess,' it ain't necessarily so. Indeed, many parents look forward to talking about this topic with the enthusiasm the tooth has for the drill.

Apprehension is understandable. Some think that they might not be sufficiently agile thinkers to respond to their children's challenges. Sometimes we lack the confidence to know what is right in our complex and conflicted culture. Some of us think our comments won't be profound or persuasive. Sometimes we agonize that our opinions might be inconsistent or might not be valid in *all* similar situations. Also, our ego, our vanity, our sense of power and authority, even our self image, can become entwined like a pile of linguini, affecting our objectivity and, frankly, sometimes our patience. And finally, let's face it, some subjects are just darn uncomfortable to talk about.

If you feel or think any of these things, as my friend Lenny says, fuhggeddaboutit! There's no need to put yourself through the rinse cycle of your washing machine. Having a conversation about right and wrong is a skill. Skills can be learned, like a hobby or sport, and this skill can be a lot more fun and a lot more rewarding.

I share my experiences talking to children about right and wrong and my suggestions for distinguishing one from the other. I also share the advice children have given me about how their parents should talk to them generally about any topic. Their comments are candid, poignant and unfiltered. A few, I confess, made my eyes watery. As you read their words, you can see in your mind's eye their earnest faces as they struggle to express difficult ideas with voices of vulnerability but also of hope.

BE OUR SIZE!

*"Praise works with only three types of people;
men, women, and children."*

–ANONYMOUS (WHO WROTE A LOT OF GOOD STUFF)

I arrived early at Erik's fourth grade class. Mrs. Nelson was seated, reading to students sitting in a semi-circle on the floor. She waived me in, finished the lesson and walked to the back of the room. I approached her empty chair, and, for no reason that I can recall, I asked the class if it would be okay if I sat down.

"Yeah!" Molly hollered. "Be our size!"

A tingling jolted up my spine. I had struck gold. Molly had said something profound, something metaphoric, something that demanded further exploration.

I asked Molly what she meant. Her nose wrinkled. Her words emerged slowly. "It's like you're the same as us," she replied. "It's like you understand us better." Clayton chimed in: "You're just talking to us instead of telling us what to do."

Hundreds of children have interpreted Molly's words. "You're not standing over us," Alexandra said. "It means," Stephen said, "you see things from our perspective." Morgan said: "To see the world as a kid sees it." Cara said. "It's that you are not so powerful." "It means to be a child with us," Ellis said.

Did Ellis really want adults to be children, I asked?

"I mean," she clarified thoughtfully, "to respect us, that we're kind of equal."

I asked children if there were specific ways that parents could talk to them so they could be "their size." Their heart-swelling answers gave instruction on voice tone, topics, vocabulary and concerns about disagreements between parent and child. Of course, the children quoted here don't speak for *every* child, but their thoughts are representative.

LAUREN: "What's an effective way to talk and get us to think about stuff? Ask questions. We might not know the answers right away but we'll start to think about it."

DAVID: "Try to think on the same level instead of using difficult language."

DIAMOND: "Get eye to eye contact. It shows us respect."

NICK: "Just ask what would happen if you did this or that."

BETH: "Talk with a calm voice and don't yell. If adults yell, the kid will get mad."

ALEXANDRA: "You should explain because kids get confused, and it doesn't feel good. You feel like you're in a little box and everyone is torturing you."

CHARLIE: "Make the sentences short and use simple words. Don't lecture."

LAUREN: "Don't keep repeating stuff."

KELSEY: "If the kid needs help, just show how to correct it."

JOEY: "It helps me a lot when you explain things to me. Don't tell me what to think."

NICK: "Talk to them as if they were your friends. Don't talk down."

SADIE: "When my parents encourage me, I feel it's not just me alone. They are helping me."

Robert Louis Stevenson said, "Use common words to say uncommon things." Note how these little children intuited the wisdom of a poet as acclaimed as Stevenson. It is easy to be clever, but real cleverness is being simple.

Amber mentioned difficulties talking with parents. "It's harder to talk to your parents about things. Some children are scared of their parents. The parents relate badly."

Paige, a verbal fifth grader, exclaimed: "I love to debate. I love to argue, but not with parents or adults."

"Why not," I asked?

"They don't listen. They just tell you you're wrong and you get into trouble."

"Yeah," Alexandra added, "Parents take things personally." I could not suppress a hearty laugh. She's right.

Stephen, a bright fifth grader said: "I feel like I have to get through a brick wall to get to my destination."

"That's quite a statement coming from a ten-year-old!" I remarked.

"I'm eleven," he sharply replied.

Sorrrrreeeeee!

One of the most consistent themes over the years is that children don't want to be treated as...drum roll...children! In 2007 I began presenting my course at the Ebert Polaris Elementary School, a glittering jewel of a school located in downtown Denver. I raised this topic in one of my first classes there.

"Don't use little words," Ari said emphatically. "We know the big words." He felt that using little words was patronizing. Emerald, elaborated with a sharp remark. "Yeah, it's like when we're given a kid's menu. I hate kid's menus!"

Children, just like the rest of us, have a sense of when they're being treated respectfully. Respect is shown when "the parent thinks about what we say." Caylin sees a lack of respect when a parent says something like, "Oh, yes, that's nice honey," and then go on to something else.

Listening and asking follow-up questions is eloquent evidence of a parent's respect for the words of the child. "It shows that the parent is making sure it knows what we're talking about." "When they ask us questions," Caylin added, "then we know they're listening and that they care." Ronald offered his advice: "Don't act like a big robot and go 'Uhuh! Uhuh! Uhuh!"

Angelo made one of the most soulful comments in all my years in the classroom. "Parents respect us when they talk about things that they're proud of or that they're ashamed of." I was perplexed. Why, I asked, did it show respect to talk about what a parent is ashamed of? His answer was profound. "It shows they can be honest and talk about the good and the bad things. It shows me that they treat me as a friend." Doesn't that answer send a little tingle down your spine? These remarks, I emphasize, were made by fifth graders!

Children feel honored and acknowledged when we talk with them. Cristina's thought is widely shared. "My mom or my dad tells me that I made a good point, and then I feel really good about that. When someone respects your opinion you feel supported." Jessie, a fourth grader, spoke in broader terms. "When they ask my opinion, it shows that they respect me. Not whatever they say goes. It's a better way to learn. Ask and talk. It's okay to disagree. If they disagree, talk about it. If they talk and take the time to explain, then they show that they care about you."

A STORY RUNS THROUGH IT

*"Feelings and opinions are recruited, the heart is enlarged,
and the human mind is developed only by the reciprocal influence
of (individuals) upon one another."*

—ALEXIS DE TOCQUEVILLE

One of the powers of language is its ability to confer values through images and analogies. Telling stories and using metaphors are two of the most effective methods of using language. Turning life's events and challenges and choices into stories, narratives and metaphors is an effective powerful tool for teaching moral values to children. As Cara said, "I like the classes. I like the stories. Don't give directions. Don't give orders and demands. Give stories."

Stories have morals and theme lines. With a little work, they can have depth and context and rich detail. They have twists and turns. They offer delicious opportunities to fashion variations and alternative plot lines. The most effective lawyers will always try to present their case in the form of a story that has vivid metaphors, vibrant themes and meaningful lessons.

I tell stories through the interactive technique of dialogue, a word derived from the Greek *dialogos*, and its roots *dia-*, meaning through, and *logos*, meaning word and reason. A dialogue seeks truth through words and reason. A dialogue is a deliberation process of rational inquiry where questions and answers guide toward education, insight and self-awareness.

The kind of dialogue I'm talking about requires a self-critical examination of one's own beliefs. The skill is to probe and extract insights, to find the truth and to develop wisdom. Dialogue encourages reasoning from the general to the specific—Was this action virtuous and, if so, why?—and from the specific to the general—I did this action. Was it virtuous?

A dialogue can be spontaneous exciting journey, with no predetermined path and no preconceived conclusions. They are moments of shared exploration, an inquiry between a child and mom or dad, grandma or grandpa, teacher or coach that deepens relationships and delights as well as educates. The give and take of ideas and the self-introspection require the child to think beyond their normal boundaries and thereby encourage the internal development of virtue.

It is not enough for a parent to have moral values. The parent should know how to articulate and communicate those values. Through dialogue, the parent helps the child develop into a moral thinker and becoming a more moral thinker is a vital precondition to becoming a more moral actor.

A dialogue with your child illustrates the virtue of taking time. Deep connections with your child are achieved through dialogue. We don't want quick statements about facts, conclusions and lessons as if we were raising our child by a Power Point presentation. There should be no attention deficit dialogue. Properly done, the interaction slows the world down and gives us time to think.

A dialogue about ethics and virtue should go beyond sound bites for it deals with complex thoughts and the brain needs time to process new information and ideas. It should give the participants a chance to tell their own stories—what's bothering you, what makes you happy, what makes you proud.

A dialogue with your child is not about winning and defeat. It is not a 'zero sum' game, where one advances at the expense of another. For several reasons, I'm against people arguing as 'devil's advocates.' First of all, to argue what you don't believe, other than posing reasonable hypothetical possibilities, risks violating the trust that needs to exist between parent and child if the process is to be credible and successful. Second, the devil has enough advocates. We parents shouldn't aid and abet that group.

I don't mind confiding that when I'm talking to my children or to the children in a class I must check myself to not be aggressive and to not 'talk like a lawyer.' Skills and styles that are effective in the courtroom—"Just answer my question." "That's not what I asked." "You're hopelessly inconsistent."—may be abusive in other places (and they're usually abusive in the courtroom also). A dialogue is like fly casting, a matter of easy rhythms rather than raw power. A dialogue with your child must be a 'smote-free' zone.

My most rewarding moments are the silences, those quiet seconds when the child pauses, reflects, and kneads her thoughts like a brioche dough and then exclaims "Oh, I get it!" or "Now I understand!" Then there is that priceless leap to a higher level of realization. Every moment can have its own magic, and you can have it also. Just remember that magic isn't magic either.

Children are not fragile porcelain dolls. They are robust, vibrant and inquisitive. They want to argue, they want to make their statements, they want to challenge and they want to be challenged. Parents say things like, "Oh, honey, you don't really mean that." or "You're saying that because you're angry."

Such comments insult the child. They don't hold the child accountable for his statements. Children lose respect for the speaker. Like airbrushing, shallow conversation hides and distorts. They can be dishonest. The child escapes responsibility for his words. Introspection and the development of judgment do not occur. Treat their words seriously and hold them responsible for what they say and they will respect you more because you are listening and evaluating. Even if their words are irresponsible, you are honoring your child by engaging them in a reasoned exchange.

Reade, a fifth grader, said to me after a discussion. "You know what I like best about your classes?" I didn't know. "You don't treat us like children. You listen to what we say and you argue back. You help us think better."

I could not have been more pleased if the great Julia Child served me a perfect meal on a platter of pure silver.

Look for the big picture, which is always conveyed through a collection of or by a bundling of little stories. As we lawyers say, stories have multiple entry points. We can talk about physical circumstances, character, training, judgment, intellect, whatever. All kinds of issues can be accessed by the same story. Just pick an issue and jump in.

Don't worry about whether you are doing well. Your children may stare at you as if they were exhibits in Madame Tussaud's Wax Museum. Don't be concerned. They are interested and they are forgiving. They will be inspired if they know you have a noble purpose. If my insights don't give you a high comfort level, then take refuge in Herman Wouk's poignant phrase, "love closes the gap where words fail."

CHAPTER 2

A CULTURE OF CONVERSATION

*"Good company and good conversation
are the very sinews of virtue."*

–IZAAK WALTON, THE COMPLEAT ANGLER, 1653

A DAY ON THE RIVER

*"The stuff of which masterpieces are made drifts about the world,
waiting to be clothed in words."*

–THORNTON WILDER

THE MOST EFFECTIVE WAY to initially engage children in a conversation is to present an issue as a dilemma, asking not only 'What's the right thing to do?' but also 'What choices did a person have?' and 'What were the likely consequences of each choice?'

Here's an example of a dialogue about an actual event that occurred in Denver several years ago. An elderly woman drove her car off Santa Fe Drive into the icy South Platte River. Some people stopped and saved the woman. Most didn't stop to help. I've used this dialogue in every class since the event occurred.

I begin this dialogue by stating the facts of the situation. Then I ask for reasons that might explain why some people helped and why some didn't. We're speculating, of course, but the children's answers are illuminating. For example, the people that stopped may have cared more about people or about the value of life than those that didn't stop. Maybe they were responding because someone had helped them in a crisis. Perhaps those that stopped knew they could be effective because they had skills or equipment that could save the woman—strength, a rope in their car, extra warm clothing—and were willing to use them.

What about those that didn't stop? Were they bad people? Maybe. Perhaps they didn't care about another person's life. But as the children continued to ponder, other possible explanations presented these people in a different moral light. Maybe a motorist was weak and infirm and knew that he could not be of any value to the rescue effort. Maybe a motorist saw that many people had stopped and figured that the matter was being adequately addressed. Maybe the motorist considered that by stopping he would only get in the way and hinder rather than help the rescue effort. Maybe a driver that didn't stop nevertheless made a phone call to the police requesting assistance from trained professionals.

We use dialogue to develop moral reasoning by engaging the intellect as well as the emotion. To say that those that didn't stop were 'mean,' 'stupid' or 'not nice' is to yield to emotional responses. They may prove true, ultimately, but we cannot reach those conclusions initially. Absent first-account interviews, and assuming the answers are honestly given, we can never know with certainty the reasoning of either group of people. But we don't need to know. We only need to be able to discuss the issues. When appeals are made only to the emotion, however, the child rightly senses a scam. The children want evidence of a mind.

Our discussion must, of course, weave the event with the issue of moral character. Which person do you want to be, the one who helps as best as she can under the circumstances or the one that indifferently drives past? Which behavior would make you most proud of yourself? Which group of people do you respect more? In this way, wisdom and knowledge and character can grow, however slowly and haltingly.

I gave a presentation to parents on talking about values to children. I used this icy rescue situation as an example. After my talk, a dad said to me, "I read the same articles. It never occurred to me to use them to talk about ethics and character to my children!"

Well, once we see the world through the lens of moral reasoning, a smorgasbord of events become viable discussion topics with our children. Thornton Wilder was right.

One of the most exciting and intellectually vibrant aspects of the dialogue process is its whimsical susceptibility to changes of directions and topic, like a paper plane in the wind. You may have specific topic when you start—why don't you clean your room—but you may end up in a delightfully different place.

The process of speaking causes new ideas to sprout. You start with the child's responsibility for keeping the room clean, then shuffle over to the matter of the respect for things and the child's blessings and good fortune for having these things, then jump to respecting the people that gave them to your child. Then, as fluidly as changing chords on a guitar, you talk about how actions influence self-respect and pride. All that from a bunch of dirty clothes and pizza crusts on the floor! It's rather remarkable.

> *"To do good deeds is noble.*
> *But to teach others to do good deeds*
> *Is more noble.*
> *And easier."*
>
> –H. L. MENCKEN

There's this quip. A tourist in Manhattan asks a cab driver, "How do I get to Carnegie Hall?"

"Practice, practice, practice," the cabbie replied.

I began teaching my classes in the spring of 1990 at Cherry Hills Village Elementary School (CHVE). Elise was in first grade. Preparing for classes encouraged me and provided a reason for me to talk with her about my topics and about life in general.

As she neared the end of high school, Elise told me "Your talking helped me think through things that I had to deal with later. I felt I got a jump over so many of the other kids whose parents don't say those kinds of things. I was better prepared."

I didn't realize it at the time but it's easier to start conversing with children when they are young, just as it's easier to get them into the habit of doing chores around the house at an early age. It becomes part of a routine and they receive the process as something normal rather than as something to be done regarding only 'serious' matters on rare occasions.

The key to success is developing what I call a culture of conversation. Elise made the fine point that when the parent begins this culture of conversation early in the child's life, "then you get used to talking about stuff with your parents."

Elise also made a very astute point, which she continues to do frequently. "If the child gets used to talking, then they trust you." After all, few actions demonstrate respect for a child or elicit its trust as much as asking for his or her opinion. In this sense, young children are remarkably similar to adults. The parent gains credibility and the conversation process gains legitimacy. It's not a matter of 'here goes dorky dad trying to lecture me on something' but rather it is a process forged on the anvil of a commitment to moral reasoning.

Joey, a second grader, acknowledged the value of the process: "We talk to our parents, and that's good, because we're spending time with them and learning from them and we're learning how to talk about things."

Julia, a fifth grader, shared how her mom comes into her room every night "to talk and ask if anything is bugging me."

Kasha described the process as quite informal: "My parents just bring up a subject and ask my opinion."

Success breeds success. And as motivational speakers instruct us, "You don't have to be great to start but you have to start to be great." They're right.

Dani, a fifth grader, explained how these conversations become a foundation for future problem solving. "I try to remember these conversations and learn from them, Mr. Sabbeth, so when I get older I can think back to what we said. That will help me figure out what to think."

Each conversation hones your technique, just as when practicing a musical instrument or training as an athlete. You get better and better, as Aristotle recognized a while ago when he wrote in his *Nicomachean Ethics*, "Excellence, then, is not an act but a habit."

Two Wolves

*One evening an old Cherokee told his grandson about a battle
that goes on inside all people. He said, "My son, the battle is between
two 'wolves' inside us all. One is Evil. It is anger, envy, jealousy,
sorrow, regret, greed, arrogance, self-pity, guilt, resentment,
inferiority, lies, false pride, superiority, and ego.*

*The other is Good. It is joy, peace, love, hope, serenity, humility, kind-
ness, benevolence, empathy, generosity, truth, compassion and faith."*

*The grandson thought about it for a minute and then
asked his grandfather: "Which wolf wins?"*

The old Cherokee simply replied, "The one you feed."

THE TIME HAS COME TO TALK OF MANY THINGS

Annie was about twelve. We were at a soccer tournament in Grand
Junction, Colorado. Wisps of clouds dotted a slab of blue sky
framed by rust-red mountains called 'the bookends.' My spirits were
high as I jogged toward the refreshment stand to get a few more bot-
tles of sports drinks. They were dashed to the ground when I over
heard a snippet of a conversation bubbling from three or four girls.

My pace slowed. They were soccer players in eighth or ninth
grade, I guessed. Their hair glistened in the morning sun as they
kicked a ball back and forth. As nonchalantly as if discussing nail
polish colors, they talked about male classmates pressuring one of
them to make pornographic movies. One girl quoted the male classmate saying something like "he thought it would be a lot of fun."
She went on about how he persisted in asking her to make a video.

Welcome to our not so brave new world.

For many parents, these words, so effortlessly and perhaps
indifferently spoken by our little angels, land in the soul like hand
grenades.

On the drive back to Denver I told Annie about this incident. I
asked if she could stand up to the pressure and to the possible
intimidation from such a classmate. "Yeah," she replied. "It's dis-

gusting. I'd tell them to get lost and I'm not interested." Then she added matter-of-factly, "Some girls let themselves get pushed around."

I'm confident that Annie would handle the situation forthrightly but I'm even more confident that she'd talk to me or to her mom about it. Then, without a doubt, the matter would be handled properly. Immediately.

Question: How is sausage made?

Answer: You don't want to know!

Well, true or not about wanting to know about sausage making, I want to know what's going on with my children. My children, and yours, are facing pressure that, frankly, I can barely fathom. Some of our children are creating these undesirable pressures.

I want to know about them. I want to be able to talk about everything with my children, and I can't if I don't know what's going on in their lives. Parents ignoring issues doesn't stop children from thinking about or from doing things. Ignorance may be bliss but it is bliss based on weakness. Generally the consequence of weakness is destruction.

This type of talking takes skill. It also takes commitment. We're not dealing with Peter Pan where you just think lovely thoughts and away we go, soaring into the cotton-candy clouds somewhere over the rainbow. We can't stop the world and we can't get off. We can, however, talk about things. Of course some topics are difficult, and that's where a history of conversation becomes such a virtue.

If you're uncomfortable about discussing a topic, here's a technique that can reduce your fears and discomfort. Say something like, "I'm uncomfortable talking about this...." or "I might not say this so well, but...." These phrases don't require great rhetorical skills. They are learnable.

Look at what such an admission has achieved. You've been honest and humble. You've transformed a weakness into strength. You've become stronger. You have become more skilled. And, by the way, you haven't said anything your child doesn't already know.

Here's a point that affirms the over-arching theme of my book.

Whether or not you talk with your child, be assured others are. Our children are subjected to dozens of competing doctrines, beliefs, value systems and enticements. Parents compete with CD's, iPods, cell phones, the TV, the radio, the Gameboys, the Walkmans, the Internet and foul-mouthed hip-hop and gangsta sewage.

Your child will choose among these competing forces based on which source is most credible. They will choose based on which source is most likely to make them stronger. They will choose based upon which source will most enhance and enrich their lives.

I want my children to choose me. Most likely, you want your children to choose you. They will not always choose based on these criteria. They will do so most of the time. Life is percentage baseball, and that's the best we can do with independent autonomous people. That's why you should start conversing early in their lives.

Be aware, be informed, that people are intentionally trying to influence your child's morality. I found it particularly disturbing ('disturbing' is not the first word that came to my mind) when I read that the King Middle School in Portland, Maine, intends to offer birth control pills and patches to students through its student health care center. Students need parental permission to access the center but not for birth control specifically. Get that? Middle School!

In Laura Ingraham's book, *Power to the People* I read about another pernicious policy where the school board in Deerfield, Illinois required freshmen to sign a confidentiality agreement promising not to disclose, even to parents, the content of the sex-ed materials.

If we parents are to have a dominant influence upon their children—indeed, any influence at all—parents have to get competitive. Competitiveness requires moral and intellectual integrity. We also have to be tough. And we have to be involved.

Let's be frank. Raising children is a daunting challenge. But we back away at the risk of great cost. We cannot behave like fawning politicians or hucksters for deodorant and interest-free credit cards. We have real children to raise, real lives to impact and real problems to address. Horrific consequences can result if we fail.

There is no perfect norm for how to talk to children. Each child is unique. Some are very verbal and love to chat; others require the effort of breaking into a vault. The topic has to be age-appropriate and you don't want to be too graphic about some descriptions.

Sometimes, a child is not communicative. I tried to strike up a conversation with Annie a bunch of years ago. I asked her feelings on some matter. Annie was silent. I tried to entice her by pointing out that Erik and Elise would have given me a cascade of words like a mini Niagara.

Annie tersely replied, "Dad, my feelings aren't that complicated." She was nine. My thoughts slithered to cleaning the garage.

With a little experimenting, the right method can be found, fulfilling our own personal formulation of the commitment to leave no child behind.

If you wait for that right or perfect time, you might wait quite a while. Right moments do not 'happen' as much as they are created. My neighbor, Paul, told me, "You have to strike when the iron is hot." One mom told me she turns off the radio when she gets into the car and talks to her child. "There is silence," she said, as if by royal decree. "They have to listen to Mom!"

WHAT I WANT

I want a lot. I want to be able to talk with my children about everything; who's pressuring them; who's threatening suicide, how they're standing up to the drug pushers, the politically inappropriate school teachers and what my children respect and what makes them proud.

I want my child to be the one that says no when offered illegal drugs or is asked to help a cheater or to make obscene movies. I want my child to return the lost wallet and to tell the police if he knows a student has a bomb or a gun in school. I want my child to call me at 2:00 in the morning to ask for a ride home rather than to drive home drunk or get into a car with a drunk driver.

I want to say 'that's my child' when listening to a jazz band or watching a soccer game, not when staring at a table in a morgue. Most parents want those things also.

I don't want passive compliant children. Unless they are strong and independent, they will yield to bullies, drug pushers, and the world's charlatans and snake oil sellers. I know my children will make mistakes. They may do foolish things. If their mistakes are made in good faith and motivated by honor and virtue, I will support them absolutely. If they are not, they'll have to hire their own lawyers.

I am most likely to get what I want if I can talk with my children. I remember comments from my mom and dad from fifty years ago that ring with the clarity of a bell finely struck this morning.

Indeed, a conversation never ends. It lingers in the mind like melodies after leaving the concert hall or memories of your child's first steps. This is how we free the angel locked in the marble, word by word, idea by idea, struggle by struggle, shaping and contouring, year after year, being the sculptor and not the stone.

Your child may, at first, look at you as if you've drizzled mustard on an ice cream sundae, but you can take this to the bank: they're listening to and absorbing everything you say. They're putting it through filters and tests, but they hear every word.

Soon they'll join in. They will join in because you are undertaking something noble and good. Your stories and your words will become bricks in their moral foundation. Not the only bricks, of course—some will be constructed of emotions and experiences— but these will be among the strongest and most durable

By your stories and words your children will remember you were there. You were present when it mattered. And they will always remember, with a smile in their souls, that for those precious moments you were their size.

CHAPTER 3

WHAT IS GOOD?

"We have the right to pursue happiness, based on the Declaration of Independence, but the one universal component of happiness is virtue, and virtue is always the same: doing good to others."

–JEAN M. YARBOROUGH, *AMERICAN VIRTUES: THOMAS JEFFERSON ON THE CHARACTER OF A FREE PEOPLE*

"Be good!"

"Be good at Aunt Tilly's this evening!"

"She's a good violinist."

"You have to be a good friend to have a good friend."

"Be a good sport on the soccer field."

"It's good to practice and work hard."

HAVE YOU EVER SAID ANYTHING LIKE THESE PHRASES to your child? Commands like these are as common as watermelon pits at a summer picnic. Their meanings, however, are often unclear. I've said words like these, and to be candid, I didn't know precisely what I was telling my child to do or not to do. The words dropped into my mind like an uninvited guest and rather than tussle and throw them out, I took the easier path and said them.

Phrases about 'good' such as "be good" or "be a good friend" are bundled with assumptions, values, expectations and history. In any given instance, those assumptions and values may be unclear. Even if they are clear, they may not be accepted. In the context of raising moral children, there is probably a broad consensus on how these assumptions and values determine what is 'good.'

It is generally accepted, for example, that being a good sport on the athletic field means following the rules of the game and excludes slamming an opponent in the back of the head when the referee isn't looking. Being good at school generally means being respectful and studious and excludes assaulting your classmates. It's understood that being good at Aunt Tilly's means being obedient, polite and not throwing sulfuric acid at the cat or taking green paper from her pocketbook.

Those assumptions, values, expectations and so forth, however, may not provide meaningful guidance for dealing with a specific situation that confronts a child. Indeed, interpretations may be conflicting. Children tell me that phrases such as 'be good' or 'be fair' or 'do what's right' often offer little useful guidance. "It doesn't help us much," Massiel said.

We may rightfully ask, for example, does 'be good' mean doing whatever someone else tells you to do? Does it mean doing whatever you think is right? Does 'be a good sport' require silent acquiescence to an opposing player's unethical conduct? Does 'be good at school' obligate a child to appease or run away from a bully or to accept a teacher's bigotry?

'GOOD!' WHAT IS IT GOOD FOR?

I stood in front of this sixth grade class for the first time. Soft December light tumbled through windows that offered an unobstructed view of the exhilarating Rocky Mountains. I felt energized.

"How do you know something is good," I asked?

Silence. Then muted muttering. Students peeled chewing gum from the bottoms of their desks. Moments crawled by like a centipede with bunions. Michelle finally spluttered, "Gee, I've never thought about that before!"

It was time to think about it. No topic is more important than defining 'good.' Only then can we distinguish good from evil and right from wrong. Only then can we act to advance 'good,' do what's right, diminish evil and avoid doing what's wrong.

A few years ago a friend sent me a small pillow embroidered with a youngster boasting a defiant impish grin sitting on Santa's knee. "Define 'Good!'" was stitched in red under the figures. Without an unambiguous understanding of 'good,' a direct 'yes' or 'no' answer could not be given to Santa's trademark question, "Have you been good this year?" Once upon a time the meaning of 'good' was understood, at least in this limited context. Now, this little fellow is suggesting that the meaning of 'good' is more like a jump ball on the basketball court.

Dictionaries define 'good' as virtuous, morally excellent, beneficial and wholesome. Aristotle viewed 'good' as the pursuit of virtue by perfecting the soul through reason, temperance and proper emotion. Ethical action led to achieving *kalon,* essentially meaning a status of the beautiful, noble or fine. Thus, the failure or inability to distinguish right from wrong or good from evil is the symptom of a deeply flawed character.

These definitions are, by necessity, generalizations and conclusions. They are not action guides or directions for behavior in specific instances. They do not provide moral judgments on life's infinite circumstances. To figure out if something is 'good,' these generalizations must be interpreted in specific actions.

Ask children why 'good' is good and more likely than not there will be a pause, an energized silence, when children hesitate and thought stops to examine itself. Then answers will dance around like oil droplets on a hot skillet.

"I help my mom with my little brother." "Helping a lady pick up groceries she dropped on the floor." "A kid was mean to my friend and I told him to stop treating my friend that way." "My family serves food at a homeless shelter." "My neighbor is a foster parent. He takes care of kids who have bad families." "My dad saved a drowning man."

These are wonderful examples of 'good,' but as James noted astutely, "They might tell us what is good but they don't tell us why." Pretty bright for a fifth grader! Why are these actions good? Maddie said that 'good' is "not only whether it is good for you. It's also whether it benefits others. Sometimes you have to go beyond yourself."

Sierra, a rambunctious fifth grader, added, "What is good depends on the circumstances at the time and in the future."

Comments like these make me feel like a chunk of a rainbow nestled on my shoulders.

Are there objective standards and tests that determine 'good' or are we stuck with something like the "I know it when I see it" test Supreme Court Justice Potter Stewart used to define pornography?

Children know that being 'good' means helping the world and specific people in it, including yourself, be better than they were before. They link 'good' to achieving virtuous consequences. Returning a lost wallet advances fairness and justice. Honesty facilitates accurate and honorable actions because they are based on truth. A foster parent advances life and decency.

Children know it's in the parents' best interests to have good children. "It's less work for the parents," Peter said. I asked him to elaborate. "Well, if you have bad kids, you have to try harder. You have to get them out of trouble."

"Yeah," Lee chimed in, "they have to hire lawyers!"

"So," I asked, "why be good?"

Andrew, a first grader, gave a memorable answer: "It makes life go easier."

I admit I chuckled at little Andrew's comment, which is generally accurate. As parents, we may well explain that doing good and proper manners and respect for others and so forth can make our children's lives easier. But, as good parents, we should also explain that doing good and respect for others are the right things to do even if it makes life more difficult.

I share a poignant exchange I had with a fifth grader and explain its significance. I had asked the class my standard question: How do you know something is good? This young lady replied, "Well, in my personal opinion, there is no good or bad or right or wrong because it's all a matter of opinion. What you think is good, another culture might think is bad." The student spoke earnestly and with intensity, massaging her words as if they were pizza dough.

This conversation occurred during the first class of the year in this school. I had not yet discussed any of the ethical principles or virtues that guide us to determine whether something is good or not good. In response to her comment, I asked: "What about slavery in the United States? Do you think slavery was good?" She answered quickly. "The slave owners thought it was good."

"But what do *you* think, I persisted.

"I think slavery was very bad," she answered.

"Okay," I said. I sensed I should move on. I called on another student whose raised hand was whipping about like a flag in a windstorm.

After the class, several students approached me to share additional thoughts. The young lady stood back from the group. I left the auditorium when the students said all that was to be said or were ushered out by their teachers. The young girl caught up to me as I walked down the hall. Speaking in a subdued voice, she said, "Sometimes it's hard to know your opinion."

Pleased that she had thought about my comments, I said gently, "Don't worry. You're just in fifth grade. You've got time to figure things out. Opinions can change."

Her next comment surprised me. Softly, drenched in introspection, she said: "You've already changed my opinion."

I admit I was moved, which, at my weight, is not easy to do. All I had done was ask a not particularly creative follow-up question. I wondered, truly, what this young child had experienced and what she intended to communicate. Instead of being angry or miffed or defensive because I had challenged her, she sought me out to clarify and to express something new.

Days later, I discussed this conversation with my daughter, Elise. She said that my follow up question had caught the youngster off guard. The student had not been accustomed to someone asking her to justify or explain her opinion. Few students are. Most likely, the child was in the habit, quite a common one, of expressing an opinion and then, literally or figuratively, plugging in her iPod or something like it and forgetting what she said. And she was used to people reacting with a smile or a shrug and no more.

The fact is the student hadn't given any thought to what she thought. Now that she began to think about what she thought, she concluded that some adjustment was necessary.

Elise observed that little children are starved for the opportunity to interact so they can explore and evaluate their beliefs and values and opinions. They want to debate ideas, so long as it's done with love and affection and respect. That's how they become more capable people. Children know the process can be bumpy and provocative, but, nevertheless, they want to grapple with the life's challenges. And they want to know why they think what they think.

A GOOD FRIEND . . . MAYBE

Learning is best achieved by relating general principles to specific actions. We examine the actions from all views as if they were sculptures. Friendship lends itself to a discussion of 'good.' The topic engages children intensely because they all have friends, they all want friends and they all want to be friends. But as we all know, friendship incorporates a cornucopia of conflicting values and emotions. Evaluating friends compels us to address issues that, often, we'd prefer to sweep under life's metaphoric rugs.

I cannot overstate the value of friends. They add beauty, joy and love to our lives. Ralph Waldo Emerson wrote "A friend may well be reckoned the masterpiece of Nature." Friends can elevate and push us toward achievement and virtue. They can also, however, destroy us. Determining who is a 'good' friend or who is acting as a good friend in a particular situation can be daunting. Yet, it is necessary, for, in extreme instances, the determination can be a matter of life and death.

My treatment of 'good' is presented through class discussions about two dilemmas involving friends. Variations of these dilemmas regularly confront our children (and perhaps the rest of us as well)The children's comments illustrate what can be friendship's masterpiece and what can be just pieces.

He that is thy friend indeed,
He will help thee in thy need:
If thou sorrow, he will weep;
If thou wake, he cannot sleep:

Thus of every grief in heart
He with thee does bear a part.
These are certain signs to know
Faithful friend from flattering foe.

–WILLIAM SHAKESPEARE
SONNETS TO SUNDRY NOTES OF MUSIC, VI.
"AS IT FELL UPON A DAY"

MY WAY OR THE 'GOOD BYE' WAY

I read this story in a magazine while standing in the checkout line at my local supermarket. I don't know if it is true. It may have been made up to teach moral lessons, just as I have been using it.

Two boys, Al and Bill, are in a toy store. Bill whispers to Al, puts some toys in his pocket and leaves the store hurriedly. Seeing the manager confront Al, Bill yells, "If you rat on me, I won't be your friend." The manager demands that Al give him the name and address of his friend or he will have Al arrested.

Don't be a rat! Don't be a snitch! Sacrifice yourself for friendship's higher calling! These commandments of friendship are appealing if you are the one making the escape but not so full of sunshine if you're the one who will be wearing bright orange clothing advertising your local sheriff's department on the back.

This story illustrates several aspects of 'good:' good friend, good behavior, good outcome and, perhaps, good-bye. When my children were in elementary school I'd ask their opinions about the topics I planned to discuss in class. Not only were they accurate barometers of whether a subject would be interesting but the rehearsal afforded me an opportunity to sharpen my arguments.

I did a practice run with Erik and Annie the evening before the first time I told this story in class. Erik was in third grade; Annie was in fourth. I was lying down with Erik on the bottom bed and Annie was on the top of the bunk bed in Erik's room.

"What should Al do," I asked?

Annie responded like a cannon blast. "Bill isn't a good friend.

He's running away and letting Al get into trouble. No one needs that kind of friend. I'd tell on Bill!" Having fully evaluated the issue, Annie turned her attention to a book on the improbable topic of green eggs and ham.

Erik was more philosophical. "I can always get more friends. I can't always get out of jail. Why should I get into trouble because of somebody that doesn't care about me?" Bill's one-way version of friendship held no allure for them.

Suddenly Erik forcefully pressed a finger against my nose.

"Oww!" I yelped. "What'd you do that for?"

"I'm putting you on 'pause,' he said. "I have to go to the bathroom!"

There you have it. I'd been reduced to an entertainment device; another gadget to be whimsically manipulated. Yet, a sliver of satisfaction tip-toed into my heart, for it meant that he didn't want to miss any of the show.

Without exception, the children in my classes focused on the inequality of loyalty. Bill displayed no loyalty to Al but demanded loyalty from him. If he obeyed Bill, Al risked paying a price and Bill would escape sanctions. Even if the two were in collusion, that outcome would be unjust. The children said they could do without that kind of friend.

Combining faith with practicality, Nicole, a third grader, concluded poignantly, "I'd tell on Bill. If he's a good friend he will forgive you because what he did was wrong and selfish, and if he's not a good friend, who needs him?"

Evaluating Al's choices was more complex. Al could tell on Bill or refuse. For the reasons Erik mentioned, the children believed, almost without exception, that Al would be a fool if he didn't comply with the manager's demand. Yet, telling on Bill did not signify that Al was a bad friend to Bill.

With elegant incisiveness, some children said that a good friend would tell on Bill. By cooperating with the manager, they argued, Bill might be taught lessons that could deter him from more serious criminality in the future. Learning these lessons at a relatively inexpensive cost would be better for Bill in the long term. Relating general principles of 'good' to these actions, moral reasoning and logic show that Bill was not a good friend to Al and that Al could be a good friend to Bill as well as serve his own self-interest.

"It is the eternal struggle between these two principles—right and wrong—throughout the world. They are the two principles that have stood face to face from the beginning of time; and will ever continue to struggle. No matter in what shape it comes, whether form the mouth of a king who seeks to bestride the people of his own nation and live by the fruit of their labor, or from one race of men as an apology for enslaving another race, it is the same tyrannical principle."

–ABRAHAM LINCOLN, THE LINCOLN DOUGLAS DEBATES

TO TELL OR NOT TO TELL, THAT IS THE QUESTION

The first story is fun to talk about and breezily lends itself to some complex thinking. This second example is true. It is more intense, the duration of the event is longer and the stakes are higher. During the off-air discussion prior to an interview, a radio talk show host described a situation regarding friendship that her daughter dealt with in high school.

A friend told the daughter that she was contemplating suicide. The friend demanded that the daughter not tell anyone about the comments or she wouldn't be her friend any more. One can only speculate as to whether the friend saw the irony of her threat in the event that the daughter honored her confidence and the friend committed suicide.

Regrettably, this ominous scenario is not infrequent. Several youngsters I know have been confronted with similar situations. When inquiring what a good friend should do, (the daughter informed responsible adults) the tendency is powerful to leap quickly to the obvious answer—you tell—and be done with the topic, just as Annie did with the Al-and-Bill story. But we parents want a dialogue; we want to probe and spelunk to develop our children's moral reasoning. The discussion process is as important as the answer. We should try to squeeze insight from each conversation as the artist squeezes pigment from the tube.

Several of the issues are stark: Do I want to be liked or do I want to possibly save a friend? What if I tell that my friend is suicidal and it turns out she was teasing me and I look like a dope?

The students' comments illustrate their compassion, their capability to tackle harsh reality and their expressed willingness to sacrifice for a 'good' higher than friendship.

CLAIRE: "If you care about someone, you'll do what is right, even if it hurts."

CHARLOTTE: "Well, you can't help someone do what is bad for him." She then thought a moment more, wrinkled her nose, and in a sky-stabbing insight said, "Well, you can do it, but it's not being a good friend. Then you have two people being bad instead of one, and everything just gets worse."

LAUREN: "It's a bad situation, because either way, you lose a friend." Then she added, "But if she's alive, well, you might get her back."

Alexandra's answer dampened the eyes: "But in your heart you will always have a friend because you did the right thing."

Many students, like Kelsey, were practical as well as moral. "Maybe you would have a friend that didn't like you any more, but you did the right thing and there is always the possibility that she will change her mind, which would not happen if she died."

SALLY: "I'd rather have a person that was alive and didn't like me than have a dead friend."

RYAN: "You have to do the right thing even if she won't like you.

This little fellow grasped a profound point: being liked or being loved is, alas, not a meaningful indicator of moral virtue.

Nicole made one of the most powerful statements in my nineteen years in the classroom: "There are worse things than having pain."

Doing 'good' in this situation requires action that will preserve life. The natural human tendency, in the face of pain or suffering or adversity, is to abandon intellect and to act based on emotion. Children should be taught to fight these impulses. But they can't fight them unless they're aware of them. Awareness is the result of analytical skill, and we parents can teach this skill through stories like this one.

Exploration of the dynamics of this relationship yields many lessons on morality that children should learn. By demanding silence regarding her suicidal thoughts as the price of her friendship, the friend has elevated compliance and obedience over 'good,' over protecting life. To be concerned, however, that someone's feelings might be hurt rather than acting to save a friend's life is to look through the wrong end of the telescope. Imagine the stinging condemnation and acid anger that would have been heaped on the daughter if the friend committed suicide and it was learned that the daughter chose to be silent about the threats!

The daughter was being asked to sacrifice her judgment to the judgment of her friend. Her friend's judgment includes, of course, her own biases and prejudices and weaknesses, which in this instance were considerable. Robert Tracinski uses the phrase 'cognitive altruism' to describe subserving one's own judgment to that of another. The daughter, on threat of losing a friend, was required to surrender her views to another in order to be nice, to be liked, to avoid anger. She was asked to subordinate her knowledge and wisdom and values to those of a troubled self-destructive friend.

We must hammer the moral deficiency in this reasoning into our children to make them morally stronger. Unless compelling reason and logic dictate a different result, children should be taught to trust their own moral reasoning and to confidently stand up to the gale forces of emotion and whim that are generated internally and externally.

Here is my rule: do what's right; worry about feelings later.

Most of us want to be liked, but that's not the end of the matter. We should have the moral and intellectual integrity to question why we are liked.

We may be liked for many virtuous reasons; generosity, high moral character, compassion, being able to make a chocolate soufflé.

But, let's face it, we might be liked for rather unflattering reasons, being gullible, pliable or weak. It's important to know which reasons apply and to judge that some reasons are better than others.

The most insidious part of wanting to be liked is that power is transferred from you to the person whose liking you desire. Questions arise. How much do you have to change, compromise, appease or distort in order to be liked? Will being liked last only until the next extortion payment is demanded?

The sooner children learn that what matters is being liked for the right reasons by the right people, the better. This understanding requires analysis, judgment and strength of character. Moral clarity counts for everything, and being liked or having someone become angry counts for very little.

The daughter could maintain her silence, of course, and hope that nothing bad happens to her friend, but, as a general proposition, hoping and second guessing are not successful life strategies. If the only thing you can hope for is hope itself, then you're going to be doing a lot of hoping and you will have about as much success as you would selling old 78 RPM records to the ten-year-old crowd. Hope is not a policy and wishing doesn't make things happen.

"Morality, like art, means drawing a line somewhere."

–OSCAR WILDE

LAYERS

"Virtuous activity is the basis for happiness."

–ARISTOTLE

Shrek said that ogres have layers. I'm in no position to argue with him. But I know this: 'good' has layers also. 'Good' is complex. It is difficult to achieve. It requires work. It requires skill. As we saw in the suicidal friend example, doing good required moral values and moral judgment. It required strength of character. It required empathy and compassion. It required intellect and wisdom. It required the actor to distinguish good from bad and right from wrong. As

Kelley, a fifth grader remarked, "It's a test of life. Not on paper, but it's a test."

'Good' is not a romantic status of innocence, like a Rousseau painting of lions and lambs and wolves and sheep smiling together in dark green foliage waiting for vegetarian dinners of tofu and soy burgers. It is not the natural inclination of the species in many instances and to the degree it is, that inclination must be realized through action if good is to be meaningful. Wanting to do 'good' and 'doing good' are as different as an ice cube and an iceberg.

Characterizing 'good' as something easily achieved or normal can create problems when trying to raise a moral child. Humanity is, by and large, frail and Paradise isn't very far from the Inferno. Teaching that 'good' flows as naturally as a gin clear trout stream fails to equip children for life's battles. That belief weakens children. It excludes or under emphasizes the requisite qualities of hard work, courage, introspection and commitment, among others, for doing 'good.' In the old 1960's lingo, that view is part of the problem, not part of the solution.

The question 'Why is there good?' is as important, Dennis Prager argues, if not more so, than the question 'Why is there evil?' The answer or answers to the first question give direction to teaching our children how to be good and how to motivate them to be good. Being good, then, reduces the 'bad' and the 'evil.'

Good and bad, right and wrong, are not always presented to us juxtaposed as pure black and gleaming white. There can the black and white, to be certain, but they are often infused with shades of gray, like a stunning Ansel Adams photograph. That's the moral challenge: figuring out the sharp contrasts and the nuances requires judgment and balancing and integrating competing interests.

The first time I taught the Al-and-Bill shoplifting story was in Erik's third grade class. After the class, as I gathered my briefcase and papers, Spencer approached me. "My head hurts," he said. I told him I was sorry to hear that and offered to accompany him to the nurse's office. "No," he exclaimed! "You don't understand. You make me think so much my head hurts." He wasn't complaining. He was proud. These are the comments that can prop up the spine.

We parents cannot risk outsourcing the meaning of good and bad; right and wrong to others, no matter how well intentioned. We must fight every day to do it ourselves. We may make mistakes, we may be 'wrong' some times, but we must continue to try. We may not have a monopoly on the moral authority to teach our children right from wrong but it's close to it.

I've discussed these stories in dozens of classes. If you talk about them with your child, you will also have the same dazzling rewarding experience I have had in every class. Use these stories and insights as starting points so that with love and patience you can hurt some heads.

Doing 'good' is the result of combining complex mental skills with an inclination toward virtue. A fan asked the great Fats Waller, the legendary pianist and composer, "Why jazz?" Fats answered, "Lady, if you've got to ask, you'll never know." Maybe so, but when our children ask us, "Why do good?" it would be preferable not to respond with a clever quip. We've got to give them persuasive answers that teach them what 'good' is, how to do it and why 'good' should be done.

CHAPTER 4

THE MORAL MEASURES

A FOUNDATION FOR
MORAL REASONING

"The world turns and the world changes, but one thing does not change.
In all of my years, however you disguise it, this thing does not change:
the perpetual struggle between good and evil."

—THE ROCK, T. S. ELIOT

I REMEMBER THE COMMENT VIVIDLY because, even at the age of ten, I sensed it was important. I had fallen off a wobbly chair on our porch and tumbled through the storm door window. After Doctor Zarchy stitched the deep gash in my wrist with a hook-like surgical needle that looked suitable for landing a trophy sailfish, he placed a hand on my narrow shoulder and said, "Whatever you do, always have a firm foundation."

That I recall the doctor's words a half century later shows adults do not forget even casual advice given to them as children. Decades later we all recall childhood insults and hurtful taunts with the intensity of a fresh wound. But we also remember, probably with greater clarity and certainly with greater joy, the words that helped us become stronger more capable people; the words of encouragement, affection and support that gave flight to our spirits like balloons breaking free from their strings.

I think of Doctor Zarchy's words not only when I notice the smooth white scar on my right wrist but also when talking to my children about the daunting and unavoidable process of growing up. For decades I have understood that his comment was about more than physical foundations. It was a metaphor for the art of living a confident and virtuous life.

Foundations are necessary for all kinds of things such as building sky scrapers, making persuasive arguments and creating ethical cultures. The most meaningful foundations, particularly when raising children, are not the chairs we stand on to change light bulbs or to look for hidden candy or the structural foundations of our homes and apartments but the foundations that form the moral architecture of our character and soul.

In this chapter I provide a foundation for moral reasoning. It is not made of brick and steel but of principles, rules and a collection of virtues.

MEASUREMENTS AND THEIR IMPORTANCE

One of the most common yet one of the most profound questions I am asked goes something like this: "If I think something is ethical, but someone else thinks it's not ethical, how do I know what's right?" The little folks that ask that question are earnest and serious. To honor their inquiry I am duty bound to give a comprehensive and serious answer.

What's right is determined by reason, logic, mastering the facts, analysis of the consequences of decisions and by evaluating whether moral principles are advanced or undermined. To the best of one's ability, morality, facts and consequences are measured. Even then, the journey toward an answer is not easy and often disagreement will not be eliminated.

If you want to have a lively chat with your children, ask how they know the speed of a car or the altitude of a flying airplane or whether they have a fever or how they know who is the fastest sprinter in the school?

Most children, even young ones, will know that a speedometer measures a car's speed; that an odometer measures how far a car has traveled; that an altimeter measures the altitude of an aircraft and that a thermometer measures body temperature. Many children will also know that a glucometer measures blood sugar and that a baseball player's batting efficiency is measured by a batting average. These facts can be known because they can be measured.

If you want to have conversations that are more thought-provoking and effervescent, ask why measurements are important?

I always ask these questions in my classes. In one brilliant phrase, Jamie, a fifth grader, expressed the essential value of measuring. "Measurements show if you need to do things differently."

"Wow!" I exulted. His answer was astute and profound, a Mickey Mantle home run blast into Yankee Stadium's centerfield upper deck (the original stadium, where I used to go).

Measurements indicate whether we need to change our behavior in order to get certain results. If you know you have a high temperature, then you can take medicine to lower it. If a tumor disappears, it may be appropriate to stop chemotherapy. If a driver knows he is speeding, he can reduce his speed a specific amount to return to the legal limit and reduce the likelihood of getting a ticket. A pilot seeing a plane coming at him at the same altitude might give serious thought to changing his elevation.

Measurements not only show if you need to do thing differently. They also show *what* you need to do differently. A sprinter that has to shave 1/100th of a second off her time to qualify for a track meet can develop a training regimen to increase leg power and improve starting technique. When the clotting time of my blood is tested, I know exactly how much more or less anticoagulants I must take to minimize the risk of a clot. A diabetic with high blood sugar will know how much insulin to inject to get a normal blood sugar level and may choose to reject a triple fudge brownie.

Measurements can also influence motivation. Ask your child how she would likely behave if she knew that she was almost good enough to be a starting forward on her soccer team or to be selected for the state marching band or if she needed one more A to make the honor roll? Her answer would probably be something like 'work harder' or 'practice more.'

Motivation is likely to increase when measurements show you are close to achieving your goal. I know that a blood clot can drop me deader than an anvil. Thus, other than around tax season, I'm highly motivated to adjust my anticoagulant dose to prevent clots. The baseball player with a .290 batting average is likely to be motivated to work harder to get the average over .300 and get paid an extra gazillion dollars.

Here's another important point about measurements: what you measure is what you get. If a company measures productivity, it is likely to become more productive. The sprinter that measures her speed is likely to improve her speed. A trucking company that wants to improve safety will monitor drivers' safety performance and traffic records. A diabetic will consistently have more normal blood sugar levels by measuring blood sugar levels.

Measurements enable us to make rational decisions about things in order to achieve our goals. Measurements provide information. Information influences choices. Improvement cannot occur without change and you cannot know how to change or how much to change without measurements.

You are more likely to get what you measure and you are less likely to get what you do not measure.

In summary, measurements do several things:

- Tell us if we need to change our behavior
- Tell us what behavior changes need to be made
- Motivate us to change our behavior
- Influence our attitudes and confidence and beliefs
- Provide us with a snapshot of the moment relating to our goals
- Create choices
- Keep us on track toward our goals

MEASURING 'GOOD'
Moral Reasoning

"Man, once surrendering his reason, has no remaining guard against absurdities the most monstrous, and like a ship without rudder, is the sport of every wind. With such persons, gullibility, which they call faith, takes the helm from the hand of reason and the mind becomes a wreck."

–THOMAS JEFFERSON

I wrote that measurements can cause us to change our behavior and enable us to know if we are approaching our goals. I wrote that measurements can motivate us to achieve our goals. Now I show how a special measurement device can instruct and motivate children to be more virtuous. My theory is that teaching children to measure 'good' will motivate them to do more 'good.'

In the previous chapter I discussed ways to judge whether or not something is good. We saw that children tend to figure out if something is good based on an alphabet soup of reasons, many of which illustrate the power parents have in influencing their children's values. "Your mom tells you that you were good." "You feel good." "You helped someone." "You did something right." "You get rewarded for what you did." "You do something and you're not ashamed of what you did." "I feel proud."

Some of these reasons—feelings, helping, rewards, fairness—may be useful for measuring good. Some may not be useful and some may not be consistently useful. Accuracy and consistency are important. The pilot with a fuel gauge that is accurate 80% of the time should not expect to reach retirement.

I am often asked, as Grace, a fifth grader, asked me in the spring of 2010, "If someone disagrees with me, how do I know what's right?" Her voice shook from the struggle to find answers to timeless questions. I answered, "How do you know what's right even if the person agrees with you?" She hadn't thought of that possibility.

I try to give guidance for answering these questions by introducing in this chapter a measurement tool or measurement structure called the Moral Measures. The Moral Measures are a collection of four ethical principles and seven virtues and skills. Collectively, these ethical principles and virtues and skills create a moral and reasoning foundation for measuring whether an act or an idea or a policy is moral or right or good. They are guidelines for sculpting reasoning, directing actions and measuring whether virtue and moral excellence have been achieved.

In Section II of this book I devote one chapter to each of the four ethical principles. In Section III I devote one chapter to each of the seven virtues and skills.

Of course, using these ethical principles, virtues and skills as measuring tools requires an understanding of what they mean, at least what they mean to most people. If a general acceptance of meaning is lacking, then we are measuring against a vacuum. If ethical principles, for example, are viewed as shapeless lumps of clay, then a handler can construct the meanings of the principles into whatever he wants. Morality then becomes no more than whim and caprice.

Such a condition reminds me of the old but stunning Bill Cosby routine about Noah and the ark, where God asks Noah to build an ark 80 cubits by 20 cubits or whatever. Noah asks God, "What's a cubit?" God isn't sure. "A cubit? Well, I used to know what a cubit is. Never mind that." God promptly moves on to other matters. But Cosby makes a powerful point: you can't build something if you don't know the units of measure. And, without measurements, you won't know if you built it correctly.

If a common understanding and agreement of the meaning of principles and virtues do not exist, then comparing actions and opinions in terms of good and bad and right and wrong cannot be done. Based upon my research and experience, I provide definitions and meanings for each of the listed principles, virtues and skills. A reader may disagree with my definitions or interpretations but there should be no ambiguity where I stand regarding them.

> *"Ethical axioms are found and tested*
> *not very differently from the axioms of science.*
> *Truth is what stands the test of experience."*
>
> –ALBERT EINSTEIN

A STRUCTURE FOR MORAL REASONING

You have to reason from a structure. Without a structure, you're left with the most flexible of all reasoning guidelines, 'Hey, whatever dude!' The Moral Measures present a structure for making moral evaluations and ascertaining moral accountability. They are, as far as I'm concerned, the controlling moral authority for determining what is good, right and just.

Business jargon uses the term 'metrics' as a measuring standard. In business, metrics tend to be very clear. Did sales increase or not? Did net operating income increase or not? Did employee productivity increase or not? Is the business losing money? 'Yes' or 'no' answers to these questions can be given with a high degree of confidence.

In sports we can tell whether one basketball player is a better foul shooter than another; in baseball whether one player is a better hitter than another. In military weaponry, we can tell whether one missile platform or one rifle model is more accurate than another. We can tell whether one jet configuration is faster than another and whether one material is more protective against bullets than another.

Much of life, however, does not lend itself to the precision of business or sports or military metrics. The reality is that there are only a few instances within our infinite human enterprises where the morality or ethics of an event or decision or policy or thought can be measured as precisely.

The Moral Measurers are not 'moral truths' or moral certainties. They don't give answers. They give guidance. The Moral Measures cannot provide definitive conclusions about some moral issues. Abortion, the death penalty and the use of torture, fetal stem cell research, the welfare state, as examples, elude immutable absolute conclusions and evaluations.

Reasoning in general, and moral reasoning, specifically, require thinking about the particular circumstances and the constituent factors presented in each situation. Each dilemma or predicament or challenge must be evaluated on a discrete individual basis. As my friend, Judge John Kane, wrote, "This process of individuation is at the heart of the moral reasoning function, just as justice demands it in a legal case."

Is it moral to try to save a drowning person? Maybe. A situation where a ten-year-old is contemplating saving a three-hundred pound drowning person is different factually and morally from one where a three hundred pound person contemplates saving a ten-year-old child.

Although the Moral Measures are a template for moral reasoning, we must keep in mind that moral reasoning acknowledges that there is no template that can be determinative of an outcome in a specific case. The Moral Measures, thus, permit us to consider issues in uniform terms although they do not predictably lead to uniform results.

THE MORAL MEASURES
PART I: The Four Ethical Principles

Part I of the Moral Measures has four ethical principles:

- Autonomy
- Beneficence
- Justice
- Sanctity of Life

By 'ethical principle' I mean a general law or fundamental truth that serves as the origin of values that guide how to behave in an ethical way. Within each principle are rules and duties and obligations to be followed to fulfill its requirements. For example, the principle of Autonomy requires that the integrity of the individual be respected. To fulfill that duty, rules such as "The Golden Rule" should be obeyed—do unto others as you would have others do unto you.

The principle of Sanctity of Life commands that life be respected. Thus, a moral duty exists to save lives through public policy such as seatbelt laws, not to commit murder and not to make pancakes with milk that has been in the refrigerator for more than seven months. The four ethical principles are the foundational laws that determine the morality of behavior and thought.

I selected these four ethical principles from the literature of biomedical ethics, relying heavily on the book, *Principles of Biomedical Ethics*, by Tom L. Beauchamp and James F. Childress. There are, admittedly, other principles of an ethical flavor floating around that I might have chosen. The Greeks, for example, had their four cardinal or principle virtues: prudence, temperance, courage and justice. I was persuaded to select the biomedical principles because of their logic, their depth and scope and because principles such as temperance and courage seemed better classified as virtues rather than as overarching ethical principles.

Application of the moral principles for judging and evaluating the ethical nature of things is accessible through the exercise of reason. That's why I emphasize 'moral reasoning' rather than trying to identify or to craft or to impose upon children rigid rules, lists of things that are right or wrong and vague bumper sticker platitudes.

I reject the simple binary notion of good and evil—that something is either all good or all evil. Nonsense. If only life were that simple! Good and evil, right and wrong, are often complex, layered and masked. That's why parents should teach morality in terms of reasoning anchored by moral principles and virtues.

Years ago, when I first began conceptualizing this section, I described the biomedical ethical principles and a few others as 'universal ethical principles,' as in honesty is a universally accepted value or that respect for life is an accepted universal principle. Mountains of literature on ethics are drenched with that 'universal' phrase. I now disagree with the notion of universality. I think I used that phrase initially out of a herd-like mentality which suppressed my independent thinking.

Certainly there are a few principles that are recognized universally—the principle that people are attracted to the strong horse comes to mind—but few, if any, are ethical principles. Many super bright writers on the topic assert that there are ethical or moral principles that are universally recognized, acknowledged and promoted. To support their claim they assert that the species is 'hardwired' to do good—everyone 'cares' about someone or something under some circumstances.

Respect for life, it is argued, is a universal ethical principle because everyone somewhere respects someone's life. Justice is a universal value, they say, because everyone believes in 'Justice' in some form or another. Maybe so. But I don't see it. Even if it were true, those 'facts' are not evidence of universal ethical values.

My meaning of universal ethical values is that a person values the principle not only for one's self but acknowledges and defends the application of those principles for others. If many people value 'Autonomy' for themselves and yet subvert it as applied to others then it's not a universal value. It's just a talking point. Everyone may value 'justice' but some notions of justice are unjust. Some notions of justice are unethical.

For whatever its worth, I conclude that universal ethical values do not exist in any meaningful sense. Individual freedom, individual liberty, equality of the sexes and for other groups of people, respect for life and the principles and rules that support them are not universally valued. Indeed, as my daughter, Annie, challenged when she was about nine years old, "There isn't even agreement on what is good!" Although a small point, it's a point worth making; something to argue over when the dessert is late.

I wish it were not the case, but it is and I am compelled to deal with the world as it is and not what I would like it to be. Not accepting the world as it is and striving to improve and elevate it are among the most compelling motivations for moral behavior. The moral and intellectual foundations for achieving those results are the unifying themes of the four ethical principles and of this book.

PART II: Sailing the Seven C'S

Part II of the Moral Measures is a selection of seven virtues and skills. The title for this second part came about spontaneously and improbably. I had been teaching at Cherry Hills Elementary School for about two years. Late one night, which often was the only time I had to attend to such matters, I was preparing for a class. Going over my notes, I noticed that several important words repeatedly mentioned began with the letter 'c,' such as character, courage, compassion and choices.

It hit me...boom! If I could find three more qualities or virtues that began with 'c,' then I would have seven (I always did well in math) and I could make a title for my teaching program that was a play on words, from the old maritime slogan of Sailing the Seven Seas to "Sailing the Seven C's." I concede that my idea fell short of Einstein's Theory of Relativity but at one in the morning it struck me as clever or about as close to clever as I'm likely to get. So, I selected three more qualities that began with 'c' and I was off sailing.

The 'Seven C's' are:

- Character
- Choices
- Compassion
- Competence
- Conscience
- Consequences
- Courage

I selected the 'c' words based their depth of meaning, ethical relevance and familiarity. Everyone makes choices. Everyone knows about consequences and everyone has some notion of a conscience. Other words that begin with 'c,' such as citizenship, cooperation, civility, commitment, courtesy, confidence and curiosity might have deserved a place in the line up and their own chapters but I shall save them for another day or for another book.

The Moral Measures supply a foundation for comparing the morality of choices and polices. They give guidance for justifying which policy or action or thought is morally preferable. I know of no system of thought that *can* provide absolute moral certainty for all things in all circumstances.

The Moral Measures can be used to make moral arguments for or against something but they will not lead to irrefutable conclusions. Except in rare instances, they will not say something is right or something is wrong. Sorry. That's just life. It's a big part of life, however, because if we teach children that there are moral absolutes that resolve all issues, we are likely to cripple them and, absent the ability to think for themselves, make them vulnerable to more aggressive and insidious forces.

The Moral Measures are not presented like fortune cookie phrases that offer rules that guarantee moral perfection. They do not eliminate the hard work of thinking. They do not displace judgment. You cannot take a moral challenge, cut and paste in a rule from the Moral Measures, make a decision and then go back to cleaning the garage brimming with confidence that you got it right.

Buzzwords and clichés are not useful in moral reasoning because they have no meaning at their core. They are weasel words. Lacking precision, it's like arguing with a puff of air. Some have written that we need chicken soup for the soul. I agree. It wouldn't hurt. But on behalf of our children and ourselves, we need more. We need tempered steel for the mind; something that can hold an edge; something we can count on. The Moral Measures provide that 'something,' that structure that we can count on to gauge the morality of our thoughts and actions and the morality of their consequences.

The Moral Measures can do for our children—and for us, too— what measurements can do generally: show us how far we are from the goal of moral behavior and guide and motivate us to do what is right. The Moral Measures can influence our attitudes, our confidence and our beliefs. Good intentions are nice, but there are only two morally relevant questions our children should be taught to ask, parrot-like, when they evaluate past and future actions: was good accomplished and is good likely to be accomplished? The Moral Measures will guide our children to the answers.

CHAPTER 5

ETHICS, MORALITY AND VALUES

"Not in the clamour of the crowded street,
Not in the shouts and plaudits of the throng,
But in ourselves, are triumph and defeat."

–HENRY WADSWORTH LONGFELLOW

WHAT'S IN A NAME?

THE WORDS 'MORAL' AND 'ETHICAL' AND 'VALUES' are tossed around as frequently and as confusingly as radio ads for credit card consolidation loans. I offer my definition of these words so the reader will know exactly what I'm trying to say. You may disagree with my reasoning but at least there will be clarity as to the disagreement. Then you can evaluate the disagreement.

'Ethics' is the philosophy and study of what is moral, right and good. Ethics guides us to what is moral based on ethical principles and ethical values. Ethics deals with honor, excellence, living a noble life and attaining happiness that results from virtuous activity. Ethics, as used in this book, is not a study of theory and nit picking abstractions.

Ethics is meaningful only to the degree that it inspires people to take action that leads to virtue and honor. The ethical person, thus, is a living conduit for virtuous behavior.

'Moral' means related or pertaining to what is good, right, proper and virtuous. It includes distinguishing between right and wrong. In his *Ethics*, Aristotle described moral behavior as action that combats evil. The words 'ethical' and 'moral' are often used interchangeably. Since I am not attempting to write an academic treatise on these topics but rather a useful guide for busy parents doing their best to raise moral children, I will also use 'ethics' and 'moral' interchangeably throughout this book.

Values, however, are a kettle of fish different from ethics and morality. Values are our personal preferences. They express what is meaningful to us. They determine what we are willing or not willing to do. Values can be moral, neutral or immoral. They span the spectrum from the greatest nobility of the soaring human spirit to the vilest sewage of the human condition.

To say that someone has values is not saying much. It is a morally neutral observation. Timothy McVeigh had values, as did Mother Theresa. Some students cheat and others don't. Some people work hard and some are slothful. Some people will help a person in need while others will not. Some societies suppress individual freedom and others do not. Some parents will make their child return stolen items to the store and others won't bother. Thus, we can draw obvious generalizations about values: all values are not moral and all values are not morally equal. A person that values all values without distinctions has no values.

The word 'tolerance' is a favorite example that distinguishes 'values' from 'ethics.' Tolerance is supposed to be a great value, a first-rate virtue that has catapulted the species out of the caves. We are told to tolerate differences, to be tolerant of different groups and classes. Every school I've been in has posters enthusiastically promoting tolerance as if it's the newest calorie-free sweetener.

Let's think about the meaning of tolerance and then determine whether it merits our respect. Tolerance means you tolerate something. You put up with it. You endure it. You don't fight against it. You exhibit only a reflexive non-judgmental acceptance. Not much greatness or virtue is displayed so far.

A rational person must conclude, then, that tolerance is morally neutral. One can tolerate the good as well as the bad. At worst, tolerance is the passivity of a disinterested uninvolved by-stander in the face of immoral behavior. Tolerance will then evolve ominously from indifference to aiding and abetting. You know the old phrase, "You're either part of the solution or you're part of the problem."

Some things should never be tolerated. Tolerance led to slavery and lynchings. Tolerance led to 9/11 and the better reasoned arguments hold that tolerance led to the Columbine High School slaughter. The train tracks to Auschwitz were built on the roadbed of tolerance. And as Auschwitz survivor, Eli Wiesel, points out, tolerance always favors the aggressor, never the victim.

Tolerance is a value but not necessarily an ethical one. Tolerance is so heavily promoted and so well received probably because it feels good—so sensitive and caring and respectful of differences—and because it avoids the hard work of moral judgment. The fact is, hardly anyone really believes in tolerance anyway, especially when it comes to tolerating the views of others that don't tolerate yours, although there are exceptions.

Tolerance, then, is a value but not an ethical one. Tolerance may or may not be ethical. Tolerance, by itself, advances nothing inherently virtuous or honorable or just. As with every action and thought addressed in this book, 'tolerance' must be measured through a moral prism. When tolerance is immoral, one is ethically obligated to be intolerant.

WHO'S VALUES, ANYWAY, HUH?

It is in the nature of our species to organize around some concept of ethical values. In his pithy book, *Being Good*, Simon Blackburn wrote "there is no living without standards of living." Without standards we are lost, unable to determine right from wrong, good from bad, friend from foe, success from destruction, the noble from the profane. Values are intimately related to a person's sense of self and are clear indicators of a person's moral character and integrity.

Although vital to our lives, in today's environment it is often treacherous to talk about ethics and values. Bring up the topic and people may look at you with knives in their eyes as if you were taking the last serving of chocolate mousse off the pastry cart. Questions are launched like cannon shot. "Where do you come off pontificating about what values are ethical?" "How dare you suggest my values aren't ethical!" "Who are you to say that one person's values are better than another's, you lawyer?" Ouch!

Most readers are probably asking those kinds of questions. They are fair and necessary. My straightforward answer is that the morality of values can be measured and compared. Whether judging an idea, an action or a culture, some values are demonstrably more moral than others. Measurement is made by applying the Moral Measures to an act or to an idea and then judging whether morality is advanced or subverted or unaffected.

Good and right and morality cannot be measured, of course, with the same precision as the speed of a jet or the size of an atom or the weight of a bowling ball. As mentioned earlier, measuring good and right and morality requires a combination of knowledge of ethical principles and virtues and moral reasoning skills.

Throughout this book I try to use logic and facts to make a case whether one thing is better than another. Also, I figure I have as much right to express an opinion on whether something is moral as those who say that I don't.

If the reader finds my thinking illogical or worse, then the reader might as well use this book to roast hotdogs or try to get his money back by selling it on Amazon.com because those are the core arguments of this book.

After my first class at Ebert Polaris in 2008, Emily approached me hesitantly and asked, "What if a culture believes in cannibalism. How can you say it's wrong?"

I replied, first, by saying her fine question would be answered by the discussions during the year. Then I explained how she might measure whether that behavior is good—does it promote Justice? Respect for Life, Autonomy and so forth.

"I might not like it," Emily continued, "but how can you say cannibalism is wrong?"

She spoke softly but with intensity as she grappled with a perplexing and profound issue. I respected her and owed this earnest young lady a thoughtful answer. I gave her an abbreviated one that would tide me over until I addressed the issue in subsequent classes.

"I say it's wrong," I replied, "because logic, reason, morality and consequences lead to the better reasoned conclusion that it is wrong. I say it is wrong because it violates ethical principles and I say it is wrong because it violates my ethical sense."

Emily winced.

That I say cannibalism is wrong doesn't stop someone from saying I'm wrong. I may be accused of violating their culture's values or practices or whatever. Well, so what? Their values violate mine. If you cannot say something is right or wrong because someone somewhere will disagree, then morality is reduced to whim, bias and opportunism. More to the point, you have empowered someone else to define your morality. Everything becomes morally acceptable because someone somewhere disagrees with you and no judgment is exercised. I reject this analysis.

Ultimately, I continued with Emily, I answered her fine question by posing these questions: What do you think is right and what do you think is wrong? What do you accept and what do you not accept? What is tolerable and what is intolerable?

Right and wrong are not matters of the wishy-washy disingenuous dodge, 'well I think it's wrong but you are entitled think whatever you want and both our opinions are morally equal.' It's a matter of what you stand for; how you see the world and what you are willing to defend.

There are those that accept slavery, pirates, honor killings, throwing gays off buildings and making folks from some groups sit in the back of buses. Okay, it's up to you. But each of us can and is obligated to make moral judgments about those beliefs and about the person holding those beliefs. Based on what I stand for, I say those things are wrong and I can support my opinion with logic, reason and moral principles better than the person disagreeing with me.

The fact that someone disagrees with you doesn't mean *you* are wrong. It doesn't mean the other person has a better argument or a more moral argument. The fact that someone disagrees with you means absolutely nothing morally, intellectually or factually other than someone disagrees with you.

When there is disagreement, those committed to moral reasoning will examine the arguments, the facts, investigate for additional facts and then make judgments based on reason, moral principles and consequences. You may still reject the other person's conclusion. That's the human condition. But rejection, in and of itself, is not a moral argument for anything.

"Woe to those who call evil good and good evil,
who put darkness for light and light for darkness"
(PROPHET HOSEA 4:6; 700 BCE)

FALSE MEASURES

I have written a chapter on each of the eleven Moral Measure principles and virtues. They show how each measurement is used to figure out whether something is or is not moral or good. Throughout this book I give examples of how other measurement devices are used to judge good or bad or right or wrong. Some of the measurement devices are imprecise or illogical. I call them 'false measures.' Since I don't devote chapters to them, it is useful to address a few of these false measures in this chapter.

FEELINGS . . . OH OH OH FEELINGS!

'Feelings' are at the top of the list of false measures. I wrote about feelings in a summary fashion in Chapter 2. Now I write about it in greater depth. I state clearly that feelings are often good and necessary. After my heart surgery, I endlessly played James Brown's classic, 'I Feel Good.' Feelings give intensity and confidence and motivation to decisions and actions. They can be a valuable indicator of right and wrong. However, as a guide to moral action, feelings are not always accurate or useful. Indeed, they may impede or sabotage moral action.

Here are classroom conversations on the use of feelings as a guide for figuring out if something is good or bad. These dialogues show how smart and thoughtful young children can be when asked serious questions.

Ask a child how she knows something is 'good' and she will likely give an answer such as "It feels good" or, as Maddie said, "You just know it in your heart."

After a few minutes of discussion, the several students chopped up Maddie's answer as if it were shoved into a Cuisinart.

"Some hearts are evil," Teresa blared, "and you shouldn't follow them."

"Wisdom is the key," Denis Prager argues, "not the heart." Wisdom's domain is the mind.

The heart is often intimately linked with feelings. Feelings are not a useful measure of virtue. Denise said, "A criminal feels good when he gets what he wants, but that's not good." Cara confided, "I feel good when I get something even when I don't deserve it." Stephen said, "A kid who cheats probably feels good when he gets a higher grade than someone who studied real hard."

Lynn asked astutely, "When are you talking about feeling good? Before you start, or during what you're doing or when it's all over, like if you get caught?" Feelings can be fluid and unreliable.

Cautiously, Gary elegantly summarized the issue: "Whether you feel good about something sorta depends on who you are." Gary brilliantly linked feelings to character and virtue.

HEAD OR HEART!

"If your head tells you one thing and your heart tells you another,
before you do anything, you should first decide whether
you have a better head or heart."

–MARILYN VOS SAVANT

One of my most compelling classes on the legitimacy of feelings as a meaningful guide to virtuous action is based on the incident when a friend got drunk at a party at my house and then wanted to drive home.

It became obvious that my friend was intoxicated. He walked out of my home, pulled his keys from his pocket and moved toward the parked cars. I stopped him outside and told him he shouldn't drive. I told him I'd give him a ride home. I told him he could stay at my house. He responded in a nasty way. I tried to grab the keys. He cursed me. He pushed me. He insisted that he was fine.

I was shaken. I was embarrassed. I felt terrible. I admit I had doubts about the propriety of my intervention. I even began making calculations with the devil: How far does he have to drive? Were the roads mostly straight? How many cars were likely on the road?

How many drunk drivers don't get into crashes?

It is easier to have a wishbone than a backbone. I made up my mind that he was not going to drive. I forced the keys from his hand and persuaded another friend to drive him home. I was angry and unsettled momentarily. I felt miserable but I was right.

During a class at least one student will point out, "Your friend will now be angry with you!" Another student will always retort, such as Katie, her face hardened like a stone gargoyle, "So what if he's angry!"

Anger can be controlling. Anger can be intimidating. Anger can be used as a weapon. But whatever it can be, it is not a useful indicator of morality. Aristotle wrote in his *Nicomachean Ethics*: "Anyone can become angry—that is easy. But to be angry with the right person, to the right degree, at the right time, for the right purpose, and in the right way, that is not easy."

It is a regrettable human tendency that people feel and think that they did something wrong because someone is angry at them. "What did I do wrong?" "Why do they hate me?" "How can I change so he won't be angry any more?" I've learned to get over it and I have tried unrelentingly to teach my children to toughen up against the anger—real or imagined—of others.

I have revisited the situation with my friend several times and have come to think of it this way: I may have saved my friend's life. I may have saved the lives of or avoided injuries to unknown innocents. How much legitimacy and attention and significance should I give to the person that directs such anger at me for those reasons? Not much, I have disciplined myself to conclude.

The only person that deserves to be angry is the one whose child or mom or whomever had been killed or maimed because I didn't have the fortitude and will to prevent a drunk friend from driving.

Who needs the brain damage from that kind of friend? Recall the comment about cognitive altruism in Chapter 3. Why abandon your morality and adopt someone else's just to avoid a bad feeling?

Standing up to someone who wants to drive while drunk or

who wants to hurt another person are not indicators that there's something wrong with you. It means something's wrong with the other person. Only a deeply morally confused person would think there is something wrong with himself when he stands up to people who want to or who are willing to risk hurting others.

This example illustrates what I mean when I argue that good parents have to make their children stronger. Our children should be strengthened to stand up to and to triumph over these emotionally alluring but morally bankrupt feelings. Burning away this moral fog through clarifying dialogues will make your child morally confident and competent.

By the way, the children always ask if I ever made up with that friend. We did, but not by openly addressing the event. We ignored it. Months passed, someone called the other—I don't remember who called first—and we went on as before, like snow evaporating without leaving a puddle.

An important point to understand is that the kinds of questions you ask—how you frame them, what assumptions you make— opens the window to your view of the world. Your questions illuminate your moral acuity.

Here's an example of how phrasing a question illustrates a moral view. Assume a mother catches her child stealing from a clothing store. The mother asks, "Don't you realize you can get into trouble for stealing?" This view is morally quite different from that of the parent that asks, "Don't you realize you are hurting other people and undermining your own character?"

WHAT KIND OF FRIEND AM I?

Emotionally powerful and intellectually profound conversations will result when you ask your child what kind of friend he wants to be. Better yet, ask your child which kind of friend he would rather have? Would your child prefer the friend that stood up to him and saved his life and kept him out of jail or out of a cemetery or would your child prefer the friend that didn't have the moral strength to stand up to him but who would visit his grave, mutter 'I should have been stronger' and maybe place flowers by the headstone every now and then?

Get your child to commit to an answer, presumably to the first option. Moral commitments make people stronger.

Let's not hold our punches: these are tough, unpleasant questions. They are, however, the kinds of questions that can make your child morally stronger, for there is no more effective way to make children stronger than to teach them to distinguish right from wrong and to develop their character so they will act on what they know is right.

More than chicken soup for the soul, such conversations can supply iron and steel for your child's moral will. If emotion and feelings are substituted for thought and analysis, the risk of descending into superficiality and appeasement increases. That can be dangerous. As people mature, they understand, or should understand, that feelings have to be constrained by reason and moral courage.

Not to get too nuanced about all of this, but the failure to grasp these lessons is to learn how to die and, perhaps, also how to allow others to die. I share a haunting exchange with Kevin, a third grader, about feelings and doing right. A couple of children at Cherry Hills Village Elementary School found it amusing to throw rocks at a bull snake that lived unobtrusively and harmlessly in the bushes by the playground. Kevin told the kids to stop hurting the snake. "They made fun of me," he lamented. "I felt bad but I knew I was right."

The little fellow then asked: "Why is it so hard to do what's right?"

I had no answer for him. I have no answer now. That the question was asked by a third grader shows how profoundly your little children can think.

COCKROACHES IN THE BATHTUB

On the radio I learned of this conversation between a father and his son. The son had committed a grievous crime. He tried to apologize to the father for the pain he caused his family. The father said,

"Never apologize for something you truly believe." I yelled at the radio, one of my favorite targets of conversation, "Are you kidding me or what?"

Phrases like 'I deeply believe' or 'I sincerely believe' or 'I truly believe' are strutted around like peacocks in full plumage. The intent of the speaker is to add moral force and intensity to his opinion. It's supposed to indicate how seriously the speaker believes something. Maybe. Fred Stocking, my extraordinary English professor at Williams College, made a memorable comment regarding sincerity. "What is sincere? A cockroach trying to get out of a flooding bathtub is sincere."

If you don't bother to think this through, the "I deeply believe" rhetoric seems more forceful than the "I believe" phrase. If you do think about the phrases, you will note how the deeply-truly-sincerely rhetoric actually reduces the power of the speaker. The 'deeply believe' add-on implies the person's other beliefs are relatively less meaningful or less significant. I don't want anyone thinking that way about my opinions and beliefs.

Lawyers, perhaps more than any other profession, understand the importance of sincerity. The appearance of sincerity is vital for effective persuasion. Thus, the observation: "Sincerity is the most critical factor in persuading the jury. Once you learn to fake it, you can get away with almost anything."

If you believe in something, fine. Make your case and see how it stacks up against competing views. Often, however, these loaded phrases are used as a substitute for morally persuasive arguments. Sincerely or truly or deeply or absolutely believing something are not valid measures of the morality of that something. An immoral belief or an irrational belief or a stupid belief does not become moral or rational or intelligent because it is deeply or sincerely or truly believed.

POPULAR! YOU'RE GONNA BE POPULAR!

The lyrics of the song 'Popular' from the musical *Wicked* are tantalizing in their advocating the virtues of popularity. However, no matter how loftily extolled, popularity is not a valid measure of morality. Morality is not a numbers game. It is not a popularity contest. This is a difficult lesson to teach. A flawed argument or an immoral argument is not repaired or does not become moral because lots of people believe it. That a lot of people do something or believe something is not an indicator of its morality.

As a general rule, we want to be liked. We want to be well-received. We don't want to be rejected. That's human nature. If lots of people disagree with you about something, you might ask yourself, "Gee, look at that! A million people disagree with me. I wonder why?" You should have the humility and moral and intellectual integrity, of course, to evaluate opposing arguments and opinions to see if your opinions should be reassessed.

If justified, you should make adjustments to your arguments and beliefs. This is how you test the timbre of your beliefs and develop opinions of greater moral integrity. But the only thing that matters is whether you are right or whether you are wrong; whether your position is more morally persuasive than an opposing position. Whether one person disagrees with you or whether one hundred million people disagree with you is absolutely irrelevant to the morality of an argument or action.

I hope to inspire my children to be among the best rather than to gain popularity by joining the indifferent, the lost and the bad. Maintaining a belief because it is popular is the moral equivalent of 'Have a nice day!' It's not a valid measure of moral content. Sometimes you have to look a person in the eye—a child, a friend, even the world—and in a measured voice say, "I don't give a darn what you think of me."

INCONSISTENCY

During their rampage at Columbine High School, one of the murderers, Harris or Klebold, shoved a pistol in the face of a terrified student—maybe more than one student—and demanded to know where the blacks and the athletes were. If your child is old enough to handle this topic, ask whether it would have been moral for the threatened student to lie if the student knew the whereabouts of the blacks or the athletes.

The moral conflict is obvious: telling the truth makes it easier for the murderers to find more victims but it might increase the chance of saving one's own life. (This added chance may, of course, be trivial. The students were killed for no reason other than existing.)

Would it have been moral to lie? Here's my answer, which I state with total confidence: I don't know.

The arguments for and against lying are equally compelling. They present a moral dilemma, a concept I discuss in the next chapter. What I do know is that in these obscenely horrible circumstances, there is no practical answer. No useful guide for behavior exists.

That there is no 'answer' does not logically or morally lead to the conclusion that there is no morality or that all morality is relative. Such conclusions are hogwash. It is irrational to take the most extreme acts of people or the most contentious issues of a culture— abortion, embryonic stem cell research, the death penalty, to name a few—and then conclude that morality and moral rules do not exist because there are no absolute answers to these moral conflicts.

As we progress through the chapters on the Moral Measures, we will see how moral arguments can support opposite conclusions. This means that moral people can disagree.

It is critical to understand, particularly regarding the purpose of this book, that the fact that we can't agree on what is moral in every instance does not mean that we cannot agree on what is moral in the overwhelming number of instances, particularly in those matters that pertain to raising moral children. To argue that there is no right and wrong because we cannot definitively know or agree upon the morality of every human endeavor is a symptom of a deeply flawed human being.

NOT SO TRICKY

To gauge how I'm doing in class, from time to time I ask if the students understand what I talking about. I ask if the concepts are too difficult. Itamer, a fifth grader, replied: "It's not difficult. It's tricky at first but then you get it." How can I know if the children are absorbing my words? Mrs. Maria Abeyta, one of the marvelous teachers at the Ebert Polaris, told me: "You know they are learning based on the kinds of questions they ask."

Sometimes, I confess, I wonder if my words have no more impact than white noise. Then a student might make an uplifting comment such as one made by Matt, a second grader. Selecting his words as if they were flecks of gold in the bottom of the pan, he said, "The class is good because I want to know whether I can be proud of what I decide."

Then I know I have reached some of the students. Similarly, you will reach your children.

The foundation of the Moral Measures serves as a prism to see the different elements of moral analysis. It's not the *only* prism, but it a useful one. Without a prism, information and challenges and decisions tend to become chaotic. If we are inclined to believe that there is some purpose in life, that life has value, then we must logically conclude that there must be a concept of 'quality of life' which has to do with excellence, honor, virtue and achievement. If we accept such a concept, then it follows logically that this quality of life can be measured in terms of realizing or achieving those purposes and values.

The Moral Measures enable us to determine whether someone is a good person. A good person is one that does measurable good; that the world is measurably better because of the actions of that person. It's not a matter of wishing to do good, hoping to do good, intending to do good or feeling that one is good. The test is quantifying whether good has been done.

Parents cannot banish fear and uncertainty and insecurity from their children's lives. We cannot slay the dragons in their lives. Our task is to teach our children to successfully address fear and uncertainty and insecurity; teach them to slay the dragons and not merely wish they would go away. It would be a dereliction of our parental duty to pretend that these negative factors do not exist and to avoid nurturing those enduring characteristics that will strengthen our children.

The Moral Measures can increase a child's faith and confidence in its reasoning and capacity for moral rectitude. The absence of these qualities can lead to crippling self doubt, easy but wrong solutions and immoral obedience.

CHAPTER 6

"Be cynical or you'll never learn anything."

—FRED SCHUMAN, POLITICAL SCIENCE PROFESSOR, WILLIAMS COLLEGE

IN 'I WONDER' LAND

AS A MATTER OF FACT!

ONE OF THE MOST COMMON QUESTIONS asked in every class is also one of the most profound: How do I know what's right?

A fundamental duty of parenting is teaching one's children to distinguish between right and wrong. Knowing right from wrong requires moral reasoning and the ability to analyze information. This chapter focuses on gathering and evaluating information.

We need information to survive. The charging bull that doesn't know there's a sword under the red cape will likely have an unpleasant afternoon. We must know the facts that are relevant to whatever we are doing. Most parents would want to know if their children's food is healthful, if the baby sitter is a child molester, whether the person at the front door intends to deliver flowers or to commit robbery and whether their child is growing to be a decent honorable person.

Parents want to know facts. They also want to know what facts mean, that is, they want to know how to interpret facts. Your child is not happy in school. Why not? Your child is an excellent student. How can you encourage her to continue that way? What can you do to protect your child from bullies on the school bus? Is a parent fair? Reasonable? Accessible? All these concerns involve establishing and interpreting facts.

Facts do not interpret themselves. Their values and relevance are determined in a context. You read that drug use in your child's school has doubled. Terrible! Is that an increase from three hundred to six hundred students or an increase from one student to two?

Isolated facts provide no basis for meaningful interpretation just as individual music notes have no beat or melody. Facts without values and context are like lobsters jogging away from their shells.

Morality is determined by applying moral reasoning to the truth in its context. Thus, we must be informed of facts and context. To assess right and wrong, we must learn the facts, not merely as a tactical life skill but as a moral duty.

In this and the next chapter I offer two skills that show how to gather and interpret facts and how to judge the morality of opinions.

Unlike my unending junk mail, moral reasoning and judgment do not blossom spontaneously. They are the result of skilled and disciplined thinking. Ask your child if it is 'good' to jump into a swimming pool to try to save a drowning person. After a few moments of discussion, your child will likely say, it depends on who is drowning and who is doing the rescuing—it is probably not good for a young child to try to rescue a flailing powerful adult.

HELP! YOU KNOW I NEED SOMEBODY! . . . MAYBE!

An effective method to teach moral reasoning is to discuss the moral components of familiar situations. I share parts of a conversation I had in Elise's second grade class about a somewhat frequent event, a person that seemed to have a flat tire on his car.

This is the question I presented to the class:

Is it moral to stop to help a motorist that appears to be changing a flat tire on the side of the road?

This discussion enhances moral reasoning and develops empathy. The children identify with the predicament of others—placing them in the others' shoes, as the saying goes. Their desire to be helped creates empathy that may motivate them to help another in a similar predicament.

Pose the question to your child regarding helping the motorist and answers will bubble forth. A typical response will be, "Yeah, sure, it's good to help people." Keep talking and you will excavate layer upon layer of thought.

As a general rule, it *is* good to help people but don't jump to conclusions. This is a reasoning skill, not a mechanism to pick out an answer and then triumphantly march off to lunch. Let's say you have a seven-year-old child and she said it was good to help the motorist. Assume that you are driving your car with your child late at night and that, for whatever reason—a disability perhaps—you cannot get out of the car but your child can.

Ask if she thinks she should help. She might bite her lower lip and say something like "I'm not sure," or "Sometimes." Those tentative responses indicate the beginning of moral reasoning.

We need information because the question provides few facts. I came up with what I thought was, to be honest, a creative method to guide the children to answer the question. I developed a bunch of different fact situations for them to consider. I created four categories of descriptions: the driver, the person on the side of the road, the location where the person was stopped and the time of day. I gave each child a piece of paper that had one description written on it.

I asked each 'driver' if it would be smart to stop to assist if confronted with each of the other descriptions. The driver might have been an eighty-year-old man using an oxygen tank or a karate champion or an armed police officer. The person on the side of the road could have been an elderly woman, a young man, even a group of young men drenched in tattoos and piercings.

The location could have been the middle of Denver's main north-south highway, Interstate 25, or a narrow dirt road in a remote area of the state. The time of day could have been mid-day or two in the morning. You get the idea. Dozens of combinations of driver/tire-changer/locations/times were possible.

TO STOP OR NOT TO STOP?
THAT IS THE QUESTION.

What would the students do in each circumstance? Ask your child when it would be reasonable or 'good' to assist and it would not. Your child will quickly realize that assisting under different circumstances poses different risks to the driver. Different risks create choices that are morally different.

The armed police officer stopping to assist an elderly woman in the middle of the day at a shopping mall is morally *different from* an elderly lady pondering whether to assist a bunch of young men on a remote road in the middle of the night with 'born to die' phrases stitched on the backs of their jackets.

Opinions will change as facts change as if they were bounced around inside a pinball machine.

Some students expressed the concern that the person on the side of the road might not *really* be changing a flat tire but rather might be trying to ensnare and inflict harm on those Good Samaritans that stopped to help. That possibility is real, of course.

Stopping to assist has risks. I challenged the students find a solution where the driver could be moral—offer assistance—and also be safe.

As the neurons begin to spark like an engine turning over, your child will suggest alternatives to stopping to help. The driver could use a cell phone, if available, to call for assistance but not physically leave his car. Certainly the driver could stop at a gas station or other business and call for help, even if he had to travel a few miles. We could identify moral options that had no risk of harm to the driver.

Ratcheting up moral reasoning skills enables the students to feel and to be more capable and competent. Liz, a fifth grader, said eloquently: "Knowing the facts is like a scale that helps you figure out the best decision."

Is it moral to stop to help a motorist on the side of the road? In the words of movie mogul Sam Goldwyn, "It's a definite maybe."

We can say, as a general rule, that it is good to help a person with a flat tire. The students learned, additionally, that the general rule should be qualified by circumstances. It is not wise or moral to place yourself in unreasonable jeopardy, a topic that will be discussed in greater detail throughout the book.

For several reasons I vividly remember that class. I thought I had developed a creative teaching method. The students were engaged. Most significantly, the school psychologist, who had attended the class, made a memorable statement afterwards. She said, "I had no idea these young children could think so deeply."

I was perplexed. She should have known the capabilities of these youngsters. I had been volunteering for less than a year and I did. I had already learned not to underestimate them.

WHAT IS THE RIGHT THING TO DO?
A Thinking Skill Helps Resolve a Moral Dilemma

*"A point of view can be
a dangerous luxury when substituted for
insight and understanding."*

–MARSHALL MCLUHAN

Every day numerous choices among competing values, preferences and alternatives confront us like an artillery barrage. Some choices are, in the greater scheme of things, somewhat trivial—have a donut or ice cream—and some are significant and can be anguishing—get a divorce, change employment, sell one's home because of debt, fight a war, represent a client you despise. You know what I mean.

The larger issue in the 'stop to help someone on the side of the road' discussion is the conflict between protecting one's self and helping someone. In the context of moral reasoning, this conflict falls into the larger category of moral dilemmas. Not all dilemmas are moral dilemmas. The decision to turn in a wallet full of cash that you found may pose a dilemma but not a moral one. There is no moral basis for keeping the wallet.

Recall the dilemma I faced with the drunken friend who wanted to drive. My dilemma dealt with a moral issue: whether to let an intoxicated friend drive. But the dilemma, although awkward and uncomfortable, was a not a moral dilemma because no competing moral principle justified *allowing* the friend to drive. I was not forced to choose between two conflicting moral principles but between right and wrong.

The essence of a moral dilemma is that competing moral principles morally justify different and sometimes opposite actions. Do you go into a burning house to try to rescue someone? Do you donate a kidney?

Abortion is an issue that lucidly illustrates the nature of a moral dilemma. Much of the justification for abortion is based on the ethical principle, Autonomy, (Chapter 9) which supports the claim that a woman has the moral right to control her body. The justification for opposing abortion is based, in large part, on the ethical principle Sanctity of Life (Chapter 12) which holds that life, including the life of the fetus, must be respected and preserved.

Although beliefs about abortion differ and lead to dramatically contrary actions, both pro and anti arguments resort to ethical principles to support their positions. The death penalty, human cloning, torture, fetal stem cell research and so forth, similarly, can be favored or rejected based on competing ethical principles.

Which belief or opinion you personally adopt will be based on those ethical principles you consider most persuasive, the facts that you find most significant and the consequences you consider most consistent with the ethics of your world view.

Aristotle wrote that there is no book of rules that describes what is and is not moral under all circumstances. Certainly, "Thou shalt not steal" does not apply to running bases in baseball.

Moral reasoning requires more than simply highlighting, clicking, dragging and dropping one moral analysis into a different situation. It would be irresponsible to teach a child such simplistic thinking. "Always do this or that…" could lead to tragic consequences. As I showed with the flat tire example, moral reasoning requires analytical skill within a moral framework.

This book is about moral reasoning yet it must be emphasized that is about moral reasoning in a current political context. Putting in the best light our species' tendency to disagree about almost everything, there is great virtue in committing to resolve morally-based differences by appealing to moral reasoning and persuasion and ballots rather than to emotion, whim, resentment and machine guns.

"Facts are stubborn things; and whatever may be our wishes,
our inclinations, or the dictates of our passion,
they cannot alter the state of facts and evidence."

–JOHN ADAMS, *US DIPLOMAT & POLITICIAN* (1735-1826)

We know morality is determined by applying moral principles through reasoning to the truth in each context. Thus, as with the drowning person and man-on-the-side-of-the-road examples, we must know the facts in order to know the truth of the situation. Only then can we reasonably reach a conclusion about solving a moral dilemma.

Mastering the facts is not a matter of amusement or abstract speculation. It can be a matter of life and death. Successful lawyers master the facts that undermine their case as well as those that support it. They will try to spin the adverse facts and argue they are not really facts, but they prepare by plugging adverse facts into their analysis.

A prepared thinker is mindful of Aldous Huxley's observation that facts don't cease to exist because they are ignored. The lawyer that is indifferent to unfavorable facts is more likely, after a trial, to get a lukewarm pat on the back from an opponent than a check. The check is better.

"It is intellectually necessary to be honest not only about
what we do know but about what we do not know.
This is not humility for the sake of religious ritual,
but necessary for the pursuit of truth, knowledge and meaning."

–DAVID E. PURPEL, *THE MORAL AND SPIRITUAL CRISIS IN EDUCATION*

I introduce the first of two thinking skills. This one teaches the importance of acquiring information in order to reach a morally and intellectually valid conclusion. The underlying theory of this skill is that we must constantly search for additional information to see if the integrity of our opinions can be sustained or if they should be modified. This skill was used in the 'stop to assist the motorist' example. Now I highlight it and use it to analyze a more complicated moral dilemma.

THINKING SKILL #1

- What do you know?

- What do you need to know?

Just as we have a moral duty to act wisely in circumstances as we know them, we have a moral duty to become informed about those circumstances. Ignorance, especially when self-imposed, can be unethical.

When discussing issues with your child, you should keep in the forefront of your mind the facts relied upon to form your opinions. Simultaneously, you should also inquire whether additional facts should be learned. Additional facts may cause you to have greater faith in your opinion or they may cause you to qualify or change your opinion.

Dialogues about moral dilemmas are effective teaching tools. They place a premium on factual analysis, test the application of abstract moral principles in fact-specific contexts and require an evaluation of the probable consequences of the dilemma's solution. Discussing moral dilemmas sharpens your child's thinking.

I share class discussions of an intriguing moral dilemma thought up, I believe, by Lawrence Kohlberg, the preeminent Harvard University professor, author and researcher in the field of the moral development of children. The dilemma drips with emotional appeals that tend to evoke reflexive shallow answers yet, for those inclined, it invites a methodical dispassionate factual analysis. I hope my students' focused and complex thinking will serve as guidelines that inspire discussions with your children.

Is it moral for a parent to steal money to buy medicine to save its dying child?

I present this moral dilemma now because I want to introduce the reasoning skill early in the book. To help move your discussions into high gear, I point out that Kohlberg's dilemma is based on the conflict between two ethical principles, Justice (Chapter 11) and Sanctity of Life (Chapter 12). An in depth understanding of the ethical principles is not necessary to master this dilemma.

I routinely present this dilemma within the first few weeks of the year to acquaint the students with the concept of a moral dilemma and to teach the reasoning technique.

As soon as I state the dilemma, children sing out, "Of course it's okay to steal to save a life!" "A child's life is worth more than money!" "You can get the money back but you can't get back the lost life!" "It's not fair that a child should die just because the parent doesn't have the money to buy medicine." A few will assert that stealing is always wrong.

The class seemed pleased. Evidently the dilemma had been satisfactorily solved by a majority. I teased them about their quick answers. "Thousands of hours have been devoted to this dilemma and you little geniuses figured it out in forty-seven seconds!"

"We're very smart," Nicki said solemnly.

Not so fast! Their answers were fine as far as they went, but they didn't go very far. At this point I usually quote the legendary acid-tongued journalist commentator H. L. Mencken: "There's always an easy solution to every human problem—neat, plausible and wrong."

Let's see how we can squeeze all the instructive value out of this dilemma. We'll start with what do we know? Not much.

- A child is dying
- It seems medicine exists that can save the child's life
- It seems the parent cannot afford the medicine
- The parent is considering stealing money to buy the medicine

That was the easy part. What facts would you want to know in order to figure out whether it is moral to steal? Sometimes a student will respond, "I don't know." When a child—indeed, any person—says "I don't know," it means that she has decided to stop thinking. I discourage that behavior.

"You do know," I always reply. I said that to one student and added, "Think now. You can take a nap when you get home!"

"I can't. I have a piano lesson."

"You win!" I sighed.

I ask 'what if?' questions to get their neurons firing. "What if the parent had wealthy relatives?" "What if the parent had a bonus check arriving in five days?" "What if the parent had an available line of credit at a bank?" We don't know the answers to those questions. They matter because as facts change, morality changes.

Here are just a few unknowns the students thought important:

- Did the parent have any money?
- Could the parent sell something rather than steal?
- Did the parent try to get a loan?
- Did the parent go to a clinic to try to get free medicine?
- For how long did the parent know the child needed medicine?
- Did the parent know the child was dying but spent money on other things like a new car or a vacation?
- Did the parents smoke or take drugs?
- Could the parent have been saving money for the medicine but didn't bother?

You can see that some of these questions reflect a high level of thinking. You and your child may think of other facts that would influence your analysis. Answers to these questions would determine the morality of the parent's decision to steal.

Timmy observed that: "It's easier to steal than to work to get the money." All agreed. The students raised questions about the parent's values. Would he steal before trying to borrow the money or getting another job or selling something? Additional facts they wanted to know were drizzled into the discussion like butter when making Béarnaise sauce.

When Julie asked how much money was stolen, a blistering volley of arguments resulted like Roger Federer battling Rafael Nadal at Wimbledon.

"What difference does the amount make?" Alexa snapped like a whip. "It's still wrong."

"Stealing a little money is wrong but it's not as wrong as stealing a lot of money," Julie retorted. "It's kinda wrong!"

"Whaddya mean, 'kinda?'" I challenged. "Take a stand! A mind is *not* a terrible thing to make up!" I went on, "So, it's wrong to steal a lot, but it's not really wrong to steal a little, but it might be okay to steal a little less than a lot, but if you steal a lot more than a little, that would be wrong?"

"Yes!" Julie said.

There you have it! From the mouths of babes.

Cautiously, as if moving a crystal vase towards the edge of a table, a student suggested that it was okay to steal from rich people. That assertion provoked a tsunami of rejection. "Something wrong doesn't become right just because someone has more money than you." "They need the money, too!" "It's still not yours to take!" "So, if someone is rich then you don't have to be moral with him? That's dumb!" "The rich person might have his own problems! You don't know."

The argument that it was okay to steal from someone rich, whatever 'rich' means, is disturbingly received with increased approval. However, thus far, in my classes, the argument tends to be left flopping like a fish on a dock.

Maddie's voice then softly wafted through the air: "It kind of depends on what 'dying' means." Her brilliant insight had the power of a blade of grass breaking through the sidewalk. She struck the mother lode! I was jubilant!

The meaning of 'dying' is the singularly most important fact of the entire exercise. Maddie figured it out. What does 'dying' mean? "We don't know how sick the child is," Maddie clarified. "You can be dying for a long time!"

Other students immediately grasped the significance of Maddie's inquiry. They became energized and asked pointed questions. "Was the child dying for a long while before the parent considered stealing money?" "How long will it take for the child to die? An hour? Five years?" Maddie had elevated the thinking level of the entire class. It was a rewarding moment.

Maddie followed up with another astute question: "How much dying does he have to be doing before the stealing is okay?" This is the kind of question that would have made Professor Schuman proud. Be cynical; avoid easy answers and always ask the tough questions. Remember, we are not looking for answers. We want to elevate moral reasoning.

The lesson here is that facts are more than different flavors of toothpaste. All facts are not equal. Facts have or can have moral weight. Some facts have more moral weight than others. Expecting death in two years is morally different from expecting death in two days. It's just plain different. The moral significance of the different facts influences the moral assessment of the act of stealing.

The critical point is that the details of the 'dying' might have created options for behavior that would have made unnecessary the immoral act of stealing. "You can get a job or borrow the money if you have some time!' Rachel observed. 'Different times give different choices," Kasha added astutely.

Morality is data intensive. Thus, children should be taught to value the fact-searching process. Is it moral for a parent to steal money to buy medicine save its dying child? It depends on the facts Once we know the facts, we can apply logic and moral reasoning to craft an answer that is most persuasive and ethical under the circumstances.

Please keep in mind that these comments were made by nine and ten and eleven-year old children. You can do for your children what Maddie did for her class—elevate their thinking simply by talking to them.

Some actions have greater moral weight than others. Standing up to a racist or a bully has greater moral value than recycling aluminum cans.

But here's the main point I unceasingly try to convey. We can quibble at the margins about the morality of stealing money to save a child's life—did the parent try every reasonable and even unreasonable option? Go to a bookie? Try to sell his blood? Beg at a highway intersection?

Honorable people can differ at the margins whether an act is moral or not, but the core issue must not be in dispute: stealing is wrong. We can argue at the margins but we should teach our children to staunchly fight to protect the core values.

Yes, we can yammer away about a hypothetical situation that, thankfully, is not likely to occur in this country. In a unique imminent emergency, I can accept that it might be moral to steal money to save a dying child. In all other situations, stealing is wrong.

We shouldn't get caught up in the theoretical and be dismissive of the real. A lot of improbable facts would have to exist before it would be moral to steal for this purpose. However, the dilemma is drenched in value because thinking it through encourages children to value facts and truth over emotion, reflexive simple solutions or rigid ideology.

The truth may be puzzling. It may take some work to grapple with.
It may be counterintuitive. It may contradict deeply held prejudices.
It may not be consonant with what we desperately want to be true.
But our preferences do not determine what's true.

–CARL SAGAN

SMOKE AND FIRE
A MORAL DUTY TO INQUIRE

Tragedy can be an effective teacher. A tragedy that occurred in the Denver area about ten years ago led to discussions infused with anger and sharp moral judgments. A fire, I think caused by the cigarette of a mother who fell asleep, destroyed her home and killed her two small children. She escaped. The home had no smoke detectors. The mom allegedly stated afterwards that she could not afford them. Apologists excused the mom's failure to get smoke detectors because she was 'poor.'

The apologists' comments evoked scathing community responses. The Boy Scouts of America, the United Way, the local fire departments and other organizations declared that they offered free detectors to anyone who asked for them. The mom should have gotten that information. She had a duty to inquire. She didn't fulfill her duty. If she had, her children likely would have survived. Information matters.

Knowledge creates awareness, and awareness triggers the moral duty to act. Thus, there can be a powerful incentive to be ignorant because ignorance can insulate from the responsibility to act. Human nature being what it is, it's more acceptable to present one's self as ignorant rather than admit to being fully informed and having done nothing.

We cannot protect our children from all harm. We must teach them how to know things on their own. Not knowing can be lethal. Not wanting to know is morally indefensible.

TALK TO ME!

These dialogues inspire and animate young children. They relish tough debate. They love to argue. They want to know why people agree or disagree with them. Katie said enthusiastically, "We exchange ideas and see things differently." "This teaches us how to think outside the box," Carlson said.

Dani described the process in a stunningly poetic way: "You give us ideas and we make attachments to them. It's like a train." She paused and pondered her words. "No, it's like a chain. The topic is the charm, and the ideas are like links in the chain that hold the charm."

Dani's words did make the eyes misty, right in front of the class. Embarrassing, I suppose. You, too, can have the same Kleenex-inducing experiences with your children.

Many times a child will begin his or her comment with words such as these: "I know that this is a stupid question...." or "This may sound stupid but...." I cut them off forcefully. There are no stupid questions or comments. Not among friends, not among parents and their children, not among people you love. Never.

Asking questions is the necessary first step to becoming informed. Only by being informed can we make moral judgments and take moral action more consistently. Morality is based on knowing the truth. The most dangerous people are those that believe lies. We see this all over the world every day. I don't want my children to be among that group. I suspect you do not either.

As with reason, truth is not the ultimate end. We seek truth and employ reason to pursue virtue. These three actions are not the same, although droplets from their separate fountains may join. Truth and reason are useful only to the extent they lead to moral behavior. Knowledge that does not lead to virtue leads to nothingness.

Examining arguments and facts require discipline, time, commitment, humility, an open mind. It's not easy. Figuring out life's problems and dilemmas is rarely simple or intuitive. It needs more than a whimsical sprinkling of common sense. Ryan, a fourth grader, poignantly said, "It's hard work and hurts the brain."

Often people make decisions fueled by the unawareness of their ignorance and ignorance of their unawareness. We can be a powerful counterforce to simplistic thinking just by asking our children what else they need to know.

ALL I WANT TO KNOW IS . . .

Sometimes getting the facts can be difficult, as can be getting to know what you need to know. One can become frustrated and annoyed. On the topic of what a child needs to know, certainly they need to know the names of their teachers and administrators. Yet, as the following transcript illustrates, that task might not be so simple.

Each year I present this re-phrased comedy sketch to my class. I choose two children to read the script. It is, of course, a re-write of the famous Abbott and Costello skit, 'Who's On First?' This routine is one of the few timeless masterpieces of comedy. I'll bet your children will laugh heartily if you do this re-formulation of the old classic. Even very little children get it. You can do a Google search and find a dozen or so variations of the original Abbott and Costello routine. You can modify the sketch to any degree you desire. I abbreviated the skit to better retain the students' attention.

THE FIRST DAY AT SCHOOL

EBERT ELEMENTARY SCHOOL
Who's In Math?

TEACHER (T): Now class, I am going to tell you the names of all the teachers at Ebert Elementary School so you can say hello to them when you see them in the hall.

Some of the teachers have very unusual names, so please listen closely. Our math teacher is named Who; the librarian is named What and our gym teacher is named I Don't Know. So remember . . .

Alexandra (A): (interrupting) I didn't understand what you said. Would you please repeat those names?

T: Of course. I said, the math teacher is Who; the librarian is What and our gym teacher is I Don't Know and, as I said...

A: I'm sorry, but I still don't understand those names.

T: Well, what don't you understand?

A: Who's the math teacher?

T: That's right.

A: The name of the math teacher?

T: Who

A: The math teacher's name?

T: Who

A: The person teaching math?

T: Who

A: Who's the math teacher?

T: That's right.

A: Tell me the name of the math teacher.

T: Who

A: Who is teaching math?

T: Yes

A: Well, go ahead and tell me.

T: Who

A: The name of the math teacher?

T: Who

A: Are you a teacher in this school?

T: Yes.

A: You know the names of the teachers and what subjects they teach?

T: Of course.

A: You know the name of the math teacher?

T: Who

A: Then tell me, who's teaching math?

T: Yes.

A: The math teacher's name?

T: Who

A: That's what I'm trying to find out.

T: Well, that's what I'm telling you.

A: You're not telling me anything. That's what I'm asking you. The name of the math teacher?

T: Who

A: That's what I'm asking you.

T: That's what I'm telling you. That's the math teacher's name.

A: That's who's name?

T: Yes

A: All I'm trying to find out is what's the name of the math teacher?

T: Oh no! What's the name of the librarian.

A: Who's the librarian?

T: Who's the math teacher.

A: I'm not asking who's the librarian.

T: Who's the math teacher.

A: I don't know.

T: That's the gym teacher.

A: Who's the gym teacher?

T: Who's the math teacher.

A: I don't know.

T: He's the gym teacher. I told you that.

A: What's the gym teacher's name?

T: What's the librarian.

A: Who's the librarian?

T: Who's the math teacher.

A: I don't know.

T: He's the gym teacher.

A: Who's the gym teacher?

T: Now why do you insist on putting who in the gym?

A: Who am I putting in the gym?

T: Yes, but we don't want him there.

A: We don't want who there?

T: That's right.

A: Who do we want there?

T: Now listen to me. Who is not the gym teacher.

A: Stay out of the gym, will you? Who is teaching math?

T: That's right. Now you've got it.

A: I got nothing!

T: It's so simple. Who is teaching math.

A: OK. Tell me the gym teacher's name.

T: I don't know.

A: You don't know?!!

T: I do know. It's I don't know.

A: What?

T: No. What's the librarian.

A: Who's the librarian?

T: Who's the math teacher.

A: I don't know.

T: That's the gym teacher.

A: There we go again. Back to him.

T: I can't help that. You mentioned his name.

A: I mentioned who's name?

T: Yes, but we're not talking about him.

A: We're not talking about who?

T: That's right.

A: Maybe this will clear up this name problem. Do these teachers get paid?

T: Of course they do. Our teachers love their work, but they still need to earn a living.

A: OK, then tell me, when the math teacher gets paid, who gets the money?

T: Every penny of it! After all, the woman is entitled.

A: Who is?

T: Yes, of course!

A: Who's entitled?

T: Certainly.

A: Who gets the money?

T: Absolutely. Sometimes her husband comes to the school to pick up her check.

A: Who's husband?

T: Sure! Why would she allow anyone else's husband to pick up her check?

A: Who would?

T: That's exactly right. You wouldn't expect her to give the money to anyone else, would you?

A: Who wouldn't?

T: Of course not. She is a very reasonable woman. Who gets all the money.

A: That's what I'm asking you!

T: Well, that's what I'm telling you.

A: Listen. All I'm trying to find out is what's the name of the math teacher?

T: What's the librarian.

A: Who's the librarian?

T: Who's the math teacher.

A: I don't know!

T: He's the gym teacher.

A: Stay out of the gymnasium, will you?

T: Well, I can't help it. I can't change their names.

A: I'm not changing anybody's name. Let's try this. Let's say I have a math assignment. I do my homework and bring it to school the next day. In order to get a grade, I have to give it to the math teacher. So, who gets it?

T: Now that's the first thing you said right.

A: I don't even know what I'm talking about.

T: You give your homework to the math teacher.

A: Then who gets it?

T: Certainly. Who gets it.

A: I don't know!!!

T: Now why would you give the math homework to the gym teacher?

A: I'll scream if you mention the gym teacher!

T: It's so simple, Alexandra. All you do is give the homework to the math teacher.

A: Then who gets it?

T: Naturally!

A: Naturally?

T: Naturally!

A: OK. So I give the math assignment to naturally.

T: No! You give the math assignment to the math teacher!

A: Then who gets it?

T: Naturally!

A: That's what I just said.

T: No you didn't. You didn't say it that way!

A: Same as you! I give it to the math teacher and who gets it?

T: Naturally! Now you've got it.

A: OK. I think I understand the names. When I want to return library books, I go to What. When I want to run around and kick a ball, I see I don't know and when I want to turn in a math assignment, I go to Who.

T: That's exactly correct!

A: And you know what?

T: What?

A: I don't care!

T: What did you say?

A: I said I don't care!

T: Oh, that's the name of our school principal!

CHAPTER 7

SMART AND SMARTER

"I shall try to correct errors when shown to be errors and I shall adopt new views as fast as they shall appear to be true views."

–ABRAHAM LINCOLN'S REPLY ON AUGUST 19, 1862,
TO NEW YORK TRIBUNE PUBLISHER HORACE GREELEY

OPINIONS, FACTS AND JUDGMENT

THAT'S JUST YOUR OPINION!" I'm sure every reader has heard those defiant words. They could have been uttered by a co-worker, a boss, a spouse, an opposing audience member at a parent-teacher meeting or even by your little cherub. The speaker often offers no rebuttal or analysis of your opinion, yet cuts off your views with guillotine-like effectiveness.

This dismissive rejection strikes me as an up-graded version of the sandbox taunt, "I know you are but what am I?" You can have a more intelligent conversation with a bag of marbles.

That someone gaseously blurts out that phrase doesn't mean your opinion must be treated like road kill. It doesn't negate the value of your opinion and it doesn't mean that your challenger's opinion is superior. It does mean you might have some work to do to present your opinion more persuasively and it does mean that you may have to dissect the flaws, if any, in your challenger's opinion. Skill is required in these efforts, and this chapter shows how some of those skills can be learned and sharpened.

Before I discuss how to deal with a challenge to or the rejection of an opinion, I make some observations about them. Opinions are critical to how we lead our lives. They motivate us. They shape our lives. They influence the way we seek approval and affirmation. They legislate who we respect and, to a large degree, who respects us. Opinions have the potency to influence whether we live or die. Our opinions are windows to our moral character.

We treat our opinions as prized possessions. We become jealous, invested, protective and defensive about our opinions. And, human nature being what it is, an opinion can become like a fortress, protecting the opinion by blocking incoming information that threatens it.

People hold onto their opinions like a drowning person holds onto a life preserver. That's why superb trial lawyers do not tell the judge or juror what to think or conclude. Rather they skillfully guide them to the opinion or conclusion the lawyers want but in a way that the judge or juror believes the opinion was derived through his own reasoning and values. Believing it to be exclusively its own, the judge or juror will fight tenaciously to defend it.

Everyone is entitled to their opinion, of course, but that's just belaboring the obvious. It's like saying you're entitled to breathe. As my brilliant contracts law professor often said, "So what?" It's a cliché, and like every cliché, it's a shortcut to avoid thinking. In fact, out of a generosity of spirit, I announce that everyone is entitled to *my* opinion!

Being entitled to your own opinion isn't a particularly useful or noble standard for guiding your life. Teaching children that they are entitled to 'their' opinion as if it were a pot of gold swinging from the end of a rainbow is not much of an endorsement of their thinking skills. It's like putting water in cupped hands. A finger moves and the water disappears. Having an opinion is morally neutral. Having one does not, without more, advance moral reasoning or develop moral character.

Rather, before one claims ownership, the opinion should be worthy of being owned. To be worthy, it should be based on logic, moral judgment, solid facts and a full assessment of the opinion's consequences. Anything short of these criteria renders the opinion entitlement trivial and risks weakening children by enabling an unjustified self-importance and potentially destructive beliefs.

A speaker has one or more motives when trying to cut someone off by saying, 'that's just your opinion." The speaker might think his opinion is better; he might think that the other person can be easily intimidated into backing off or abandoning his opinion or the speaker doesn't want to be bothered with the hard task of defending his opinion out of laziness or because he intuits that his opinion is inferior.

> *"Talk sense to a fool and he calls you foolish."*
> —EURIPIDES

MAY THE FACTS BE WITH YOU!

A lawyer may, in thunderous tones, proclaim, "Ladies and gentlemen of the jury, these are the facts!" Well, if you say so. But what does that bold assertion mean? What's a fact? And if something *is* a fact, what is the fact's significance? Facts are things that actually exist. A 'fact' is reality. Facts are provable by empiricism, testing, scientific inquiry, reason and experimentation and accepted as such by rational minds.

Most of us will accept as 'fact' that there are fifty states in the United States of America and that the Declaration of Independence was signed on July 4, 1776 and that Germany invaded Poland in September 1939. It is a fact that the earth revolves around the sun and not around my next door neighbor's daughter, Karen, despite what her father says.

Establishing some facts can be complicated. It is a 'fact' that seatbelts save lives overall, but it is also a fact that sometimes, in specific instances, a seatbelt can increase the risk of injury or death. It is also a fact that things once thought to be 'facts' turned out not to be facts, such as the sun revolving around the earth. Some day it may be proved to be a fact that steamed broccoli with tofu causes colon cancer, which would be fine with me.

Facts and truth do not depend on your point of view. No reasonable parent would accept such a proposition. Facts and truth are not obstructions that you trip over like junk littering the garage. Facts are the path to truth. According to an article in Fortune Magazine a few years ago, super investor Warren Buffet was asked whether he was troubled or bothered when writers called him a 'has been' and that he was finished as an investor when he missed out on the hi-tech investment boom.

> "Never," he said. "Nothing bothers me like that. You can't do well in investments unless you think independently. And the truth is, you're neither right nor wrong because people agree with you. You're right because your facts and your reasoning are right. In the end, that's all that counts. And there wasn't any question about the facts or the reasoning being correct."

Opinions are different from facts although an opinion can also be a fact, which gets a little confusing. It is both an opinion and a fact, for example, that security was inadequate at Columbine High School in Colorado prior to the attacks.

Opinions are conclusions about the significance and values of facts. An opinion is the result of applying principles, values and logic to facts. It takes more than a string of facts to make an opinion, just as it takes more than a pile of pearls to make a necklace.

Some facts have more value than others. For example, the fact "he has a gun" is a more important fact than "he seemed to be joking when he said he'd shoot the students." Reaching an opinion by determining the existence of and evaluating facts is what lawyers call 'weighing the evidence.'

SUPPORTING YOUR OPINION

I was watching some of the extraordinary athletes in the 2008 National Basketball Association playoffs and managed to get into an argument over who is the greatest current NBA player. We narrowed the field to two: Kobe Bryant of the Los Angeles Lakers and Lebron James of the Cleveland Cavaliers.

Who's the better player? Well, Kobe is so dynamic, such a leader, great under stress. Lebron is all of these things also, and doesn't have the team support and on and on. Well, one can argue endlessly, throw nachos and pizza crusts and soda cans at colleagues watching a game and get nowhere near a resolution, which may be part of the joy of the exercise.

It's fun to argue and yell and scream and be emotional, but the consistently most effective way to persuade and to support an opinion is to argue based on the facts. Study data such as points per game, minutes per game, rebounds, blocked shots, three-point shots, foul shots, shooting efficiency, assists and so on.

Who is better player? I don't know. To be honest, I don't care. I just like watching them play. How you weigh and evaluate the facts is up to you—whether rebounds are more significant than blocked shots—and reflects your judgment and values, but at least *identify* the facts so that you are judging with common criteria.

It is vital to teach and constantly remind a child —anyone, actually—that thinking is a skill. It is a technique. Thinking is the result of a process. Any thinking worth doing is not a matter of whim or impulse or emotion or feelings. Thinking takes work.

Several elements determine the quality of thinking when forming an opinion. These elements include, but are not limited to, the facts, how the thinker relates the facts to each other and the morality of the link between the facts and the opinion.

Here's an example illustrating the morality of the link between facts and opinions. Assume a school bond issue will be presented to the voters. A meeting is held to debate the proposal. At the meeting, all the folks in favor of the bond meet in the front of the room; all opposed meet at the back. A reporter interviews only the people in favor of the bond proposal and writes, "The bond proposal is popular. Everyone I spoke to is in favor of it."

The facts are accurate but the link between the facts and their implication is unethical.

When I talk about 'facts' that form an opinion, I mean that that the quality of an opinion and the integrity of its logic and its morality are determined by how facts are used. The following criteria for analyzing how facts are used are dominant but not exclusive:

- The facts that support the opinion

- The facts that are ignored when forming an opinion

- How the facts are linked to each other

- The value given to each facts in the opinion, and

- The consequences of the opinion based on the facts

Here's another useful guideline on the relationship between opinions and facts. Speaking in generalities and failing to supply facts and examples to support the generalities can be useless at best and dishonest and manipulative at worst. Generalities can have value, of course, but without specific examples, no rational judgment can be made concerning their wisdom, values, usefulness or integrity.

A person might say, "People don't respect us as much as they used to." What meaning should be given to that assertion? Without specific examples of which people don't respect as much, how much they respected us before, why they don't respect us as much now, the values of those that allegedly don't respect as much and why we should care whether those people respect us, the assertion is meaningless and may be no more than manipulative demagoguery.

FASTEN YOUR SEATBELTS!

"I know that I am prejudiced in this matter,
but I would be ashamed of myself if I weren't."

–MARK TWAIN

Most class discussions are like pleasant jogs in the country, exhibiting a few bumps and up-hills and, of course, you always have to watch where you're stepping. This dialogue with a fifth grade class at CHVE about the "that's just your opinion" topic more closely approximated a football tackling drill. It was one of the most bombastic discussions I've had, but it was memorable for several reasons.

The discussion encouraged students to expand the breadth of their reasoning and to see beyond themselves. It showed, also, how conversation topics flow into unplanned new ones, thereby enriching the experience. It showed that these talks can be delightfully humorous and that you can have a lot of fun with them.

The conversation started unremarkably. We were discussing the moral aspects of wearing safety helmets when bicycling or roller blading or skiing. A key point students came to understand was wearing safety helmets had impacts beyond the safety of the user.

Wearing helmets reduced the number and severity of injuries, which, in turn, reduced demand for medical care, required fewer ambulances to race dangerously through red lights, lowered insurance premiums, reduced family and taxpayer costs and, of course, resulted in healthier children. You can, doubtlessly, think of other benefits. Without going out on even the most fragile limb, we agreed that wearing safety helmets was 'good.'

Although he admitted the benefits, Reide questioned whether wearing safety helmets should be required by law. "There should be the right to decide whether to wear the helmet. It's a matter of freedom," he exclaimed. "I should be able to do what I want!" Freedom, of course, is most enticing when someone else pays for its abuse.

Not persuaded by Reide's libertarian freedom argument, Lauren pounced as swiftly as a brown bear impaling a salmon. "That's really dumb!" Her eyes narrowed. Her hands formed fists. "Then you end up injured and you see a doctor like my father (a neurologist) and he tells you that you're crippled or dead!"

The reward for me is students thinking of similar examples and evaluating real-life applications of their hastily-expressed generalities.

Conversations evolve, of course. Note how Reide re-directed our discussion on the morality of helmet laws to freedom of choice. My intuition told me to go with what is often referred to as 'the flow.'

Grant cleverly challenged Reide to reject laws that had been accepted by society. "What about seat belts? That affects your freedom. Are you saying there shouldn't be seatbelt laws?"

"Well, we should be able to choose...." Reide's voice disappeared like sand in the wind.

Then I got into trouble.

"It seems," I said to Reide, "your opinion wasn't very persuasive."

The class erupted with hurricane force. Andrew lashed out, "You have no right to tell us our opinion is wrong or isn't good."

Recoiling at his injunction, I replied confidently. "Really?" Never mind that saying something is not very persuasive is not the same as saying it is wrong or not good. "If I accept your reasoning," I said with an edge, "then you have no right to tell me that I have no right to tell you that your opinion isn't good. Got it?"

Momentarily quiet, Andrew looked as if, as writer Sir P. G. Wodehouse might have written, all the lime had been squeezed out of his light. His silence was short-lived. Leaning forward like a threatening tiger, he exclaimed, "Everything is an opinion. Yours isn't better than anyone else's."

"Well!" I exclaimed in Jack Benny fashion.

Stephanie banged her petit hands on her desk, and, in a voice appropriate for rounding up cattle, yelled, "You have no right to disagree with my opinion. It's my opinion. You can't overrule my opinion!!" Her red face could stop traffic. She didn't simply respond to my comments. She went after them with a hatchet. "That's freedom of speech!"

Suddenly these little moppets had become constitutional scholars, throwing around theories of rights and freedoms like rice at a wedding. I stood there, a model of reason. "I'm not trying to limit your speech," I purred. I knew I couldn't do that with dynamite. I did ruefully chuckle at yet another example of a speaker demanding freedom of speech for herself while denying it to others.

Stephanie had unknowingly used a classic and effective debating technique: misstate the original issue—the right to challenge an opinion—by creating a straw argument—freedom of speech—then defeat the straw argument—I cannot limit her speech—and then declare yourself the winner of the original argument—that I can't challenge her opinion. It's a useful skill, mastered by politicians and most four-year-olds.

I wouldn't fall for the tactic. Moreover, since she wanted to get snippy about all this freedom of speech stuff, I pointed out that freedom of speech applies only to the government limiting speech. For better or worse, I was *not* the government.

Stephanie was unmoved. "It's my opinion and you can't disagree."

Kate interrupted. "He always thinks about arguing. He's a lawyer!"

Was there ever a profession more misunderstood?

With sandblaster intensity they continued to yell about my not having the right to judge their opinions. Little Samantha saved me. She stood, dramatically slapped a hand on her desktop and said authoritatively, "Quiet in the court! Quiet in the court! Let's take a brief recess."

I laughed heartily. The moment was, as some credit card advertisement says, priceless. And educational.

A lot of big issues were packed into that little ten-minute "you can't overrule my opinion" discussion. We saw how students challenged opinions. Some arguments were patched together as if by duct tape rather than by reason. Others were based on logic, analogies and experience. We also saw how children tried to insulate their opinions by resorting to hand-pounding emotion.

But there is no avoiding reality: opinions will be judged and judgment and consequences and history will show that some opinions are, in fact, better than others.

"Yes", I said. "I believe in evidence. I believe in observation,
measurement, and reasoning, confirmed by independent observers.
I'll believe anything, no matter how wild and ridiculous, if there
is evidence for it. The wilder and more ridiculous something is,
however, the firmer and more solid the evidence will have to be."

–ISAAC ASIMOV

EH, WHAT'S UP, DOC?

"It must be 'criminal' justice indeed that should condemn a work
as a substitute for not being able to refute it."

–THOMAS PAINE, *THE RIGHTS OF MAN*

In the previous chapter I offered a two-question skill to improve reasoning: 'What do you know? What do you need to know?' That skill taught that facts were important, offered guidance on how to get the relevant ones and showed how different facts have different moral significance. Now I address what we should do with those wonderful facts once we get them.

Facts can be used pretty much like anything else in life: they can be used honorably or they can be abused; they can be used logically or they can be used in a sloppy manner. In this chapter I offer a two-part skill on constructing an opinion. Once the opinion is created, this skill can serve as a guide to evaluate and compare the logic and integrity and morality of competing opinions.

REASONING SKILL #2

- What is your opinion?

- What are your facts?

This skill requires linking facts to opinions. When facts and opinions are clarified, the consequences of those opinions can be discerned more accurately. Well-crafted opinions and clear understandings of consequences will give what economist Thomas Sowell described as "a systematic way to analyze ideas, derive their implications and test those implications against hard facts." With this method, Sowell argues, we can distinguish rhetoric from reality, that is, distinguish words and hype from what's really going on.

This skill can accomplish several desirable goals: strengthen the justification for our opinions; increase the value of our opinions; persuade us to adopt a better opinion and reject an inferior one and teach us how to defend our opinions and identify the flaws in opinions that challenge our own. As our opinions become more credible, moral, rational and defensible, our moral character increases.

Here's a key point: by using this skill children begin to see a relationship between the moral character *of* an opinion and the moral character of the person *expressing* the opinion. They soon realize two fundamental truths: we have the *right* to judge other people's opinions and we have the moral *obligation* to do so.

A collection of class discussions shows how I used this two-part skill to evaluate opinions. I hope my examples inspire you to give them a spin with your child.

One day, while my students were haranguing me with their opinion that I wasn't entitled to my opinion that rejected their opinion, I sought refuge in art to defend myself. I picked up a book on Italian art that happened to be lying on the teacher's desk. I leafed through the pages and found a photograph of Michelangelo's "God About to Touch and Give Life to Adam." I knew I had found the evidence to make my point. This painting is on a section of the ceiling of the Sistine Chapel in the Apostolic Palace in the Vatican City. Michelangelo began to paint the ceiling in 1508 at the request of Pope Julius II.

While the photograph was passed around the class, I drew an approximation of Bugs Bunny on the chalkboard, crooked teeth and floppy ears and all.

Which was the greater work of art, I asked, my Bugs Bunny or Michelangelo's "Touch of Life?"

Here are some student comments. "They're the same if you think they are." "You can't judge the difference." "One is no better than the other." "It's just your opinion."

I confess I was dismayed. This reasoning is darkly troublesome. Would they find no difference between freedom and slavery? Between representative democracy and totalitarian fascism? Between a culture that suppressed women and one that elevated them? Are those differences merely matters of opinion?

I was pulled back from the brink of despair when a few students said something like, "Are you nuts? The Sistine Chapel is much better!"

Abbie's critique rejecting the students' relativism was as poetic as it was profound. "The Sistine Ceiling represents something important. You judge it by the effort, the talent, the meaning of the art." This quote has many qualities but one of the most significant is providing insight into the judgment, wisdom and expressive skill of young children.

Comparing the artistic qualities of the Sistine Ceiling with my haphazard drawing of Bugs Bunny might seem silly, but serious points can be made. First of all, to say comparisons are not possible because it's just a matter of opinion is a cowardly cop-out that avoids the hard work of thinking. There are differences between the two works. Those differences can be identified. They have artistic significance. Rational judgments can be made about them.

TAKING AN OPINION APART

An opinion is often built upon a group of separate underlying beliefs, each of which addresses some part or fragment that is necessary to form the larger opinion. I call these underlying opinions 'sub-opinions.' These sub-opinions are based on facts and collectively these factual assumptions form the foundation of the main opinion. Think of an opinion as a house and the sub-opinions as individual bricks or walls that make the house.

Continuing the house-brick-wall imagery, it is obvious that some bricks or walls are more important to the integrity of the house than others. Some bricks or a wall, or a group of them, if removed or if defective, will cause the house to fall down. So it is with sub-opinions. Some are more important than others and when some of them are discredited, the final larger opinion loses credibility and may fall apart.

Here's an example of sub-opinions used in an analysis of a legal issue. Let's say a judge has to decide whether a pre-nuptial agreement should be enforced. In order to reach that opinion, the judge has to form a bunch of sub-opinions, which is done by looking at the facts and 'weighing the evidence,' that is, determining the implications of those facts. These sub-opinions might also be called 'facts,' but I don't want to make an issue here of the distinction between facts and an opinion that becomes a fact.

The judge has to 'find' as a fact or form an opinion about several issues, such as whether both parties were fully informed about all the important elements of the agreement, whether there was full disclosure about each person's assets, whether one person intimidated or coerced or unduly influenced the other and whether the resulting agreement, under present circumstances, is 'conscionable' or fair to some degree.

Only when all of those sub-opinions are determined—there was full disclosure of assets, etc.—can the judge give an opinion on the ultimate issue of whether the pre-nuptial agreement should be enforced. Here's the point: in order to form an opinion on whether or not the pre-nuptial agreement should be enforced, the judge has to believe a bunch of other things first.

We can see the application of sub-opinions in determining whether my Bugs Bunny drawing was less than, equal to or better than Michelangelo's "Touch of Life."

To engage in reasoning, generally, and to engage in moral reasoning, specifically, the first task is to gain clarity about the sub-opinions. When a student says, "You can't judge them" or "It's just a matter of opinion," the student is accepting several sub-opinions, whether or not the student realizes it.

Identifying some of these sub-opinions will illuminate how the reasoning was done in a particular case, whether the reasoning was logical and whether the reasoning was, in fact, reasonable.

Here are just a few of the sub-opinions that would be held by the students that could not make a judgment comparing the two works:

- skill does not matter;
- balance and proportion do not matter;
- rarity of technique and competence do not matter;
- intellect and design and effort do not matter;
- blending colors does not matter
- the judgments of scholars and experts over centuries have no greater value than the instantaneous opinion of a ten-year-old
- the application of paint, color, balance and technique mastered over decades has no greater value than my nine-second artistic effort

Talk to your child to see if you can figure out additional sub-opinions.

Once the sub-opinions have been identified, we can evaluate them individually. We can make judgments about the argument, for example, that design, use of color, balance and proportion are all meaningless. We might conclude, for example, that such an argument is intellectually and morally bankrupt.

We can determine whether other sub-opinions of the non-judging student have been overlooked, such as overlooking the variable "decades of study, practice, trial and error and improvement do not matter." We can then figure out whether that additional sub-opinion weakens or strengthens the larger opinion.

By evaluating the sub-opinions, we can better evaluate the primary opinion. If we find flaws or errors in the sub-opinions; if we determine that the sub-opinions are irrational or foolish or unethical, we can conclude that the "two drawings cannot be judged" opinion is foolish or irrational.

If we conclude that technique and balance and proportion *do* matter and that intellect and design and effort *do* matter, then we can reasonably hold the opinion that Michelangelo's work is *better than* mine. Not only can we reasonably hold the opinion. We can reasonably *defend* the opinion.

We can also say that that opinion that Michelangelo's work is better than mine is *a better opinion than* the opinion that the two works cannot be comparatively judged. This distinction is vital. The first opinion is better supported by facts, logic, reason and history. That opinion can be better defended. We can, thus, judge that the opinion "They're the same if you think they are." is weak, untenable, unpersuasive and not supported by the facts.

Note what I am *not* saying. I am not saying that everyone *must like* Michelangelo's art more than mine or that it is *wrong* to like my drawing more than Michelangelo's. That's a matter of personal taste. I am only discussing the comparative value of opinions. Certainly someone is entitled to prefer an inferior work but the person should acknowledge that what he or she likes is inferior artistically to the one that is not preferred.

Michelangelo's masterpiece required decades of training, boasted extravagant treatment of color and light and featured design and balance and proportion of the highest order. It was a work of genius.

Mine lacked all of the above.

It is important to grasp that a reasonable opinion that is poorly reasoned or poorly expressed will have diluted value. A student's opinion that the "Touch of Life" is a better work of art—It's better because I say so—that has no factual or reasoning support will not be worth much even though it is the more logical and defensible opinion.

Another point merits emphasis. There must be a shared reality and common reference points to evaluate or to compare opinions. In the "Touch of Life" example, some shared values would include valuing work, beauty, discipline, the acknowledgment of artistic elements and so forth.

To evaluate Michelangelo's work requires shared values, common knowledge of art history, technique, light, color, balance and so on. Those that lack that knowledge cannot make useful judgments about the quality of Michelangelo's work. It is easy to be confident in your opinion when you know nothing.

The same reasoning process applies to valuing values: if you do not value the same things, comparison and moral judgments are impossible. Those inclined to ignore the issues inherent in comparing values invite the end of rationality and objective inquiry. Some folks are quite at ease with that. They are called 'relativists.' Everything is just a matter of 'constructs' and 'theories' and personal experiences and perspectives. I am not at ease with that thinking.

If someone were to say, "You're just imposing your values," the deceit of the speaker should now be obvious to all. It's the same as the 'it's just your opinion' condemnation. Imposing your values is a value just as attacking someone for imposing their values is an expression of values. The accusation ignores or diminishes the substance, the facts, the moral analysis and the reality of the issue. Everything is reduced to 'your values.' Don't fall for the trick. The accuser is hiding in a cave of morally sloppy words.

It is vital that our children understand how the world really works. Some facts are more important than others. Some opinions are better than others. Some opinions, irrespective of their inherent merits, are better reasoned than others.

These skills will help develop children's moral and intellectual judgment. Lacking such judgment, children become vulnerable to being pawns in the hands of others who might not advance their best interests. They are at risk to those who might not be moral enough or intelligent enough to know our children's best interests. Ignoring this reality will not serve them well over the long run and may bring a lot of harm and pain to them and to others.

CHAPTER 8

THE MORAL DUTY TO JUDGE

*"Man, once surrendering his reason, has no remaining guard against
absurdities the most monstrous, and like a ship without rudder,
is the sport of every wind. With such persons, gullibility,
which they call faith, takes the helm from the hand of reason
and the mind becomes a wreck."*

—THOMAS JEFFERSON

TRUTH, KNOWLEDGE AND BELIEFS

I T IS HELPFUL, between the Bugs Bunny discussion from the
previous chapter and the following one about Blackstone's
Ratio, to think about the meaning of knowledge. What is it?
How do you know you have it? Is there value in having knowledge?
If so, what's the value?

Epistemology is the branch of philosophy that addresses knowledge and beliefs, the difference between them and their relationship to truth. It explains how beliefs can be supported and proved or refuted. It is built largely upon the thinking of the Greeks. Plato developed a model for relating truth, knowledge and beliefs, illustrated here:

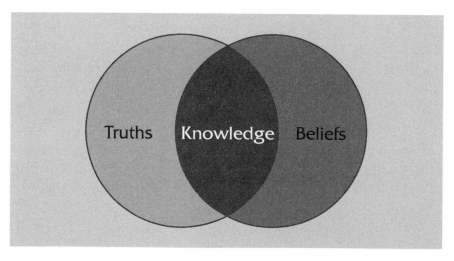

You can see that all that is true is not believed and not all beliefs are based on truth. Knowledge is a belief that is based on truth. This diagram illustrates what we all know: truth exists whether or not someone believes it or agrees with it or knows it.

Thomas Aquinas, the 13th century Italian priest, philosopher and theologian, pointed out, "it is true for all that the three angles of a triangle are together equal to two right angles, although it is not known to all."

Knowledge, Plato concluded, is belief that can be explained or justified or proven in some way. That is, to cut to the core, knowledge, which is based on truth and facts, can be distinguished from false beliefs.

You might believe, for example, that a drug made you better. Did you get better because of the drug or was your improved health a coincidence? Do you have knowledge that the drug made you better or do you have only a belief? You might believe it is good to tell children they are wonderful because it increases their self esteem and thereby makes them into stronger more compassionate people. Fine, but what is your evidence? Do you have knowledge or only belief?

In his dialogue, *Gorgias*, Plato, through Socrates, speaks with Gorgias about persuasion and its relationship to truth. Gorgias was an expert on rhetoric, the skill of persuasion. Socrates distinguishes between 'having learned' something and 'having believed' something. He and Gorgias agreed that what is learned is different from what is believed.

Knowledge, which is what is learned, is belief based on the truth. In *Gorgias* Socrates referred to belief not based on truth as 'false belief.' Thus, two categories of belief exist: belief with knowledge and belief without knowledge.

Socrates points out in the dialogue that those who have learned as well as those who have false beliefs have been persuaded to arrive at their beliefs. Significantly, Socrates gets Gorgias to admit that persuasion can be the source of false beliefs as well as of knowledge. Socrates asks Gorgias, "Shall we then assume two sorts of persuasion, one which is the source of belief without knowledge, as the other is of knowledge?" Gorgias agrees.

Since persuasion can cause false beliefs not based on truth, Socrates challenged Gorgias on the morality of persuasion. Socrates got Gorgias to admit that persuasion only gives belief about the just and the unjust, as an example, but gives no knowledge or instruction about them. Socrates viewed persuasion with great suspicion because of this moral deficiency.

Socrates' point goes to the heart of moral reasoning because it acknowledges that people can be persuaded to form beliefs—have opinions—that are not based in truth, whether about the just and the unjust, good and evil, a war or legislation or a school policy, all without knowledge of the facts.

To avoid false beliefs, we have a moral obligation to be fully informed about how we get persuaded and about what we get persuaded. I grant that agreement on what is 'knowledge' may not always exist. Indeed, there is often disagreement about what is truth in any situation. Disagreement challenges knowledge and truth but does not eliminate them.

Earlier I made my case that the existence of disagreement doesn't negate the existence of morality. Similarly, I argue that disagreement regarding the truth does not negate the existence of truth. Aquinas was right. Rather, disagreement compels the moral quest for further information and for the discerning analysis of that information.

The best one can do is to gain knowledge by continuously seeking the truth and by persistently applying reason, logic and empiricism to what you think are the 'facts.' This analysis of belief, knowledge and opinion is relevant to raising ethical children. If children are to gain wisdom and moral clarity and to act virtuously, they must develop reasoning skills to gain knowledge and to distinguish knowledge from false belief.

Teaching children they can know what is 'right' or 'good' or 'ethical' only when there is substantial agreement on it—when an idea is popular or generally accepted—is dangerously flawed. Agreement does not transform false belief into true belief. It is the equivalent of teaching children to believe in the Tooth Fairy.

Such advice will make children insecure, dependent on the thinking of others and undermine their confidence in their own moral reasoning. It increases their vulnerability to folks that appear more confident, more aggressive and who are intolerant of their children's views.

> *"When the facts change, I change my opinion.*
> *What do you do, sir?"*
>
> –ECONOMIST JOHN MAYNARD KEYNES'S
> RESPONSE TO CRITICISM THAT HE CHANGED HIS MIND.

AN ADVANCED DIALOGUE
PROTECTING THE INNOCENT

> *"The foolish and the dead alone never change their opinions."*
>
> –JAMES LOWELL

Moral reasoning is about gaining clarity about the moral implications of reality. It is about generating knowledge and rejecting false beliefs. It is about compelling a person to take the most morally justified action under the circumstances. The dialogues on the stopping-for-the-motorist and the steal-money-for-medicine topics were examples of moral reasoning.

Throughout my classes I present an array of topics which require and thereby continuously call upon the students' moral reasoning skills. We practice constantly, like a tennis player perfecting her serve or a musician perfecting his tone.

Some issues or dilemmas are more complex than others and demand higher levels of thinking. Here is a complex dialogue that relates knowledge and false beliefs to moral judgment. It relates to justice: punishing the guilty, protecting the innocent and the practical consequences of the Quixotic search for perfect justice.

Admittedly, the topic and its analysis are difficult, maybe even uncomfortable, yet they resonate with young children because the issues are known to them and strike a chord deep in their sense of fairness. The topic also leads to compelling and passionate discussions. It pits emotion against reason and beliefs against truth. I have seen discussions provoke dramatic changes in students' views about the justice system as their thinking progresses from emotional idealism to a hard-nosed real-world analysis.

The conversation topic is referred to as 'Blackstone's Ratio,' named after the 18th century English jurist Sir William Blackstone.

"Better that ten guilty persons escape than that one innocent suffer."

Blackstone wasn't the first to come up with a formula that offered to trade the freedom of a gaggle of guilty people for the avoidance of wrongful punishment of one innocent person. My research indicates the idea originated with Chancellor Sir John Fortescue. In 1470 he wrote in his massive treatise *De Laudibus Legum Angliae, A Treaty in Commendation of the Laws of England*, that "Indeed one would much rather that twenty guilty persons should escape the punishment of death, than that one innocent person should be condemned and suffer capitally."

Fortescue's statement is different from Blackstone's. Those differences have moral significance. Fortescue refers to guilty people escaping the death penalty and the innocent person being spared from the death penalty. Those facts are specific. Blackstone's criteria for escaping are ambiguous. Agreeing with Fortescue and rejecting Blackstone can be morally consistent.

Fortescue's statement spawned many variations on the theme. Presumably Blackstone's version was one of them. For example, on October 3, 1692, regarding the Salem witch trials, Increase Mather wrote, "It were better that Ten Suspected Witches should escape, than that the Innocent Person should be Condemned."

Blackstone's Ratio is perceived as a virtuous acknowledgment that protecting the innocent should be so highly valued that it justified incurring an extreme cost. One can easily get tennis elbow patting one's self on the back for one's willingness to pay such a high price for protecting the innocent.

We shall see if the spotlight of analysis shows whether Blackstone's phrase elevates justice or if it is a simplistic emotional rhetorical flourish that violates its own logic. We can then judge whether implementing this ratio would be prudent public policy or whether it would subvert the protection of innocent people.

What do you and your child think? Is it better to have a bunch of guilty people escape than have one innocent person suffer? I bet you will experience with your child what I have in my classrooms— that layers of opinions get peeled away and change as we discuss Blackstone's Ratio in a focused way.

I've asked hundreds of children what they think about the statement. Almost all agreed with it initially. "It's wrong to punish an innocent person." "It's not fair to have an innocent person suffer." "That's not justice."

Well, maybe.

Let's dig in and see what treasures of analysis we excavate. Remember, the purpose of the dialogue is to serve as a template for your own discussions. You can emphasize or disregard any facts you desire.

Evaluating Blackstone's Ratio requires examining the facts, which may support or undermine it. We must also consider the consequences if the policy were enforced. Let's use the two reasoning skills to analyze the statement: What do we know?/Need to know? and What is your opinion?/What are your facts?

There are only two facts: ten guilty people escape punishment and one innocent person avoids suffering.

Before reaching a conclusion about the morality of Blackstone's Ratio, there are a lot of facts we *don't know* but need to know. There are also lots of facts not mentioned in the ratio that we can logically assume exist.

One of the first points—a very sophisticated point—many children made was how is it known that the 'innocent' person that will avoid suffering is actually innocent? If the 'system' knew the person was innocent, then an innocent person would be made to suffer intentionally. That would make Blackstone's statement absurd.

If that's not the case, then the person's innocence is a matter of probability. The issue then becomes a matter of risk analysis: what risk society should take and what price should society pay to avoid convicting a person that might or might not be innocent.

If subjected to the withering cross-examination of my students, Blackstone would have to concede that his proposition involves releasing a lot of admittedly guilty people in order to avoid the suffering of a person that *might* be innocent.

But let's not be too persnickety, whatever that means, and let's assume we are dealing with a truly innocent person. If this kind of dialogue appeals to you, it can be a lot of head-scratching fun. Now let's go a level deeper. A singularly important group of facts we don't know relate to the kinds of crimes the ten guilty people committed.

Fortescue's statement refers to twenty people facing the punishment of death. As a general proposition, in merry old England one did something rather bad to face a death sentence. The severity of Blackstone's miscreants is not identified.

But it is imperative to raise the issue. What crimes might have guilty folks committed? Jay-walking? Speeding fifteen miles per hour over a posted limit? Bombing an airliner in mid-flight? Child molestation? Reasonable people would conclude that the category of crimes matters and we don't know these facts.

We also don't know what crime the innocent person would be punished for. Bouncing a check? Failing to pay sales taxes? Watering the lawn on an unauthorized day? Murder? Not doing tax withholdings for a babysitter? The wrongful punishment—the suffering—inflicted upon the innocent person for bouncing a check would be quite different from the punishment for committing murder. We don't know what punishment the innocent person faces.

One reasoning skill is to reason from an abstract generalization to the concrete specific case. We cannot begin to rationally evaluate Blackstone's ratio because these critical facts are unknown. In its actual implementation, Blackstone might be advocating that ten rapists, mass murderers and child molesters (not examples I use in class) escape in order to avoid the suffering of a person wrongfully accused of failing to have his auto insurance card.

Does the nobility of Blackstone's Ratio begin to lose its luster?

Kacie, a fifth grader, grasped the moral significance of these differences. "If ten really bad people go free and the innocent person is, like, jailed for being a bad driver, then letting them go is really unjust."

Now we peel off another layer of analysis. Consider all the future crimes that the ten guilty escapees will commit against innocent people. If criminology studies are accurate, as a general rule, criminals are caught for only a small percentage of their crimes. So, perhaps dozens of future innocents will be hurt or killed by these ten escaping guilty folks.

All this future criminality against innocent people will be part but only a part of the price paid for avoiding the wrongful punishment of *one* innocent person.

Consider also the injustice inflicted upon their victims when those ten guilty fellows escape. Imagine a family member savagely victimized by a criminal who now is allowed to escape as a precaution against the suffering of an innocent person.

There's still more to talk about. If you want to spice up your discussion, play around with the numbers in the ratio and see if you can determine the outer limits of the Ratio. Blackstone says it's okay to let ten guilty people escape. What about twenty? How about one hundred? Ten thousand? Blackstone's number is whimsical and not linked to any measure. Where does it stop?

Why not completely eliminate punishment? Then there would be absolute *certainty* that no innocent person would suffer. Is abolishing the justice system a reasonable price to pay for the perfect protection of the innocent?

Well, almost perfect protection of the innocent. We can logically conclude that tens of thousands of innocents would be harmed if all guilty people escaped.

Here's a paradoxical question: would this quest for perfect justice lead to the greatest injustice?

Socrates said one of the greatest evils is the injustice of failing to punish the guilty. Note that Blackstone gives no moral value to the injustice inflicted upon the innocent victims of the ten guilty people that will escape punishment.

Some of the consequences of the ratio include, therefore, the injustice of no punishment for the guilty, the injustice inflicted on the victims of the ten guilty folks and the future violence these ten will inflict on other innocents. If the released guilty people are particularly vile, their future crimes against the innocent could be horrific.

The reality is that innocents will always suffer or are likely to suffer. We must analyze which innocents suffer, how many will suffer and how grievously. Clearly, Blackstone has a bias. He favors protecting the wrongly accused innocent over dozens of past and future innocent victims. They don't concern him. Which group is likely to suffer more? My insights are no better than yours, but the issue is worth discussing.

And, by the way, do you think Blackstone would receive with enthusiasm all those escaped chaps running around his neighborhood, mingling with his kids at the ice cream shop or following the missus around as she shops for tea and scones? My guess is he'd back off a bit and add a few qualifiers to his expansive statement. High minded moral abstractions tend to become less abstract when applied to oneself.

I share a poignant classroom moment. Kacie, quoted above, also said, "I wouldn't mind being punished a little if it saved someone's life." She meant she would be willing to be the wrongly suffering innocent if her suffering kept ten heinous people from escaping and hurting others.

I share Kacie's comment for several reasons. Certainly I won't hold her to her words in the unlikely event she is confronted with such a choice. But I remember her earnest face and her folded hands as she leaned forward to make her statement. Her words were measured, the product of thought. She didn't speak whimsically or jokingly or self-righteously. She spoke from the heart. She was grappling with a difficult topic in a serious manner. Her comment shows that your children, also, have a limitless capacity for moral thinking and decency. We just have to help them along.

What to do with all this analysis? Remember that our goal was to see if we could logically and morally evaluate an opinion, in this case, Blackstone's Ratio, by investigating the facts supporting or undermining the opinion and by judging the opinion's consequences.

Here's where I think we end up when evaluating Blackstone's Ratio. If you *accept* Blackstone's opinion, then you must, by definition, accept the following sub-opinions. I am certain you can think of others:

- That avoiding the wrongful punishment of one innocent person (we don't know for what crime) is *more moral* than punishing ten guilty people (who may have committed horrific crimes)

- That avoiding the wrongful punishment of one innocent person is *more moral* than avoiding the injustice committed against the victims of those ten guilty people that will escape

- That avoiding the wrongful punishment of one innocent person is *more moral* than preventing the infliction of future violence on dozens of innocents

- That making a decision without knowing the facts that allows guilty people to escape is a moral decision.

When we look at the facts and look at the consequences, we can now make moral *judgments* about Blackstone's Ratio because we have separated knowledge from false beliefs. We can have what Dennis Prager describes as "clarity," meaning we know the facts and the implications of the facts before we agree on or form an opinion about the issue.

Is Blackstone right or wrong? Who knows? It's up to you, but after this analysis perhaps you will have greater clarity about what you are agreeing with or rejecting and why. Should someone dismissively say, "Well, that's just your opinion," you now have a basis to respond to such a vapid challenge.

You can discuss facts and consequences and judgments about them. You can engage in moral reasoning even if the other person cannot. Attacking someone else's opinion is not a substitute for having your own.

As a pronouncement that protects the innocent, I find Blackstone's Ratio falls woefully short. Yet, Blackstone's Ratio has value. It is inspirational. It should motivate us to continuously strive to improve the mechanisms for justice—skilled honest police and investigators, honorable skilled prosecutors and defense lawyers, moral intelligent judges insulated from political pressures, laws based on moral principles and so forth.

Blackstone's Ratio is useful to the extent it compels us toward those conditions. Moral people working in moral institutions, however, provide the best protection for the innocent. Freeing the guilty does not.

OPINIONS-R-US

"All truth passes through three stages.
First, it is ridiculed.
Second, it is violently opposed.
Third, it is accepted as being self-evident."

–ARTHUR SCHOPENHAUER (1788-1860)

Returning to the dialogue in which Andrew and Stephanie blasted me for disagreeing with their opinions, several perplexing questions arise. It is a curious phenomenon that some people want the freedom to express anything and everything but don't want to permit others to express opinions about their expressions. They judge quite harshly those that reject non-judgmentalism.

Even more curious, and, frankly, quite ominous, is that in their protestations about non-judging, they fail to see at least three grand ironies:

• That deciding not to judge is a judgment;
• That by judging everything as equal, they reduce their opinions and thus, themselves, to meaninglessness, and

- What appears to elevate and dignify—respect, tolerance, acceptance—actually ends up trivializing. What was a virtue in the abstract turns on itself and becomes a poison.

If everything is equal, if nothing can be judged, then there are no standards. There is no excellence. There is no right and wrong; no good or bad; no better or worse. We are beyond good and evil, as Nietzsche wrote. We are empty.

Most curiously, I ponder why children say things they absolutely don't believe? "You can't judge." "All opinions are equal." "Good is whatever you think." and so forth. They don't live their lives that way. They judge everything and they change their judgments as quickly as CD's at an overnight party.

They have opinions on everything, from who should be president to who is a friend to who should be the starting quarterback for the Denver Broncos to what kind of shoes are 'in' or 'cool.' And children are very assertive and confident in their opinions, so much so they remind of the quip from some mass media pundits, "often wrong, never in doubt."

Teachers tell me they are not surprised by these attitudes and beliefs. The children are merely mouthing what they have been told to believe, kind of like lip-synching a song and having no idea of the song's meaning. Critical thinking is discouraged, many teachers lament, because it is considered improper to judge others.

Judging 'devalues' others, the argument goes. Acknowledging right versus wrong becomes a source of conflict and, worse yet, inequality. The person who judges becomes the troublemaker. Disagreement becomes divisive, one of the greatest modern sins, so divisiveness must be extinguished as if it were a fire in the kitchen.

The capacity to make judgments is what separates us, by and large, from the primal ooze. Making judgments is a moral duty. Some beliefs manifest in our culture do not spring from virtue or excellence.

Children know that kind of thinking compromises their ability to make moral choices and judgments. It erodes their self-confidence. They know it makes them weaker. They know they will be less capable to deal with an often harsh and brutal real world.

Children resent those that inflict harm upon them. Being six or seven or ten years old, often there's not a lot they can do about it. They have few options but to trust and have faith in their parents. There's a lot, however, we parents can do to earn and sustain our children's trust and to make them strong. Teaching them to distinguish between truth and false beliefs and to make moral judgments are high on the list.

THE FOUR ETHICAL PRINCIPLES

CHAPTER 9

AUTONOMY

REFLECTIONS IN A MIRROR

*"Act as if the maxim from which you act were to become
through your will a universal law of nature."*

–EMMANUEL KANT

I WATCHED MY MOM DIE. I also watched her live. She was a nuclear reactor continuously combusting. She hiked The Cotswolds in southern England, stood at the base of Mount Everest in Nepal and, bathed in moonlight, meditated on a mountain top on an Indian reservation in New Mexico. She watched whales in Alaska, probably shouting that they were eating too many seals and krill and needed wheat germ to balance their diets, otherwise they'd get fat, just like her oldest child, (me) who is starting to look like them. She tutored ex-cons in reading until one of the ex's conned her and sometimes she slipped a pastry or two into her pocketbook as she left a luncheon.

My mom could be a little rough around the edges. Smiling impishly, she sometimes asked waiters if the salad dressing could be on the side rather than slopped on the lettuce and if the chef could please substitute brown rice for the white rice, which is poison and causes cancer and shouldn't be served anyhow.

My mom chose to live an opinionated robust life. Now cancer ravaged and diminished her once vibrant body and she had to choose the terms of engagement with the unhappy process of dying. She stopped chemotherapy a few months before the end. The treatment made her nauseous and it wasn't defeating the cancer. All pain, no gain. Not a good deal.

After considering the probable outcomes of each treatment protocol, all supported by studies, test results and X-rays, my mom said, essentially, 'No mas!' as prize fighter Roberto Duran famously said to stop a fight against 'Sugar' Ray Leonard. Roberto knew he was beaten just as my mom knew her fight was over.

During her last weeks I fed my mom pain pills and warm broth instead of chicken and tofu. Two weeks or so before she passed on I brought her chocolate ice cream.

"It's not low fat," she noted disapprovingly.

"You're worried about fat, mom? Spit out the fat!" I yelled.

Her lawyer, Suzy, had all the legal stuff prepared. No heroic measures, no feeding tubes, no experimental drugs, no forced hydration were to be used. My mom had made those choices long before the cancer began its assault. She chose how she lived and she chose how she would die. She exercised her Autonomy.

FIRST AMONG EQUALS

Autonomy is the first of the four ethical principles in the Moral Measures. Its lead-off position is the banal consequence of beginning with the letter 'a' but perhaps its alphabetical primacy is also a fateful indicator of its moral primacy. Autonomy is the foundation of individual liberty and the first ethical line of defense against tyranny. To a large degree Autonomy is the ethical basis for the three other ethical principles in the Moral Measures.

The English word Autonomy is derived from the Greek roots 'autos', which means 'self,' and 'nomos,' which means rule, governance or law. Autonomy commands that an individual has the moral *right* to self direct or self-legislate his life and destiny.

Ask your child to name words that have the syllables auto in them. Likely she will mention words such as 'automobile,' 'automatic,' 'autograph,' autobiography' and 'autopilot.'

Analyze the words and you will decipher that they have in common that the 'self' or the thing exercises power or authority. The automobile driver determines where the car goes. The driver can stop for pizza or pick up a hitchhiker or change the intended destination. A passenger on a bus or a jet or a train cannot exercise such power. The automatic machine and the autopilot on the jet operate independently on their own.

TWO SIDES OF THE AUTONOMY COIN

"If I am not for myself, who will be?
And if I am only for myself, what am I?"

–THE TALMUD

Autonomy is usefully thought of as the two sides of a coin. One side represents the right to have one's Autonomy respected and the other side represents the duty to respect the Autonomy of others. As Emmanuel Kant phrased it, we are both sovereigns and subjects. To honor your Autonomy, other folks must be honest with you, but you have a moral duty to be honest with them. I often refer to this duet of rights and duties as the 'bookends of life.'

Kant's phrase quoted at the beginning of the chapter has several versions. Probably the most familiar one is the old Golden Rule: "Do unto others as you would have others do unto you." Another and perhaps less elegant way of phrasing Kant's statement is "Would you like everyone to behave the way you behave?" This concept of the 'bookends' extends Autonomy beyond the 'self' to the 'other.' This reality is not trivial because, to all the world, *you* are the *other.* So, it's not just about 'me;' it's about 'us.'

English philosopher John Stuart Mill expressed the core principle of Autonomy in this statement from his treatise, "On Liberty:"

> "In that part (of his conduct) which merely concerns himself,
> his independence is, of right, absolute. Over himself, over his
> own body and mind, the individual is sovereign."

Mills' words are true as far as they go but, in practical terms, they have limited application. Few matters 'merely concern' only the self. All else, and that includes almost everything, engages others. My mom's medical directive and her right to be informed of her prognosis perhaps concerned only the 'self.' In the real world, the fibers of our lives are woven into a much larger fabric.

Good manners, for example, demonstrate how the rights and duties required by Autonomy extend beyond 'me' to 'others.' Lynne Truss, in her best-selling book, *Talk to the Hand*, writes of rudeness:

"So the collapse of manners stands for a vast and under-acknowl-edged problem of social immorality. Manners are based on an ideal of empathy, of imagining the impact of one's own actions on others." Manners are justified, in large measure, by the Autonomy ethical principle.

In fact, there are two levels of the rights-duties polarity. One level has to do with the rights and the duties that each individual has on his or her own behalf. The second level has to do with the duties that others have to honor another individual's Autonomy.

As an example of the first level, the principle of Autonomy holds that a person has a general right to be treated with dignity. So, for example, a person should not be the target of a racial slur. Thus, making a racial slur is unethical. Defamations based on such irra-tional criteria degrade a person's integrity and compromise its abil-ity to self-direct his life. Ellis poetically explained the ethical defect in racist remarks. "It's like you put someone in a box and you don't see the whole person."

The person making the slur violates the recipient's Autonomy. The right to dignified treatment incorporates a duty to take action to enforce that right. On the other hand, the person has an ethical duty not to violate the Autonomy or dignity of another person. Thus, there is a moral duty not to make racial slurs against some-one else. A more general statement can be drawn from this kind of example: no one has the right to commit a moral wrong.

The doctor-patient relationship illustrates both levels of the rights-duties interaction. The patient has a right to be fully informed so that it can exercise its Autonomy in making an informed decision regard-ing care. Thus, the doctor has a corresponding duty to inform the patient. But there is more. The patient has the duty to assert and pro-tect its rights. The patient, thus, has the duty to become informed. The patient has a duty to take action. The patient has a duty to help direct its care. The patient that sits like a pet rock and pays no attention to some of the doctor's information or that does not seek additional infor-mation or that mindlessly consents to treatment violates its own duty to itself under Autonomy.

Getting a second opinion, or a third or a fourth to achieve a comfort level necessary to make an informed decision fulfills Autonomy's ethical duty *to one's self*. In the doctor-patient example, the *right* to be treated as an autonomous human being is hollow unless the autonomous individual acts to advance that right. Having a reasonable diet, driving only when sober, self-defense, wearing seatbelts and bike helmets are all duties to one's self based on the Autonomy principle.

As these examples illustrate, you have to know what you're doing. Autonomy therefore requires the development and use of several qualities and skills, including self-reliance, independence, education, courage, engagement and being informed. Those who lack these qualities or abandon them risk morally compromising their Autonomy and, by default, granting to others the power and right to think and act on their behalf.

I'm not talking about the sick, the infirm, the disabled and those that cannot take care of themselves. Our children, of course, cannot fully exercise their Autonomy. Parents must do it for them as their surrogate or agent. One of the key benchmarks of adulthood, how-ever, is the committed exercise of one's Autonomy.

An effective way to explain Autonomy to your child is to talk about a typical visit to the doctor. I mentioned the doctor-patient relationship above and will now expand on the example. Keep in mind that the most effective dialogues link abstract ideas like Autonomy to real-world personal experiences. Here's the progression of points I use in my class discussions:

- First, the doctor asks, more or less, why are you here or where does it hurt?

- You give an answer and the doctor examines you. Stick out your tongue. Take an X-ray. Give the arm that got chopped off.

- The doctor proposes a treatment. We'll give you chemotherapy. We'll put the broken bone back in place. We'll pop in an artificial heart valve.

Next are the key points for understanding Autonomy:

- The doctor describes the risks and probable outcomes. For example, my mom's doctor told her that chemotherapy would only prolong her life for a short while and not cure her.

- The doctor then gives you a choice: to accept or reject the treatment or accept some of the treatment or choose a different treatment.

- The doctor then must receive your permission to begin treatment. With little children, the doctor will ask for the consent from an adult—a parent or a guardian.

In summary, before being treated, the doctor will—or should—inform about your condition, describe the proposed treatment, inform you about the risk of side effects and of the probability of success. Then you decide what to do. The result of this process is called informed consent. Informed consent is the ethical core of Autonomy regarding medical care. You have a right to be informed—meaning others must respect your Autonomy by providing complete information—and a right to decide what to do after being informed. Your Autonomy cannot be meaningfully exercised if you are not fully informed.

If you choose, you can just say no to the treatment, grab a few stale mints from the dish by the receptionist and walk out of the office. It's up to you.

Two days after I was hospitalized, Dr. Kowal said to me, more graciously, of course, but basically, "Here's the deal, Michael. Your aortic valve has been eaten away by bacteria. Your heart can't pump blood into your artery. Soon you will have congestive heart failure. Blood will pool in your lungs and you will drown. You have about a month to live. Replacing the heart valve will save your life. Anything you'd like me to do?"

"Do the surgery." I muttered. "Wake me when it's over."

WHAT TO DO? WHAT TO DO?

Autonomy is a complex subject, but if we explain it simply, which is different from simplistically, children will understand the concept in the abstract as well as in its application. Here's part of a dialogue on Autonomy and informed consent I had with a fifth grade class. Note how the conversation gently meanders like a little trout stream into new territory and how each section offers an unexpected big catch. New topics are built upon previous ones as the conversation progresses.

"What would you do," I asked, "if you needed medical treatment for a life-threatening problem?"

Some children said they would pray or cry. Brent focused on facts. He'd go to the hospital and talk to another doctor. "I'd want more information." Jared understood the relationships among information, choices and probabilities. "Truth helps you make better decisions. I'd need to know what will happen and what *might* happen to me."

The core of Autonomy is self-determination and self-regulation. Note how Karen's few words captured Autonomy's essence. "If you don't know what can happen, you can't control your life." Thus arises, Julie explained, the need to be informed. "How can you make decisions about your life if you don't know the facts?" Peter took the thinking a step further, expressing the need, indeed, the duty, to find the truth. "If you don't know the truth, you won't take the necessary steps to help yourself."

Stephanie grasped the relationship between knowledge and self-empowerment. "Getting the information is like standing up for yourself. That's how you do it!" Sarah's comment showed that these little folks do comprehend the larger concepts, such as the trade-offs inherent in making choices. "You might decide you don't want the surgery if something bad can happen and you don't want to take the chance."

Stephanie's analogy between doing well in school and taking care of yourself led to this priceless exchange. "It's like looking up information for your homework so you don't get a bad grade."

Finding the parallel amusing, Tommy blurted out, "You mean dying is like a bad grade?"

"Yeah," Stephanie roared. "Really bad!" Laughter filled the classroom.

YOU DO AUTONOMY FOR ME

Joey made a comment that caused the conversation to flow into an intriguing bend in the verbal river. His began, "When I was a kid...."

Paige leaped on his words like a cougar. "You're still a kid!"

Unflustered, Joey shrugged. "When I was a little kid...." Joey recounted that his parents made medical decisions for him when he severely burned his hand years ago. "I guess my parents took care of my Autonomy." His insight was spot on.

Joey's comments raised the issue of honoring a person's Autonomy when a person cannot exercise it himself. Sometimes through age, disability or some other incapacity, a person cannot act to enforce its Autonomy. This sometimes vexing issue is explored comprehensively in the Sanctity of Life chapter.

The short answer is that the law recognizes a concept called "substituted authority," which means that another person—a parent or an agent—is authorized to act on a child's behalf or on behalf of a person that is unable to exercise its authority. In my mom's case, another person had the legal authority to make end-of-life medical decisions, including the decision to refuse further medical treatment.

Joey was correct. Under the principle of substituted authority, his parents did 'take care of' his Autonomy. We see in these following comments that children want to grapple with challenging moral issues and moral dilemmas. As the students repeatedly told me, don't treat us like children. We can handle difficult subjects. I respected their Autonomy and told it like it is, more or less, for the most part and so on.

Rosa asked about the right of a person to refuse medical treatment such as a blood transfusion when that treatment could or would likely save its life. This issue presents an ethical dilemma where the Autonomy principle conflicts with the Sanctity of Life principle. Recall the 'steal medicine to save a dying child' ethical dilemma, where Sanctity of Life conflicted with Justice. Rosa asked, "Does the person have the right to decide to live or die?"

Indeed the person does, as long as the person is considered to be mentally competent and able to make a reasoned decision. The principle of Autonomy provides moral justification for a person to refuse medical care, even when that medical care can save its life. Note that this circumstance is different from refusing medical treatment to prevent prolonging life, the kind of situation that might have but, blessedly, did not confront my mom.

My students continued to ask probing questions. Abbie directed the discussion to a more complex issue when, rolling out her thoughts carefully as if they were pastry dough on marble, she asked, "What if a child needs a blood transfusion but the parents don't believe in transfusions? Can the parents stop the doctor from giving the transfusion?"

Seeing children think thoughts and raise questions never previously considered is a source of great joy. Abbie's question was such a source. I strive to avoid quick answers that give the illusion of absolute authority or wisdom, in large measure because I have neither, and also because it would be unethical. Recall that any subject can be taught unethically, including ethics. Rather, I try to respond in a way that allows the issue to marinate in the children's minds as we reason together toward a moral resolution.

Abbie's provocative question addressed the conflict between the substituted authority of the parent and the Autonomy rights of the child. Obviously, we cannot know whether or not a two-month-old child would decide to have a potentially life-saving blood transfusion. Similarly, a twelve-year-old is not legally allowed to make a decision that might lead to its death. That's why the principle of substituted authority was created.

The law assumes and requires, however, that the agent act in the best interests of the principle, in this case, the child. Society, through its laws, presumes that a person would choose to live.

Although the principle of Autonomy allows a parent to take risks and make decisions regarding its *own* life that might prove fatal, the principle does not allow a parent to impose those beliefs and consequent actions upon the child.

In this rare instance, the Golden Rule—do unto others, etc—is disregarded because obeying the parent's 'doing unto' would violate the child's Autonomy. The parent that would reject a transfusion is not permitted to impose that choice on its child. The government, usually through a judge, will intervene and substitute *its* authority for that of the parents' and require treatment that holds the greatest likelihood of saving the child's life.

By the way, even professionals such as lawyers are sometimes challenged to honor a client's Autonomy. For example, a colleague of mine, while preparing a will, asked the client, "Do you want to be buried or cremated?" The client replied unhelpfully, "Surprise me!" (thank you, Henny Youngman!)

I hope my presentation of these dialogues has done justice to the intellect and curiosity of the wonderful children in my classes. They are bright, inquisitive and committed to learning how to figure out for themselves what is right and decent and honorable. Your children have the same motivations and are no less capable of such profound insights and vibrant discussions.

WE HOLD THESE TRUTHS TO BE SELF-EVIDENT

So fundamental is the principle of Autonomy to the primacy of the individual that our Founding Fathers made it the heart of the political philosophy of the United States. Autonomy is the ethical foundation for one of the greatest statements ever created by our species, The Declaration of Independence. The Declaration, adopted by the Second Continental Congress on July 4, 1776, declared the American Colonies free of British rule. The principle of Autonomy underscores the several individual rights defined in this famous sentence:

We hold these truths to be self-evident, that all men are created equal, that they are endowed by their Creator with certain unalienable rights; that among these are Life, Liberty and the pursuit of Happiness.

That these rights, life, liberty and the pursuit of happiness, among others, were unalienable means they were not given by the government or the State but were endowed by something higher. The legitimacy of these rights, the Founders believed, was so obvious that they were described as self-evident. These unalienable rights are sometimes referred to as 'negative' rights because they are inherent by virtue of the individual's existence and thus can only be taken away, and, if taken away, only done so by an illegitimate political system.

Irrespective of one's beliefs regarding a creator, this proposition is an unsurpassed affirmation of an individual's Autonomy. Ayn Rand illustrates how individual rights are a version of minority rights:

The smallest minority on earth is the individual. Those who deny individual rights cannot claim to be defenders of minorities.

We know that rights have corresponding duties, and the Founders recognized that these self-evident unalienable rights also carried with them important duties. Citizens had the duty to be informed, educated and self-reliant; to be what The Federalist Papers referred to as "an active and engaged citizenry."

Autonomy was expressed through action, by a robust individualism and sense of self, a pioneering vigor and the principle that you received that which you merited, because receiving more than you merited meant taking from the labors of another person's Autonomy. Autonomy can, therefore, usefully be considered society's moral connective tissue.

Autonomy is the basis of human dignity. Liberty, for example, may be a self-evident right, but liberty is concerned with more than the self; more than self-realization or self-expression or self-direction. Taken alone, those are the values of a narcissist. To be virtuous, liberty must have intrinsic moral limits and be balanced by personal responsibility, the other side of Autonomy's coin.

There is also another aspect of Autonomy which some enviably bright thinkers call 'the psychology of Autonomy.' If I understand the concept, the psychology of Autonomy means an active dedication to create one's own dignity through virtuous action based on the notion that *you* are responsible for your life. Numerous variations of this theme are stated throughout this book. This psychology commands the stoic pursuit of physical and mental and emotional independence and rejects victimization and delegating to others the chores of life. Perhaps my best expression of this ennobling psychology is the introductory quotation in the Choices chapter.

Regrettably, a negative counterpart to the psychology of Autonomy exists, the psychology of decline, the other side of the metaphoric coin. Fundamentally the psychology of decline is evidenced by the willingness to give up one's Autonomy, often incrementally and subtly, and sometimes under the delusion that this decline is actually for one's own good. This psychology of decline has profound moral implications.

Some limitations on Autonomy are morally justified, such as prohibitions against rape and other assorted criminal conduct. We have seatbelt and helmet laws that, I am persuaded, do more good than harm. But other encroachments of Autonomy, of differing degrees of subtlety, individually and collectively raise an ominous specter of moral decline.

Encroachments that dictate who you can have in your clubs, what cars you can drive, which light bulbs you can use, which grocery bags you are permitted, which doctors you can see and for what purposes and how much the doctor can charge, how much of your earnings you can keep, unaccountable government officials acting like a resurrected monarchy, school admissions and job offers unrelated to merit, state policies favoring some industries and punishing others, influencing access to information and which media programs one should listen to and what they should be permitted to say, how many fries you can have with your hamburger and controlling the content of soda pop and pretzels and butter, who can watch your children, how your property may be used and whether one is permitted to defend one's property or one's family or even one's self. All this and more represent the subversion of liberty and Autonomy in the delusional menacing pursuit of a risk-free life and are but a few indicators of the psychology of decline.

I think it was Mark Steyn, (I may be wrong and, if so, I apologize for not giving proper attribution) who expressed the relationship between declining Autonomy and the moral consequences of the psychology of decline. With the psychology of decline, the values of individual liberty and freedom, of merit, achievement, indeed, self respect, change. As Autonomy diminishes, other forces become stronger and virtues once held in esteem such as hard work, independence, self-reliance, sacrifice and postponed gratification lose their luster because they are not rewarded and not respected. Thus, they are abandoned. My Justice chapter provides an example of moral psychology's decline.

Think about rudeness, mentioned above, and you will recognize that its acceptance is an indicator of the moral implications of the psychology of decline. Here's a straightforward example of the psychology of decline that can engage even young children and make profound points.

A person walks to a grocery story. The sidewalk or grass or asphalt has garbage and litter on it—fast food packaging, soda cans, newspapers, politicians' campaign literature. The person doesn't pick up any of the trash. There may be several explanations for this behavior. One may be simply that the person doesn't care. That explanation has significant moral implications. Another explanation is the old "I didn't put it there so why should I pick it up?" mind-set. But another likely explanation is that picking up the trash and litter and junk is someone else's job—the property owner, the government, criminals on work release programs, whatever. This mind-set also has moral consequences.

The traveler might not be aware of the underlying motivation to leave the refuse and garbage. The reasons may have become buried long ago in the person's psyche. But the result—not picking up the garbage up—impacts the person's moral psychology. The individual accepts the garbage and litter; accepts the incremental social decay and sees no relationship or does not care about the relationship between its actions and his community. This psychology subverts personal and civic responsibility. And separate from technical responsibility, it undermines civic virtue and the sense of community.

I don't want to push the point too hard, but the same mentality that ignores the soda pop can, when taken to its logical extreme, leads to slums and blight and social disorder. The concepts of moral attitudes and moral psychology are relatively sophisticated, but your children, even the little ones, will understand their core aspects and will enthusiastically welcome discussing them.

The psychology of decline acts like a fine pin hole in a large balloon inflated with helium. Just as the balloon descends deflated as if exhausted, the virtues that have energized and liberated the human spirit and which have led to the greatest human achievements begin a death spiral, to be replaced by mediocrity, indifference and emptiness.

Revisiting the coin metaphor, the other side of achieving greatness and dignity is accepting responsibility, often tedious and sometimes risky, whether studying for a math exam, practicing the piano or jump shots or defending liberty and freedom. If you don't nurture greatness and liberty, you will lose them and all else that has been accumulated and granted to you from the past.

Tension between freedom and constraint will always exist, just as there is tension between rights and responsibilities. People love the rights and freedom parts but often tend to skate away from the responsibility and obligation parts. Thus, in the real world, Autonomy can exist only to the degree that it is protected by a moral community. Individual Autonomy can flourish only when institutions value it and protect it and when citizens honor it for themselves and for others. Absent these forces, prattling on about rights is about as useful as a wolf yelping at the moon.

*"No man is an Iland, of it selfe; every man is a peece of the Continent,
a part of the maine; if a Clod bee washed away by the Sea,
Europe is the lesse, as well as if a Promontorie were...And therefore
never send to know for whom the bell tolls; It tolls for thee."*

–JOHN DONNE

We want to raise autonomous children; children that are strong and independent and capable of becoming strong independent adults. The child that appreciates the 'rights and responsibilities' bookends and acts accordingly will have developed a profound moral sense and be well on its way to becoming a morally autonomous adult.

I close with a child's statement that readers may find valuable if they are inclined to discuss this topic. I've asked hundreds of children what parents can do to respect their children's Autonomy. Char, a fifth grader, gave one of the most illuminating answers. "Parents show us respect when they talk seriously to us." Parents can have no better guideline.

Char's statement pretty much sums up my motivation for writing this book. If you want to honor your child's Autonomy, and to increase the odds that your children will honor yours, talking about Autonomy is a great way to start.

CHAPTER 10

BENEFICENCE

"Every object rightly seen unlocks a quality of the soul."

—RALPH WALDO EMERSON

A MATTER OF DUTY

EVERY DAY IN DENVER I see selfless goodness, kindness and decency; people donating to charities, tutoring children, volunteering at schools and hospitals, giving their time and their resources. The annual Marine's 'Toys for Tots' program is always successful. The Denver Police Orphan's Fund, The Barbara Davis Diabetes Center, the many Santa's Helpers at the Denver Children's Hospital, Concerts for Kids, children's sports associations and dozens of other worthy activities flourish because of countless acts of selfless decency.

A few years ago, as Thanksgiving approached, a radio talk show host asked for donations of turkeys for homeless shelters. The *next day* I called the station and asked where to deliver my frozen bird. The receptionist told me that five thousand turkeys had already been donated, exceeding the system's capacity. Mine wasn't needed. "Think of us next year," she graciously said.

Weeks later, thousands of dollars were raised in *a few hours* for surgery for a dog savagely maimed by an assailant. Greater Denver is a hospitable area and I'm fortunate to live there, but I don't think its decency and compassion are unique. Most likely your community's generosity is equal.

This chapter is about Beneficence, the second ethical principle of the Moral Measures. I explore its meaning and applications and share examples of how a few seemingly ordinary people brought this principle to reality in extraordinary ways. Several children's comments illustrate wonderful expeditions of thought as they grapple with this moral duty.

ON THE ROAD

I was about seven years old. I was riding my bicycle on my quiet street in East Rockaway, Long Island when I hit a patch of loose gravel and took a nasty tumble. I was wearing short pants (I haven't worn shorts since) and a T-shirt. Lying in the street, observing blood congeal on my knees and arms and the scratches on my new bike, to the best of my recollection, I screamed. Phyllis, my neighbor and Richie's mom, came to my aid. "Are you okay?" she asked.

"Never felt better," I replied. "Rays of a loving sun are caressing us and all is right with the world! Why do you ask?" Perhaps those were not my exact words. I was yelling. Maybe crying. I was not beyond such behavior. Phyllis walked me to my house and bid me adieu. My mom cleaned my wounds and gave me a doughnut. She added, in typical motherly fashion, 'Be careful!' I assured her I would. Then I asked for another doughnut, the one with chocolate sprinkles. My recovery was swift.

It was nice, right and decent for Phyllis to help me, of course, but...drum roll...was she morally *obligated* to help me? Phrasing it another way, would Phyllis have been *wrong* or *unethical* if she did *not* help me? If there was a duty to help me, what ethical principle created that duty?

For guidance, we look to the principle 'Beneficence.' It derives from the Latin, *bene facere*, meaning 'do good (to)'. 'Doing good' or 'the act of being kind' are general definitions. Synonyms include altruistic, humanitarian, neighborly, public-spirited, philanthropic, mercy, charity, kindness, grace, generosity and good will.

These synonyms are essentially accurate but they omit what I suggest is the most important component of Beneficence, the concept of moral duty. The core of the principle is the moral obligation to do 'good' or to reduce or avoid harm. Beneficence, then, is more than charity or mercy or kindness. It is the moral obligation to be kind and charitable and good.

I've talked about my bicycle incident in class to introduce the concept of ethical duty. Consistently my students have said that Phyllis should have helped me. When I asked why, they said they didn't know. When I hear such responses, I think of Inspector Clouseau's nasal voice saying, 'Ah, the old I-don't-know ploy!' When students say 'I don't know,' it often means they don't want to think. Follow up questions are thus required to get them thinking. Certainly, such a duty seems logical, does it not?

We agree Phyllis was nice. We agree she was good. All agreed with Jonathan comment, "It's the right thing to do." Now ask your little ones if Phyllis was ethically *required* to help me. Emphasize the word *required*. I'm not talking about being good. I'm talking about doing something she was *supposed* to do.

For guidance we re-visited the old Golden Rule. You don't have to be a lawyer to understand that 'Do unto others as others would do unto you.' doesn't mean 'Please give some thought to doing unto others as....' or 'Maybe you should, if you are so inclined at the moment, do unto others as....' or 'If you're not going into a meeting or playing a video game please spare a moment and do unto others as....' or 'If there is no way you could suffer or pay a price, then do unto others as....' You get the point. The Golden Rule means 'Do it!'

Shirleen's 'Golden Rule' answer didn't hit the target's center but was close to the mark. "Yeah, you would want someone to help you if you were hurt!" Of course, helping me was the right thing to do and I would want someone to help me, but I was determined to keep the focus on the issue of moral duty and not on what I would like.

In a burst of insight Lynn captured the essence of Beneficence. "Well, if you can help, you should do it." Lynn brilliantly linked moral obligation to ability. If you can, then you should! But Lynn also realized that if you *can't* do something, then there is no duty to do it and, by inference, there is no duty to try to do something. There's a lot of elegant moral philosophy in that third-grader's nine words.

When Phyllis saw me sprawled out in the middle of the street, oozing blood like grapes in a wine press, she not only had an opportunity to be nice but also a moral duty to help. She could, so she should.

Additional examples will illustrate the components of moral duty, but before I give them, I will explain the general meaning of 'duty.' I draw upon the law of torts, which deals with defining duties—the shoulds that folks are required to do—and the consequences for failing to perform those duties.

Legislatures and courts define duties generally in terms of social benefits, predictable harm and the practical burden of preventing the harm. Courts try to craft consistent formulas for determining whether a duty exists. They consider an aggregation of factors that include the risk of harm caused by the behavior at issue, how useful the behavior was that led to the injury, the degree of burden that would be created by guarding against the injury and the consequences of imposing liability on the behavior.

This collection of factors may impress the reader as unduly technical or obtuse, but that's the way it is. None of these criteria are easily measured and people can reasonably (or unreasonably) disagree on their importance and implications.

The failure to perform a duty is phrased in several ways: 'violating' or 'breaching' a duty. Liability—legal responsibility—results when a person didn't do what he was supposed to do and that failure caused harm to someone or something. In tort law, once a duty and a breach of that duty have been established, the next issue is determining the cost or damage caused by the failure to perform the duty.

An automobile driver has a duty to stop at a red light. A driver that ignores the red light violates or breaches that duty. If that driver then slams into a car that was legally going through a green light, then the violation of the duty to stop for the red light leads to liability or responsibility for the harm caused to other driver and/or its property. Three aspects of liability are present: the duty, the breach of the duty that caused harm and the harm.

However, let's say it's two in the morning and no other car is on the road and a driver goes through—ignores—a red traffic light. There would have been a duty and a violation of that duty but if the violation caused no harm—no crash or injury to another—then the violator would have no liability for damages although the driver would be liable for violating a traffic code provision, usually a fine, points against a driver's license and, in extreme cases, a jail term. Based on my limited experience, under these circumstances it is singularly unhelpful to emphasize to a police officer that no other person or car was in the vicinity.

Let's analyze a more complex issue of duty. Assume a bank has an ATM machine placed in an unlighted part of the building's exterior. A customer is robbed withdrawing money at one in the morning. Is the bank liable to the crime victim because it breached a duty to have adequate lighting near the ATM? The first issue is determining whether there is a duty to have lighting or more lighting where the ATM is located.

Refer to the four criteria mentioned above. What do you think? Does society benefit from having ATM machines well lit at one in the morning? If so, how much does society benefit? What is the cost of that benefit to the bank and to its customers? Did the customer have an obligation to avoid the darkened area at one in the morning? Was the deficient lighting a cause of the robbery? Would more lighting have prevented a robbery at one a.m.? How much lighting can be required before the requirement becomes unreasonably burdensome to the bank? Who knows?

In all fairness, it is quite a mental and linguistic struggle to provide rules that tell us what we should and should not do regarding the gazillion things that our species does. Applying these criteria, however imperfect they may be, most of us would likely conclude that a person has a duty not to smoke a cigarette when pumping gas into a car and not to fly an airplane while drunk.

Similarly, a boat owner has a duty to provide life preservers and gun owners with young children shouldn't leave loaded guns on the kitchen table next to the rye bread and smoked turkey.

We can apply these duty criteria to Phyllis to determine if she had a moral duty to help me. Helping was not a great burden to her; helping injured children lying in the street is socially useful; the risk of harm to me lying in the road was significant and imposing such a duty on neighbors would likely not cause anti social behavior. It is unlikely, I suggest, that such a policy would encourage neighbors to hide in a closet every time they heard a child scream, although, I suppose, if neighbors started getting sued for failing to help screaming children, it could.

For our purposes then, let us speak in terms of moral duties and not legal duties and let us further agree that not all moral duties become legal duties. Based on those criteria, I am confident most folks would agree that Phyllis had a moral duty to help me. Her behavior would have been unethical if she did not.

With this foundation of understanding about duty, we can explore more complex dimensions of Beneficence. The best way I know to move a conversation to a logical conclusion is to think about the relevant facts. Recall that facts determine morality and that morality changes as facts change. Think of the discussion about helping the motorist on the side of the road or saving the drowning person. Facts also determine duty and, similarly, duties change as facts change.

Just because you *can* do something doesn't mean you are morally *obligated* to do it. The commands of Beneficence are not infinite. Recall the criteria used by courts. Phyllis might not have a duty to enter a burning building to rescue me—it depends on the facts— and I concede she would have no duty to help me if I were injured on the peak of Mount Everest while she was having a mocha latte at base camp, even if she could hear my screams from up there.

A duty may exist in one situation but not in a slightly different one. The art is to teach what I call "the power of the particular," which means understanding that duties are fact-specific. We must calculate the benefits and risks inherent in the specific situation when figuring out whether Beneficence commands us to act. Only in this way can we teach our children how to become moral thinkers rather than to act reflexively and without thought.

There is another aspect of Beneficence that deserves mention. We are duty bound to help others but no one has a moral *claim* to our moral obligations or to our charity. If a panhandler approached me and demanded I produce my latest tax return so he could calculate how much I morally owed him, some florid words would tip toe from my otherwise circumspect lips.

No one has a moral right to my charity. Absent a legal obligation, no one has a claim on the Beneficence of anyone else, and legal obligations can also be unethical.

BLOOD, MARROW AND TEARS

Here are segments of class discussions that involve Beneficence. The first pertains to the common and noble act of donating blood. Is there a moral obligation to have a vein punctured so your blood can spew out for the benefit of someone else? The 'What do we know? What do we need to know?' reasoning skill will guide your children toward a moral conclusion. Many readers have given blood, I bet, and even if not, the process is sufficiently common that it can be knowledgably discussed. I think these observations can be taken as facts:

- Pain is rare and, in any event, brief
- Giving blood takes a few minutes
- The risk of harm to the donor is essentially non-existent
- The benefit to the donor is substantial
- Afterwards you get a glass of juice and sometimes a cookie

Are we obligated to donate blood, as Phyllis was obligated to help me? Well, first of all, sometimes there are other facts to consider before reaching a conclusion. I cannot donate blood because I take anticoagulants. It would be dangerous to me—something about my puncture site not healing quickly enough. Also, the anticoagulant would have to be filtered from my blood, which apparently isn't cost effective.

Separate from unique situations such as mine, ask your child whether donating blood is an act of charity or is a moral duty? Would it be *wrong* not to donate blood or would it be just *good* to do it? To guide your thinking, I offer my own answer at the outset: I don't know. Ethics experts can't agree, so my uncertainty doesn't bother me.

But getting the answer isn't the goal anyway. Moral reasoning is—teaching your children to analyze an issue so they may have confidence in their own conclusions, even though their conclusions may change.

Here's a variation of the blood donor example. A dad needs a kidney transplant and his daughter is a perfect donor match. Is she morally obligated to donate a kidney to her dad? Let's look at the facts. Medical treatment in the United States is unsurpassed in safety and pain control. The risk to the daughter would be minimal, and the benefit to the dad would be considerable. Yet major surgery is involved and, as we know from indelicate bumper stickers, bad things happen. For whatever its worth, I suggest the better argument is the daughter has no duty to donate a kidney. You may reach a different conclusion. That's your business.

Here's another variation of a medical donating situation. The young daughter of a neighbor was diagnosed with Type 1 Juvenile Diabetes. The dad offered to donate part of his pancreas to his daughter in the hope it would replenish her insulin-producing cells. The doctor told the dad that such the surgical procedures would be unethical. Why? The dad's pancreas would be rejected by the daughter's immune system, not only rendering the pancreas useless but also risking the daughter's life. Additionally, the surgery posed substantial risks for the father. Since no benefit would result and the risks to one or both lives were substantial, it would be unethical for the doctor to perform the surgeries.

Despite great intentions, once again, Beneficence does not require an action just because it can be done. The reader should now realize that the duties required by Beneficence can be quite subjective. People may view risk and pain differently. That's the human condition. My interest is teaching children to do the analysis. How they end up on any given issue is their business. I have faith that once analyzed thoroughly and dispassionately, most people will make ethically-based decisions, even though I might disagree with some of them.

BEATING THE ODDS

Two of the most inspirational and motivating stories I share with my classes illustrate how Beneficence can be as expansive as the human spirit. Alex, the son of one of my dearest of dearest friends, at the age of five, was diagnosed with Acute Megakaryoblastic Leukemia, a rare and particularly virulent form of leukemia. Death was imminent. The only hope for a cure was a bone marrow transplant, a risky procedure with speculative results.

Given the perniciousness of the disease, the donor's marrow had to be an almost perfect genetic match, a statistical improbability on the order of winning the Powerball lottery. As death slithered closer, a data bank search yielded a marrow donor who, against all odds, fulfilled the genetic criteria. The marrow transplant was a stunning success, a miracle in every sense of the word and a transcendent testament to modern medical technology, hard work and a dash of the divine.

My friend developed a friendship as deep as the ocean with the donor, Rex, a civil engineer and lay Baptist minister in Alabama. I was honored to meet Rex several times. He is modest and unassuming, soft spoken and gracious.

I learned donating bone marrow is a complex medical procedure. The potential donor first undergoes several medical tests. After passing the tests, extracting the marrow requires the donor to be placed under general anesthesia, a procedure saturated with risks. A needle is injected deep into the pelvis and the marrow is withdrawn. Soreness and pain are experienced for several days.

I asked what motivated him to take those risks on behalf of a stranger.

Sitting on a couch in my friend's home, Rex sipped a soft drink and replied slowly. "It's very simple, really." He paused to fit the words to his ideas. "How do we make the world better? Not knowing the person is hardly important. We are all family! How could I not help?" He took a breath and smiled. "Helping others brings dignity to my life." His gentle words hit me like a linebacker.

I sought my students' opinions about this man who endured pain to save a person he never expected to meet. Julie's sparse answer was one of the most eloquent and life-affirming. "It's worth it to have some pain to save another person."

I confide I get weepy writing about Rex, doubtless, in part, because he saved the life of my friend's child. Yet I am equally compelled to share the story of a family I have not met but whose Beneficence is as vast as the Milky Way galaxy. My information is taken from local newspaper articles.

Robin and Bob Zaborek, a Denver-area couple, adopted a Downs Syndrome baby born with pulmonary hypertension. When told that the infant was also missing her left hand, Robin responded, "No problem!" I question whether I can grasp the unbounded enormity of their hearts. They *could*, so they *did*, and they did because they believed they *should*. This is Beneficence to the hundredth power.

It is comforting and reassuring to talk to children about people like Rex and the Zaboreks. They become inspired and, I think, motivated to pursue virtue and to sacrifice for something larger than themselves. They empathize with these marvelous people. "It would be very difficult to raise a child like that," Amanda said of the Zaborek baby. "They have to have more love and courage than regular parents." Ruby added, "Raising such a child wouldn't be as much fun."

I couldn't constrain myself. "You think it's so much fun to raise you little creatures?" Giggling, the children admitted that they could be demanding. "Sometimes I'm a real pain," Patrick acknowledged.

One measure to gauge whether I'm connecting with the children is whether they relate my words to personal experiences. Almost always they do. One little fellow talked disarmingly about his friend who has Downs Syndrome. "When we were little, she could do everything about the same as we could and we had fun. We played soccer together. But," he paused and bit his lip, "now that we're older it's very difficult to play with her. And I know it's hard on her parents."

One night, seated near a crackling bonfire, my scoutmaster made a statement that, even though I was only eleven or twelve, I sensed was insightful: "No man is as tall as when he stoops to help a child." Rex and the Zaboreks and those like them were not stooping, of course. Quite the contrary, they were flying as close to the angels as humans are capable.

These conversations are valuable because they portray sacrifice and decency and evoke empathy. People that rise to meet great challenges serve as admirable role models. I know that, in some small way, the child leaving the classroom after such conversations is not the same child that entered it.

> *"Make yourself useful to somebody."*
>
> –RALPH WALDO EMERSON

JUST WONDERING AROUND

In our rambling discussions about Beneficence, the topic of giving money to panhandlers always arises. Children are not certain whether giving money is beneficent, that is, helpful, or whether their generosity furthers improper behavior such as alcoholism or drug use. They also wonder if they are being hustled under false pretenses, induced by heart-breaking statements scribbled on battered cardboard signs about needing insulin or visiting children not seen since the Koran War and so forth.

The panhandling discussion probes the relationship between Beneficence and uncertainty. My role is to promote thinking by asking questions rather than providing answers. I will never know whether money I give will be spent on broccoli or heroin, on insulin or on cigarettes. A dialogue is justified nevertheless even though the issue has no resolution. I confess I react spontaneously and inconsistently, giving based on whim, emotion and gut instinct.

Another intriguing topic relates Beneficence to selfishness. The argument alleged is that doing good is motivated by the selfish desire and impulse to feel good about yourself. This concept will provoke fascinating conversations with your children.

The likelihood is that your children will say something similar to fifth-grader Lilli's appraisal of this 'good is selfish' argument, which displayed a degree of practical reasoning that escapes a lot of academics. "Well, I guess it's selfish, but if you're good just to be good and you don't have any expectation, then it's not selfish." Examining thoughts she'd not previously considered, Lilli concluded, "It's not selfish to want a better world."

I do not purport to be a deep thinker, but my appraisal of the 'doing good is selfish' argument is, Who cares? If the Zaboreks and the Rex's and those that donate blood and treasure and fight crime and tyranny are selfish, then let selfishness reign throughout the land!

LOOK WHAT I FOUND!

A couple of years ago I went to a mobile phone store to get a new charger. I arrived early. I went to the entrance and pulled on the door but it was locked although employees were inside. I retrieved my keys from my pocket, walked the few paces to my car and got in to wait for the store to open. A moment later a young woman with a little boy—maybe five years old—knocked on my car window. The boy, her son, had found a twenty-dollar bill where I had been standing. He gave it to his mom.

"I think this is yours," she said. Indeed it was. I thanked them and offered a reward to the little fellow, who sported a big smile.

"No thank you," she said. "It was the right thing to do."

Beneficence inspires us to do heroic deeds when we can but it also obligates us to do those little acts of kindness and decency that give dignity and joy and honor to our lives. Beneficence increases social efficiency. People view the world more optimistically when they can count on being helped when they need it. One day's blood donor is another day's blood recipient. We even have a duty to be happy, according to Dennis Prager, an astute observer of culture, which includes the duty not to inflict our misery on others.

Beneficence and its offspring—civility, kindness, generosity of spirit and courtesy—cannot be legislated or enforced, at least not effectively. Some institutions try to do so, with predictably obscene and immoral consequences. The imperatives of Beneficence create what Lord Moulton described as "obedience to the unenforceable; those moral principles which have no legal sanction... obedience to the unwritten law which all decent, honest, and honorable persons everywhere submit to as being right."

Beneficence is a matter of personal character. You do what you can under the circumstances. The duties imposed by Beneficence remind us that we are in this life together; that we need each other. To love humanity is one thing. Doing something that betters humanity is quite another. Your children are likely the same as the hundreds I've talked to for two decades. They want to "make a difference in the world," by which they mean, "make the world a better place."

When your children tell me they want to do something good, I believe them. Teaching the duties of Beneficence is an effective way to help them fulfill that goal.

I'd like to think when life is done

That I had filled a needed post,

That here and there I'd paid my fare

With more than idle talk and boast;

That I had taken gifts divine,

The breath of life and manhood fine,

And tried to use them now and then

In service for my fellow men.

–EDGAR A. GUEST

CHAPTER 11

JUSTICE

THAT'S NOT FAIR!

*"I think aesthetics is at the base of all meaning;
not the improvement of skills and effectiveness, but achieving
those fleeting moments when craft and determination produce
beauty and virtue. Why else bother?"*

–THE HONORABLE JOHN L. KANE,
UNITED STATES DISTRICT COURT, DISTRICT OF COLORADO

THAT'S NOT FAIR! The accusation rips at the heart of most parents like a serrated knife. It's one of the great sins, right up there with nuclear weapons proliferation and not using the proper dressing on your child's salad. Most of us want to be fair. Fairness is an indicator of decency, virtue and moral judgment. On the personal level, it's a sign that we are 'good' and wise. On the societal level, it is a fundamental value that increases society's tensile strength and durability, lubricates its functioning and, by and large, keeps the barbarians at the gate.

Children understand fairness in practical terms such as treating people based on what they've done or applying consistent standards to the same behavior or taking the time to learn the truth about something. It is unfair, one child told me, when her brother's friend messed up the house and she had to help clean it up. It's unfair to be grounded for a month for saying a dirty word. It's not fair to punish the entire class because an unidentified child wrote dirty words on the chalkboard. Racism is unfair because it demeans people for reasons unconnected to behavior or attitude or accomplishment.

Your children will have a seemingly endless list of examples of unfairness. A coach gave her own child more playing time during a game than your child even though your child is the better athlete. One child gets home from school earlier than the other and eats all the cookies. To avoid the squabbling, the mom stopped buying cookies and no one gets them. That's not fair!

Sometimes the unfairness relates to responsibilities. Regina, a fifth grader, explained her predicament. Her younger brother "acts up and doesn't do his chores." Her mother says, "You're the older sister. You should control him. You should know better." But when Regina tries to do so, the younger brother defiantly yells, "You're not my mom!" and continues to act improperly. "I can never be right," Regina lamented. "It's not fair."

Some examples are deliciously candid. Ryan said his little sister starts fights but he always gets into trouble. "My mom says it's my fault because I should set the example. But why should I get in trouble when usually it's not my fault!" 'Usually!' Priceless!

Being fair is a matter of Justice, the third ethical principle of the Moral Measures. Justice is the foundation for ethical behavior as water is for life. Its many dimensions incorporate equality, merit and enforcement. We read and hear about 'Justice' in many contexts: bringing someone to justice, creating social justice, the justice system, justice being done or not being done, the virtue of a democracy based on justice, among others. Given the word's many uses, defining Justice can be challenging. To help readers talk about Justice, I address these questions:

- What is 'justice?'
- How do we know if it has been achieved?
- How do we protect it?, and
- How do we promote it?

I talk about Justice on the 'local' level; our homes, schools and communities, where the rubber hits the road, as some might say, and where parents have the most influence. I leave grand universal applications of Justice to others. Ask a child to define 'Justice' and you will likely get an answer similar to Abbie's: "Justice is why we punish people for doing morally wrong things." You might also get an answer such as Ellie's that refers to the legal system: "We have the law to accomplish justice."

Every now and then your child might have an extraordinary insight as did Dillon, a fifth grader, which goes beyond systems and punishment and shines a light on Justice's essence: "Justice seems to be balancing the good and the bad, the right and the wrong." My soul glows when children speak so profoundly. Dillon's intuition happened to echo the Greek concept of Justice: bringing opposite forces into balance. The change of seasons, the cycle of growth and decay, hot and cold and birth and death involve the encroachment or extension of one opposite into the other of the pair.

This concept of opposites was metaphorically extended into human behavior, such as evil encroaching into what is 'good.' As applied to human society, the encroachment of one behavior into the opposite had a lawless quality. Thus, the Greeks spoke of the encroachment of one opposite on another as injustice (αδικια) and of the due observance of balance between them as justice (δικη).

Little Dillon, of course, didn't know about the philosophy of the Greeks, but his words show that true wisdom can bubble forth in dialogues with your children. I have been the joyful recipient of it hundreds of times. Plato's dialogue *Gorgias* deals with Justice and rhetoric, the art of persuasion. Seeing a relationship between injustice and evil, Socrates asks: "Does it follow that injustice and doing injustice are the greatest evils?"

"Yes," Gorgias answers.

Saint Augustine, the fifth century philosopher and theologian, offered a definition that linked Justice to merit: "Justice is that virtue that assigns to every man his due." A person is entitled to get what he or she is due, whether benefits or punishments, based on achievement and moral right.

In addition to merit, Justice is linked to equality. There is the notion, for example, that there should be equality before the law. Atticus Finch, the heroic lawyer in the masterpiece novel, *To Kill a Mockingbird*, referred to justice as "the great leveler."

That doesn't mean that all people should be treated equally. Few would argue, I hope, that the guilty should be treated the same as the innocent. Aristotle wrote: "It is thought that justice is equality, and so it is, but not for all persons, only those who are equal. Only equals should be treated equally."

Combining concepts of equality, merit and moral right, I suggest this definition of Justice: equals should be treated equally and unequals should be treated unequally.

"We the People of the United States, in Order to form a more perfect Union, establish Justice, insure domestic Tranquility, provide for the common defence, promote the general Welfare, and secure the Blessings of Liberty to ourselves and our Posterity, do ordain and establish this Constitution for the United States of America."

–PREAMBLE TO THE CONSTITUTION OF THE UNITED STATES

GETTING A KICK OUT OF JUSTICE

It was late in the afternoon in March, 1990. The air was crisp as chilled apples, the snow-capped Rocky Mountains were dissolving into a blue-red sky and I was blessed to be on the field at West Middle School coaching Elise's first grade soccer team. I had been out of the hospital six weeks or so. When I ran or bent over the halves of my breast plate, sawed in half during surgery and then stapled together, grinded against each other, creating a sensation in my chest of bricks sliding down a pile. It didn't bother me. I was lucky to be alive.

My players did a 'cut move' drill to develop foot speed and ball control. They formed two lines. The attacking line faced the goal and the defending line faced the first line, their backs to the goal. One at a time, an attacking player dribbled toward the defender. As the defender advanced to kick the ball away, the attacking player was supposed to fake sharply to the left, tap the ball to the right with the outside of her right foot, then accelerate or 'cut' to the right around the defender who, hopefully, was caught leaning in the opposite direction. The attacker would then have an open shot on goal.

Margot, my fleet-footed center forward, made her cut, beat the defender and with authority kicked the ball into the goal. Sarah went next, made her cut but kicked wide of the goal. I told Sarah to kick again. Margot turned toward me, an impish smile on her freck-led face. "That's not justice, Coach Mike! She had her shot!" Margot had paid attention in class.

SHOW ME THE VIDEO!

I always discuss these two examples in my Justice classes: one about cheating, the other about bullying. The cheating example is based on an actual event. The bullying example is based on actual events but is combined into a fictitious situation. School-related examples are effective teaching devices because children identify with the sit-uations and become more engaged.

I begin with the cheating example. A fifth grade teacher saw a child look at other students' exams and copy answers on his paper. The teacher told the student what he saw, ripped the student's paper in half and said the student would receive a 'zero' grade. The stu-dent did not protest his innocence or object to the punishment. At the end of the school day the intercom blared instructing the teacher to report to the principal's office. The mother of the cheater sat in the office, sautéed in indignation. The principal asked the teacher to describe the incident. He did.

The mother demanded evidence of cheating. The teacher repeated his observations and her son's response. The mother then asked, "Do you have a video that shows him cheating?" Taken aback, the teacher replied, "Of course not! Cameras are not installed in classrooms."

"Then you have no evidence!" the mother exclaimed defiantly. "Nothing that will hold up," she added with an ominous edge, unsubtly hinting that her lawyers would descend upon the school like locusts if the matter were not resolved to her satisfaction.

With a spine that even a jellyfish would find pathetic, the prin-cipal concluded that no clear evidence of cheating existed and instructed that the student take the exam again. Feeling that his integrity had been run through a trash compactor, the teacher vowed he would not enforce any policy against cheating. "Let the darn (not his exact word) parents raise whatever kind of kids they want," he told me years after the incident. I know this teacher. He is dedicated, honorable and credible. He had nothing to gain by falsely accusing a child.

I first discuss the morality of cheating and then whether this principal's actions advanced or subverted Justice. "Cheating is wrong because the cheater takes something that is not his!" "The cheater is getting something he doesn't deserve." "Cheating is taking the easy way to get something that's not yours." We may reasonably conclude that cheating is unjust because it violates the rule that things should be obtained based on moral right and merit. People that act unequally—cheat and don't cheat—are treated equally in the grading process.

As the conversation chugs along like the happy little 'I Think I Can' engine, somewhere down the line a child's comment adds a new and sometimes surprising dimension to the conversation.

"It's unfair to the cheater!" Caroline said.

Surprised, I asked for clarification.

"Because that student will probably cheat on other things also and never grow up to learn anything. He'll keep doing it and some-day will get into a lot of trouble!" Megan elaborated: "If you cheat when you're little you'll probably cheat all your life."

Note the child's view of cause and effect: the failure by adults to hold the child morally accountable will likely lead to more and perhaps worse immoral behavior. I hope I have the skill to capture even a hint of the eloquence and insight possessed by these wonderful little children. If given the opportunity, your children will also speak such thoughtful inspiring words.

Let's now trundle from the immorality of cheating to the principal's influence on Justice. I start by using the "What do we know? What do we need to know?" skill.

We know these facts:

- Based on specific behavior, the teacher concluded the child was cheating
- The child did not deny he was cheating

- The child didn't object to the teacher giving him a zero on the exam
- The child's mother dismissed as meaningless the teacher's observations
- The child's mother dismissed as meaningless her son's silence
- The mother would only accept evidence of cheating that she knew did not exist
- The mother intimidated the principal with the threat of legal action
- The principal deferred to the parent and undercut the teacher
- The cheater was allowed to take the test again
- An honorable teacher abandoned his anti-cheating policy

For brevity's sake let's agree that there is not much else we need to know. I concede it is theoretically possible that the teacher was hallucinating on LSD and only *thought* he saw the student cheat and that at that same instant the accused student was almost comatose from low blood sugar and couldn't defend against the teacher's wrongful accusation. However, these events are not likely.

The children were offended by the principal's abandonment of his responsibilities. "He's supposed to make people obey the rules." "Cheating is wrong and he didn't punish him." Justice was not accomplished, Sophie pointed out. "The unequal cheater was treated as if he didn't cheat." "Yeah," Candace added, "He got away with it."

Not only did the cheater avoid punishment. He actually *benefited* by cheating. Allowed to take the test again, he would know the questions and answers. "Now he'll really do better than the honest kids," Jason said. Light bulbs of comprehension glowed in the students' minds. Shannon exclaimed: "Now I get it! The honest kids got treated unfairly! They ended up worse!"

The beauty of the sustained unhurried dialogue is that thoughts can evolve through re-assessment. For example, the students soon realized that the principal's subversion of Justice had consequences beyond the cheater. When injustice can be committed with no penalty, immorality becomes rational and attractive. "Now the kids will know there is no such thing as cheating because getting caught doesn't mean anything," Stuart said, then adding, "You're dumb if you don't cheat!" In the principal's morally perverse world, honor becomes a liability. By failing to confront injustice, the principal aided and abetted it.

Assuming this school was like every school I've been in, the halls are plastered with posters exhibiting the sayings of inspirational people; gushy poets, civil rights leaders, philosophers, politicians, entrepreneurs, athletes, all extolling virtue and character and honesty and all that jazz. What juxtaposition between the school's advertised values and what it actually does!

Answers flew at me with hurricane force when I asked the children's opinion of the cheater's mother. Julie said emphatically, "The parent didn't care about her kid." Julie elaborated, "Letting the boy get away with cheating is going to hurt him and the mother knows it. The child will get taught bad things, not good things. The parent was more concerned about herself, that people would think her kid was bad." According to Stephanie, the mother was "was not protecting the kid." Regina concluded that "the mother was helping injustice."

Of course, justice was the last thing the mother wanted. In my many years as a criminal defense lawyer, never did a client say, "Mr. Sabbeth, I ask for justice," as Bonasera pleaded to Don Corleone in The Godfather movie. Quite the contrary. People want injustice—but they want the injustice to be in their favor, and the more extreme the injustice in their favor, the better. Criminal defendants want a lot of things—to be acquitted, to get a lenient jail term, to get convictions reversed on appeal, to have opposing witnesses disappear—but Justice is notably absent from the list.

The mother's demand for 'evidence' was seen as insincere and manipulative. "The mother knew there was no video of the class. The teacher saw him cheat. That should be good enough!" "The parent was just trying to push the principal around!"

Some students wondered why the mother didn't ask her son if he cheated. Tate gave a credible explanation: "The child probably wouldn't tell the truth with that kind of mother." Truth is often undesirable, but even so, I was shocked by the mother's aggressive ruthlessness. She employed the typical fall-back weapons of unethical persons: lies and shamelessness.

I asked if any student had been in a similar situation and if so, how did their parents handle it? Andy admitted that he got caught shoplifting gum 'a while ago.' "My parents made me apologize in person and write a letter of apology and I lost my allowance for a month."

"Did they do the right thing," I asked?

"Yes. They wanted me to grow up to be good." Andy was proud of his parents. Marcus then made a statement that hit the old ball out of the park. "That's how parents show they care about us. Making us do what's right."

There's a saying that virtue is its own reward, but let's be honest. In the real world that reward often doesn't go very far, particularly when the competition cheats without penalty. The cheater knows cheating is wrong. There is no misunderstanding. Rather, the cheater makes a dispassionate calculation that the possible gain is greater than the risk of punishment or the amount of punishment.

And why not? Many people are rewarded for cheating. Other students do it. Successful business people do it. Politicians do it. Athletes do it. In such an environment, not cheating becomes foolish. When incentives to cheat exist, cheating will increase. Paraphrasing Michael Corleone talking to his consiglieri, Tom Hagen, "It's not about morality. It's strictly business."

Sometimes I hear creative rationalizations for cheating. One student said, 'If I cheat, I can get good grades, get into medical school, become a doctor and then help a lot of people." Pretty slick, huh? Cheat your way to virtue!

Now is as good a time as any to dispel some nonsense regarding one tired moral evasion: the "everyone does it" rationalization. The statement is dishonest. Everyone does *not* cheat. More significantly, even if everyone cheated, so what? The 'everyone does it' drivel is not a moral argument that justifies cheating. It's like the mindless blather for not committing crimes: "Crime doesn't pay." So what if it did? Would crime then be moral or a good thing for folks to do? And by the way, for whatever it's worth, crime often pays quite well.

One of the larger and more despairing implications of this cheating example is that if one aggressive mom can so effortlessly cause a squishy principal to throw Justice under the bus, what else is the principal willing to appease? Tolerate a little bit of drug dealing? A lot of drug dealing? Attacks on teachers? Ignore bullying and gang wars? Will that craven domino game of appeasement end, yet again, in horrific tragedy, where, amidst piles of flowers and teddy bears and heartfelt cards, everyone wails, "We're shocked! We never thought it could happen here!"?

"I would agree with St. Augustine that "an unjust law is no law at all."
Now, what is the difference between the two? How does one determine
whether a law is just or unjust? A just law is a man made code that
squares with the moral law or the law of God. An unjust law is a code
that is out of harmony with the moral law. To put it in the terms of
St. Thomas Aquinas: An unjust law is a human law that is not rooted
in eternal law and natural law. Any law that uplifts human personality
is just. Any law that degrades human personality is unjust."

–Dr. Martin Luther King Jr.,
A Letter from a Birmingham Jail, April 16, 1963

AND JUSTICE FOR ALL

I discuss this bullying example each year because it raises a whole truck load of interesting issues that go to the core of Justice. Sometimes I present it as a little skit, in which the children enthusiastically role play, and sometimes I simply tell them the facts.

Here are the facts:

Bob has a history of bullying. Jeff is an honor student and
decent guy. Outside, Bob sees Jeff. Bob demands that Jeff walk
ten steps behind him because Bob doesn't like the way Jeff is

looking at him. If he doesn't obey, Jeff is in for a lot of pain. Jeff says, "Get lost, you jerk." Bob punches Jeff and slams him to the ground. A teacher arrives. She says that Bob was unruly but that she can't determine who started the fight. She said both students violated the school's 'zero tolerance' policy by provoking or hitting one another. Thus, to be fair, both students will be suspended for five days.

This story has several issues that relate to Justice, but I address the two I think most important:

- The issue of 'equal wrongs'
- The standards used to judge

ALL WRONGS ARE NOT CREATED EQUAL

Recall my definition of justice: treating equals equally and treating unequals unequally. To achieve Justice, therefore, you have to figure out whether people acted in a way that makes them equal or unequal. Thus, figuring out what is 'just' requires moral reasoning and factual analysis.

Regarding Bob and Jeff, asked if Justice was done, the children's initial opinions were like these: "Both students are wrong. Jeff called Bob a name, which is wrong, and Bob hit Jeff, which is wrong." "Jeff should have obeyed Bob in order to avoid a fight." "Jeff knew Bob was a bully so he kinda knew he'd be beaten up if he didn't obey." "If Jeff just obeyed he wouldn't have gotten hurt."

What do you and your children think of those answers and their implications? I found them disheartening. Note how the children immediately defaulted to the easy non-analytical position that both students were 'wrong.' As if being asked to wash dishes, they scrambled away from the key issue: whether both students *equally* wrong.

I pressed on.

If the boys were equally wrong, then the equal suspension would be Justice. If they were *unequally* wrong, then the equal suspension was unjust. Let's revisit the thinking skill: "What's your opinion? What are your facts?" In order to support the opinion that both boys were equally wrong, you have to believe that calling someone a jerk was the equivalent—physically and morally and in terms of provocation—as punching and slamming a student to the ground.

It is fascinating to see how some children—anyone, really—will contort an issue to avoid making a moral judgment. For example, so committed were many students to the idea that both students were 'wrong' that they created a psychological argument to show that Jeff harmed Bob! "Well, words can hurt on the inside," Monique said. True enough. Assume a parent repeatedly said to her child something like "You are a worthless. You will never amount to anything. I wish I never had you." I agree those words would 'hurt' the child.

Jeff said nothing of the kind, of course. A critical teaching skill is staying focused on the facts. Don't wander into the infinite space of "What if...." and "Yeah, but...." We are not dealing with the abstract idea of whether words can hurt. We are dealing with two limited issues: could the word 'jerk' hurt under this circumstance and, even if it did, was it the moral equivalent of a brutal physical attack?

Once these issues were analyzed in greater depth, the students' answers changed dramatically. Max, a fifth grader said eloquently; "There are different levels of evil; some bad things are worse than other bad things. Taking my sister's teddy bear is not as bad as flying planes into the Twin Towers." All the children agreed: "Yeah, they're both wrong, but the bully is more wrong. He should be punished more." Max concluded, "Well, I'd let Jeff go."

The students reassessed their earlier opinions. Monique now said, "Calling someone a jerk isn't really a big deal." Without exception, every child would rather be called a jerk than be beaten. So much for equal harm.

The teacher's failure—indeed, indifference—to figure out how the fight started was, in Socrates' words, a great evil. The failure of adults to stand up for children is a greater evil. It's fine to be fair, but when wrongdoing is rationalized, then fairness becomes a cover for injustice and cowardice.

Let's study the moral implications of the teacher's behavior. By saying both students were wrong and by imposing equal punishments, the teacher held that calling a name was morally equivalent to a physical beating. Of course, the teacher can believe whatever she wants, but most rational people would agree that the two acts are *not* the same. The teacher valued unethical 'equality' over Justice.

There is simply no intellectual or moral depth to such reasoning. If everyone is wrong, then no one is wrong. Avoiding tough thinking is, of course, seductively alluring. What a wonderful world it would be when no one is wrong and no one ever has to stand up for any moral principles! The process is based on emotion. It is intellectually and morally lazy and cowardly. Creating false equivalencies is not moral leadership but moral abdication.

I confess it was deflating that several students accepted as legitimate Jeff not wanting to be intimidated yet they faulted Jeff for not being sufficiently sensitive to Bob's demands *even though* they conceded Bob's demands were wrong. They considered Jeff responsible because the fight could have been avoided if he had obeyed Bob. Curiously, the youngsters accepted Bob's bullying nature, and thus, in some twisted way, excused him from responsibility, as if to say, 'we can't change Bob so let's work on the other guy.'

Dismayingly, this lofty non-provocation standard anchored around Jeff's neck was NOT applied to the bully. Many students said Jeff shouldn't have provoked Bob by calling him a jerk but only a few students said, initially, that Bob shouldn't have provoked Jeff by his intimidating demand that Jeff walk somewhere else.

In Bob's mind, Jeff was provoking him merely by *existing*. Bob was waiving his mood around like a pistol, yet the children didn't hold him accountable for not controlling his feelings. They didn't require the bully to respect Jeff's feelings but they required Jeff to respect the bully's feelings. They expected Jeff to be sensitive to Bob's mood but they didn't demand that Bob be sensitive to Jeff's mood. They demanded total obedience and defenselessness from Jeff yet they held Bob to no such standards.

My students are not bullies, yet, it is perplexing that many were initially harsher on Jeff than on Bob. This is the 'blame the victim' mentality on steroids. Once their double standard was exposed and its moral implications brought to light, however, students quickly concluded that Jeff had little, if any, responsibility for the fight and that the teacher's resolution was unjust.

Why, I wondered, did the students default so quickly to a moral inversion where the victim is held as accountable as the aggressor? Why did the children reflexively require the victim to accommodate the aggressor? I do not have definitive answers but I suspect answers reside in the murky 'moral equivalence' and non-judgmentalism mindsets that increasingly pervade our culture.

The logic of these belief systems proceeds as follows: name calling is a 'wrong' equivalent to a physical assault. Thus, since all wrongs are equal, non-judgmentalism holds that the victim is no different from the aggressor. Since the victim is no different from the aggressor, in this morally upside down ideology, standing up for one's self becomes escalation and provocation. Facts and moral reasoning just get in the way and become annoyances.

THE TRIAL

Justice was achieved delightfully and humorously in one memorable sixth grade class. Two students were fighting in the playground as I entered the classroom. After some final shoving and yelling, Karl and Joey ambled into class. Although the fight was benign by today's standards, some lessons can be learned from the skirmish.

I conducted a trial to determine who started the fight. The class would be the jury. Joey stood on my right, Karl on my left. The trial began with my singularly brilliant question. "Joey, how did the fight start?"

"Well," Joey began.

Before another syllable could escape his lips, Karl interrupted. "This isn't fair."

Consumed by curiosity, I boldly inquired, "Huh?"

Karl explained. "Joey's gonna tell his side of the story and he won't tell the truth because he doesn't want to get into trouble!"

I smiled. Tranquility caressed me like a summer's breeze. I felt that joyous tingling of the spine experienced only by testosterone-infused trial lawyers when they hear a statement that is thoroughly fatal to the opponent's case. I played the situation as if landing a tarpon.

"Karl, you don't think we should believe Joey?"

"No," Karl snapped.

"We shouldn't believe him because he wants to get out of trouble?"

"That's right. He just wants to get out of trouble."

"Joey has a motive to lie?"

"Yes."

"We shouldn't believe Joey because he's biased against you?"

"Yeah."

"Joey's not likely to tell the truth?"

"That's right."

"You're certain about what you're saying?"

"Yes."

"You've given your answers plenty of thought?"

"Yes."

"Well, my dear Karl, aren't those the same reasons we shouldn't believe you?"

Pause. More pause.

"Ooooops!"

The class cracked up with laughter. Karl rolled his eyes, his face red as an over-ripe tomato. Then he giggled. The trial ended with apologies and a handshake, and, lamentably, no legal fees.

JUSTICE IN THE FAMILY

This may surprise a lot of parents but little children talk with approval about getting punished for lying, for being nasty to parents and for disobeying them. They respect punishment. They might tinker at the margins regarding what is fair—being grounded for a week versus nine years—but they respect the imposition of consequences for wrongful behavior. Their reasoning is logically solid. "Well, we did something wrong!"

I insist that my children be fair—with me, their mother and their siblings and with the rest of the world. However, I know that these little ones are calculating like Pentium processors how many cookies everyone's had in the past seven years, how many shirts and socks everyone's left on the floor, how many times each child has cleaned up the mess from the dog, how many minutes each person has watched the TV programs he's wanted and who had more candy. They're always figuring out what's fair.

I share an insight into fairness and Justice that took a while to penetrate my foggy mind and even longer for me to stiffen my spine to act accordingly. I have come to understand that it is unreasonable to expect that other people will always be reasonable when they respond to someone's unreasonable behavior. That means, if you act unreasonably, it is unreasonable to expect that others will always react reasonably to your actions, if you get my drift. Once I grasped this dynamic, I saw the ironic double standard: the unreasonable person expects—indeed, demands—that others be held to a higher standard than his own. Those that are unfair expect others to be fair; those that are unreasonable expect others to be reasonable.

The vicious rapist or murderer expects the judge and jury to be fair and reasonable although such constraints were of little concern to the actor during the crime. The school bully expects to be treated reasonably and compassionately although such traits were not shown to its victims. This belief has the potential for justifying a curious and perverse result: that the immoral unreasonable aggressor can claim to be a victim of the actual victim's unreasonableness. In an equally perverse way, the aggressor makes a claim to dictate the moral standards to be used against him by the victim.

Of course, when dispensing justice, we parents and the 'system' must be reasonable and fair, whatever that means under the circumstances. But one should be aware of the system's vulnerability to moral abuse.

I distill these ideas into this workable lesson which I teach to my own children and to my students: don't get into situations where you are at the mercy of other people's reasonableness or unreasonableness. Fairness and justice cover a range of responses. If you don't want to be subject to the judgment of someone else's notions of fairness and justice, do the right thing.

Once I became aware of this dynamic, I gained a sliver of inner peace. I know what's unfair. Being inflicted with leukemia is unfair. Starving to death in the Sudan is unfair. Getting hacked to pieces in Darfur is unfair. Being crippled by a drunk driver in a car crash is unfair. Leaping to your death from the Twin Towers is unfair. Having your home washed down the street in a hurricane unfair.

So, for most of the whining I hear, my sense of things is, get a grip and knock it off! On rare occasion, I've told my children, "If you think I've been unfair, be my guest, but whine quietly. I'm taking a nap."

I try to be fair. I listen to my children's grievances. I try to understand their reasoning. I explore my response options. I try to be aware of my biases. I expect to have the humility to make adjustments if I am wrong. But I have come to understand that honesty is the most important ingredient in being fair—honesty in analysis and in moral judgment. Such honesty takes work and courage.

Justice is valued not because it is practical or because it works. Justice is valued because it is the foundation for the noblest aspirations of the species: liberty, freedom and inalienable rights that advance the singular dignity of the individual. Most parents want to determine Justice and to have the backbone to enforce it. As the great Gershwin wrote, "Who could ask for anything more?"

CHAPTER 12

SANCTITY OF LIFE

TO LIFE!

"To Save a Life is to Save the World Entire"

–THE MISHNAH, BOOK OF JEWISH TRADITIONS

SHORTLY AFTER THE COLUMBINE HIGH SCHOOL KILLINGS in Colorado I made several presentations to personnel in the Littleton Fire Department. Many of the firefighters had been involved in rescuing wounded students from the grotesque assaults. My talks explained how my moral reasoning skills could be worked into the department's existing fire safety school programs. I asked several participants what motivated them to risk their lives going into burning buildings to save strangers. It's their job, of course, but why choose such a treacherous a job?

Eric, a tall muscular man with an athletic bearing, answered matter-of-factly: "Life is precious. Life is sacred. You have to try to save it." Not a lot of flowery prose in that sparse reply. A similar opinion was expressed by a fire fighter entering the World Trade Center engulfed in burning jet fuel. "People are dying in there. I have to help." Using simple words to express profound ideas, these firefighters expressed the core of the Sanctity of Life principle: the duty to protect life because life is sacred and precious.

Sanctity of Life, the fourth ethical principle of the Moral Measures, is the unifying principle that justifies all other ethical principles and virtues. It holds that life is worth valuing and that valuing life is the unique quality that defines one's humanity.

Ask your little ones what valuing life means and dozens of comments will sprout like wheat on our fruited plains: respecting others; taking care of pets, saving a drowning person, donating blood. Keep pressing and your child will give answers of greater depth and nuance: adopting children; being a foster parent, being a competent doctor, working to create life-saving drugs or donating organs after death.

Your children will quickly grasp that Sanctity of Life is the foundation for Justice and for almost all the laws. The right to self defense, wearing bicycle helmets and seatbelts, having speed limits on the highways, laws relating to murder, requiring drugs to be adequately tested, licensing drivers and airline pilots, improving air and water quality and thousands more are derived from the Sanctity of Life principle.

I talk about Sanctity of Life in several contexts. My discussion selections are intended to help children identify the principle as they leap through the day and to develop their ability to apply the principle when confronted with situations that challenge or compromise respect for life.

SHE WAS JUST A KID!

"If you have tears, prepare to shed them now....
Oh, what a fall was there...
Then I, and you, and all of us fell down."

–WILLIAM SHAKESPEARE, *JULIUS CAESAR, ACT 3, SCENE 1*

Occasionally students will ask, sometimes forcefully, to discuss a specific event. Usually it will be something in the news such as the Columbine High School killings, the Oklahoma City bombing, the murder of Denver police officer Bruce Vander Jagt by skinhead Matthaues Jaehnig. Of all the events that spurred a demand for a discussion, the death of little Jessica Dubroff in a plane crash was most poignant and, in a sense, most personal. Jessica's death directs a spotlight on the high cost of ambition married to weak character. Teaching about Jessica would, I hoped, honor the spirit of a remarkable child.

A Google search taking 0.021 seconds will provide all the relevant facts. I highlight the most important ones. Jessica was a spunky fifty-five pound seven-year-old girl. Assisted by her father, Lloyd Dubroff and a pilot, Joe Reid, Jessica was attempting to set a record as the youngest person to fly an airplane coast to coast and back. Jessica trained at Half Moon Bay, California, which was at sea level altitude.

On April 11, 1996, Jessica, along with her father and Joe Reid, took off from Cheyenne, Wyoming in a Cessna Cardinal 177B, a light single-engine plane, which was dangerously overloaded. Gusting winds at take-off were up to 30 knots, visibility was minimal due to rain and thunderstorms were reported northwest of the airport. Tower controllers reported wind shears. The pilot of an airplane that took off minutes before Jessica's plane told controllers he had encountered perilous flying condition and the crew of a United Express commuter aircraft elected to delay their takeoff.

The thin air at Cheyenne's six thousand foot altitude adversely affected the plane's performance by reducing its horsepower, making it more difficult to lift the heavy load and more difficult to control compared with performance at sea level. Joe Reid and Lloyd Dubroff insisted on taking off. The plane crashed moments later. All were killed.

I admit I feel a chill of caution talking about a situation where a dad caused the death of his child. The emotionally charged topic could easily descend into useless generalities—life is full of risks or sometimes adults are foolish—and I had to avoid taking cheap shots at the adults that, although accurate, would not be conducive to developing thinking skills or enlightenment. It would be unethical to instruct—indeed, even hint—that my students should sometimes disobey their parents.

My opening question in class is did the dad and Joe Reid honor the Sanctity of Life principle? We summarize the numerous facts, the most notable being that they were known by the adults. Hunter, a fourth grader, voiced the thoughts of the class. "For sure, the father and the pilot would know all that." Then we deciphered the unambiguous implications of the facts. Hunter continued. "They shouldn't have tried to fly. It was a stupid risk."

Face taut, half standing at her wooden desk, Jane shouted, "They didn't care enough about the life of the girl..." Jordan interrupted with an opinion piggybacked on a tone of exasperation, "The grown ups didn't even respect their own lives!" Lloyd Dubroff admitted, "We're trying to set a record." But they faced a time constraint. Jessica would become eight in May, a few weeks away, and no longer qualify for the record. It didn't take long to whittle down to the heartwood. The adults recklessly took an unreasonable risk to gain a record.

Ruby evaluated the adult's values by saying, "Breaking a record isn't as important as living." Karin added, "There was a lot of publicity. They were under a lot of pressure. Everyone was watching them. They didn't want to fail."

Another significant fact was that Jessica's father was financially in trouble and had been aggressively wooing advertisers for the record-breaking event. Although it was discomforting, the students unhesitatingly acknowledged that the adults valued things more than they valued Jessica's life. "The grown ups thought money was more important than the kid," Ellie said with a hint of disgust. They risked their lives for money and lost both.

The youngsters were capable of processing all the facts and reaching logical conclusions. They also reached moral conclusions. Joe Reid was the target of the students' most pointed contempt. Levi expressed the predominant opinion in the class. "The pilot had the experience, the information, the authority and the choice. He was a coward. He knew the risks but he didn't stand up to the father."

THE DISCUSSION GAINS ALTITUDE

I've repeatedly experienced a student making a comment that elevated the class if I kept the conversation moving long enough. That's what happened when Megan made the fine point that "Jessica probably really wanted to win the record. It must have been fun flying all over the country!" Megan's point was that Jessica most likely agreed to take the risk regarding flying the pane.

Jessica probably wanted the record as much as her father. The students said that the quest must have been 'cool,' 'fun,' and 'really exciting.' The students believed that if she were asked what she wanted to do at the time of take-off, Jessica probably would have said, "Dad, let's go for it!"

However, no matter how enthusiastic or committed to breaking the record, the students grasped that Jessica had to rely on the judgment of Reid and her father. They concluded that the adults should have acted in a way that valued life more than 'cool' or fame. No doubt Jessica was enthused and motivated to fly the plane, but recalling our discussion about Autonomy, we see that the adults had to make decisions on her behalf, and their decision failed to respect Jessica's autonomy.

Jessica, a seven-year-old child, could not have possibly grasped the risks involved. Also, she could not waive or release her dad and Reid from the moral duties they owed her, no matter how cool it was to zip around the country in an airplane. Just as no rational parent would place its child in a nest of rattlesnakes just because the child wanted a pet, the failure to abandon the flight violated the Sanctity of Life principle.

By the way, the class reasoned that even if she didn't want to take off that afternoon, it was unrealistic to expect Jessica to stand up to her father or to Reid. Camille, with a voice like a feather in the wind, reasoned, "If the pilot wouldn't stand up to the father, how could Jessica?"

If you were to ask the dad or Reid whether either cared about Jessica, I'd wager that each would reply with self-indulgent indignity, "How dare you ask!" Well, so they cared! So what? As we shall see later, caring can be an easy cost-free sentiment. In any event, caring was not the issue. The issue was permitting caring to be trumped by factors such as money and fame. If the adults cared, it didn't do Jessica much good. Caring is not a substitute for moral judgment.

Jessica's father violated a parent's single most sacred duty: the duty to protect the child. The dad and Reid had a moral duty to protect their own lives, of course, but they had the moral right to choose whether to be reasonable or to be jerks. They had the moral right to take whatever risks they desired. It's up to them. The adults did not, however, have the moral right to subject a captive child to the unreasonable risks they chose for themselves. Doing so violated the Sanctity of Life principle.

Jessica might have wanted to take off in that storm but note the exquisite applicability of third grader Molly's jewel-like words. "Sure we want to do stuff that we shouldn't do. That's why we have parents!"

Children expect moral leadership from their parents. For example, the brother of a friend of one of my children had a high-powered air rifle. The children were eight or nine years old. I was told the boy sometimes shot the rifle irresponsibly. I didn't let my child visit that house any more. My child was relieved that I imposed limitations that my child would not have imposed on his own. Exercising moral authority is the essence of parenting.

I WANT TO KNOW!

When I think a topic might be disturbing, such as the Jessica topic, I ask if they'd rather not talk about it. Never have students said 'no.' If it's relevant to their lives, they want to talk. They're getting information from the Internet, radio, TV, Twitter, Facebook, from friends and from their parents. Nothing is hidden. If I do have a discussion, I am reassured when students tell me, with pride, by the way, that they had already discussed the topic with their parents.

Look at the beautiful poignant phrasing Isabella, a fifth grader, used to describe the criteria she expects from parents. During a Jessica discussion, she said, "Parents should talk to us about unhappy things. But, tell me honestly what happened. If you just want me to feel better, that's dishonest."

Olivia added, "It's like when parents say you did well and you know you didn't. It's as if the parent said, 'We don't expect much from you.' We don't like that."

Char, a fifth grader possessed of rare verbal skills, spoke of the value of discussing difficult subjects. "Those kinds of conversations make you more informed. This is how we know to be ready; how to be prepared. But," she cautioned, "don't overload us on depressing or unhappy things. Then we feel that bad things will happen to us. Tell us in a gentle way."

Her message was, I believe, that the parent should not speak like a French chef that smothers the food's taste with heavy sauces. Be forthright, be attentive and let the topic express itself rather than blanket it with dismissive or frightful words or with impatience.

Fifth grader Max, one of the most articulate children in my twenty years in the classroom, spoke unflinchingly of the need to know the truth, however distasteful. "I want to be treated as an adult. I have to know that there are horrible people in this world; that this world is not perfect. Not telling us the truth is one of the worst things you can do to a child." Do his words bring tears to your eyes? They do to mine!

Children want to grapple with the tough issues. They know it's the only way they can become stronger and more competent. They want to be spoken to as serious young people, whose opinions matter, whether or not they agree with their parents. This is what loving a child requires. Children measure our love by whether we make them stronger.

Life is complex, often unfair and, more often, unreasonable. When you can brush your child's face with a tender caress and, with love and logic, share your values, your thoughts, your doubts, and with words and eyes, let her know you will help your child become strong and confident, then you are an educator. Indeed, you are something greater. You are a parent.

VARIATIONS ON A THEME

Two other class discussions illustrate two points: the ease with which Sanctity of Life obligations can be disregarded when interacting with someone close and meaningful to you; and how its values may become fragile when challenged by opposing values and forces.

TO LIVE OR NOT TO LIVE: THAT IS THE QUESTION

Many readers will have some knowledge of the death of Theresa "Terri" Schiavo. For those inclined, a quick Google search will provide information sufficient to follow this discussion.

On February 25, 1990, at the age of 26, Terri collapsed in her home. To my knowledge, the cause of the collapse has not been determined precisely. Respiratory and cardiac arrest led to extensive brain damage. Terri was diagnosed as being in a persistent vegetative state, meaning that there was little or no brain activity. Kept alive by a feeding tube, she was institutionalized until her death on March 31, 2005.

The Terri Schiavo case is another emotionally difficult and morally complex matter that young children, nevertheless, fearlessly discuss. I won't talk about, of course, the messy conflict-of-interest financial issues or the graphic medical details or the political and legal nuances of the sordid competing interest groups that used this comatose woman like a rag doll. Those issues are irrelevant to my purposes.

Terri's unintended rise to local, then national and then international attention began in 1998 when her husband and guardian, Michael Schiavo, petitioned the Pinellas County Circuit Court to remove her feeding tube. Removing the tube would lead to Terri's death within a week or so. His claim was based on the argument that Terri, if given the choice, would not want to live in a vegetative state. He was attempting to exercise Terri's autonomy on her behalf.

Robert and Mary Schindler, Terri's parents, opposed removing the tube, arguing that facts existed which did not justify letting her die: that she was conscious, that she recognized and responded to them and that she suffered no pain. Thus, allowing her to die could not be justified on the basis of ending painful suffering. Although their positions were in opposition, Michael Schiavo's argument and that of Terri's parents were based on the principle of Sanctity of Life.

Terri had not signed a 'living will' or a medical power of attorney such as the document signed by my mom, which stated her wishes or instructions regarding treatment in such catastrophic circumstances.

The battling parties took the matter to court. The court ruled that the feeding tube could be removed, based on two findings or conclusions regarding the facts: that prior to her collapse, Terri had made "credible and reliable" statements that she would not want to be "kept alive on a machine" and that there was no rational basis for expecting that she would recover from her condition.

I talked about two aspects of Sanctity of Life in this tragic situation: the right to life and the concept of a meaningful 'life.' This juxtaposition is captured in the statements of two students. "They really weren't respecting her life when they allowed her to die," Lauren said softly. In words draped in anguish, Jack responded, "But who wants to live like that? That's not really life, is it?"

I simplified the themes and emphasized that one's moral conclusions depended to a large extent on what 'facts' you accepted as true. Recall that as facts change, opinions change, and as facts change, moral analysis changes. Causing Terri's death by removing her feeding tube arguably violated the Sanctity of Life principle.

On the other hand, and it's amazing how many hands there can be in these situations, keeping her alive denied her a dignified life, also violating the Sanctity of Life principle. Keeping Terri alive or not keeping her alive, again depending on the facts one chose to believe, also could have violated the principle of Autonomy.

How does one 'respect life' in this perplexing situation? Since the judge didn't know what Terri 'wanted,' many children thought that the legal system should default to keeping her alive. Others argued she was not 'alive' in a way that she would want to live and justified removing the feeding tube.

It is important to grasp what is happening here in terms of morality and analysis. The issue of respect for life is being transformed into the issue of quality of life. Yet, they are not the same. Respecting life and valuing life are different from evaluating a life's 'quality.' Different standards apply and each standard leads to different consequences.

Quality of life standards are subjective. Note that the life that does not have sufficient 'quality' becomes a life with no value, and a life without value will not be protected. This analysis is particularly significant when the person making the decision about 'quality' is not the one who is going to die.

Sanctity of Life/quality of life conflicts can lead to Orwellian beliefs such as what is best for society is therefore best for the individual. Individual rights and freedom are thus subordinated to the vague betterment of the masses or the collective. Some rather horrific outcomes have resulted from such beliefs.

Euthanasia, for example, in some countries, for an array of reasons not always morally based, is increasingly inflicted on the aged, the infirm and on damaged children. Once this logic is accepted as legitimate, morally perverse consequences become more likely. Some professors, paradoxically referred to as 'ethicists' drawing paychecks from allegedly prestigious universities, argue that disabled new born children should be killed. Fortunately, there are more Zaboreks than such ethicists, at least at the moment.

We should be on guard against this devolution of 'sanctity' to 'quality' of life and be very astute in our analysis of the facts in order to reach moral conclusions. As Reverend Richard Neuhaus, editor-in-chief of *First Things*, warns, "then the unthinkable becomes.... justifiable, until it is finally established as the unexceptional."

I discuss the Terri Schiavo case because the vibrant dialogues expand the children's breadth of moral reasoning. I don't direct the students toward a resolution. I dare not suggest that one result is 'right' and one result is 'wrong.' It's not my business. But I know the ethical issues raised in the Schiavo matter are and will continue to be contentious ethical topics. Our children should become better informed and better skilled so they may be better prepared to fight for life's sanctity.

WHAT IS HONOR?

Conversation topics are all around us. With a little guidance, you can find them on TV, newsstands, the Internet, visiting with friends or in your private lives. One intriguing topic popped up when I was flipping through a newspaper while standing in a supermarket check-out line or going from one radio station to another trying to avoid commercials. I don't remember.

The facts were simple. A mother wanted to become a nurse. She didn't speak or understand English very well; couldn't read or comprehend the books and papers assigned to her in nursing school and couldn't fulfill basic class requirements for her nursing certification. Her daughter helped her mother cheat on school exams and writing her mother's papers and did whatever else she could do to complete her mother's schoolwork.

I've already written about cheating, so I won't re-visit the issue. This situation is distinct from the class cheating example, though, because the daughter justified her dishonesty by appealing to her culture's alleged requirement that a child must honor its parents. In this case, honor was demonstrated by cheating and lying.

It would be a curious culture, indeed, that demanded lying and cheating to enable parents to get into a position of trust where they might injure or kill innocent people. Cultural mandate or not, we can evaluate the morality of the daughter's actions. Could honoring a parent in this situation violate the Sanctity of Life principle?

Your children might not be as candid with you as they were in class if you discussed the situation with them, but the topic is so intriguing it's worth parents giving it a whirl.

If you've managed to endure this much of my book, you can probably accurately guess what my students thought of the daughter's behavior. Their analysis would likely be no different from that of your children.

Lori captured the issue's essence: "The daughter is trying to not have her mother work hard, and I can understand that, but the mother isn't learning to be a good nurse. That's the problem."

By enabling the mother to avoid the hard work of mastering her profession, the daughter positioned her mother to be a liar, indeed, to be a living lie that could do great harm to innocent people.

Kelsey believed that the justification of honoring her mother was an excuse for the daughter's weakness. "The daughter should have said 'No, I can't help you this way.' There are other good ways the daughter could help her mom."

It is noteworthy that if the daughter had refused to cheat for the mother, no student would have interpreted that refusal as a sign of disrespect toward the mother or as a failure to honor the mother. Indeed, to the contrary, as Jasmine, a third grader, said, "It shows you care enough about your mother to be strong. It shows that the daughter wants to help the mother not do something that is wrong."

"It's just the opposite," Marcus added. "It shows the daughter respects and cares about the mother so much that she won't do something that will hurt her. And she cares about the other people also."

Elise recognized the ethical and character issues. "It might seem like she's hurting the mother now, but she's really doing her a favor. And she's protecting innocent people who are counting on her to know what she's doing."

The daughter and her mother conspired to violate the ethical principle of Sanctity of Life. The students also expressed the insight mentioned in the school cheating example: if the mom cheats this time, she'll probably cheat again.

The nurse/daughter situation presents another illustration where feelings dominated moral conviction and moral thought. In such a situation, morality has no content. It is no more than the hollow cocoon that remains after the moth has flown away. The cocoon may be intriguing but, alas, it is empty.

We parents should not spare our children the agony of thinking and the torment of understanding required for reasoned deliberation. Good intentions and good motives are not enough. When severed from moral behavior, they can be destructive.

> *"To have ideas is to gather flowers.*
> *To think is to weave them into garlands."*

> —ANNE-SOPHIE SWETCHINE,
> 19TH CENTURY RUSSIAN FRENCH WRITER

SAYS ME! STREET

Leo, my auto mechanic, told me about the rules he imposed when he bought a trampoline for his children. "No using the trampoline unless at least one parent is home." His children protested: "What's the difference if you're gone or you're in the house or if you're across the yard at the neighbor's house?"

Leo replied that a parent needed to know what was going on. "But if you're in the basement...but if you're in the garage...but if you're sleeping...."

Well, the 'but' stops here! "I brought them into the world," Leo told me. "I have a duty to protect them. I had to learn how to talk persuasively to them to do what's right."

The likelihood was that, at any given moment, Leo or his wife would be watching the children. Leo also knew that more likely than not his children and their friends would not be as rowdy if one of the parents were home and being monitored, even if only inter-mittently. Leo made it clear that if his children and their friends did-n't obey his rules, he would get rid of the trampoline.

To be honest, sometimes I feel that it's parents against the world and that we have a tough fight that shows no signs of abating. We have to be strong, for ourselves and for our children.

In her no-punches-pulled book *The Death of Right and Wrong*, Tammy Bruce writes that hip-hop, gangsta rap, murder-and-torture-filled video games inures our children to death and horror and thereby undermines if not extinguishes the nobility of life. "We have been behind the Looking Glass," she wrote, "where everything is the opposite of what it should be."

Advancing Sanctity of Life doesn't happen just because someone says, "Respect life!" It is meaningless unless you have the character and will and skill to act to advance the principle.

For example, my children's teachers in Cherry Creek and Littleton High School respected Sanctity of Life principles by being competent, by restraining their biases, by intervening against bully-ing and by demanding excellence. My doctors and nurses respected Sanctity of Life by being prepared, maintaining their professional education levels and by coming to work sober and rested.

The firemen and police who save lives do so not only because they value life but because they have mastered life-saving skills, as we saw with the rescuers during Hurricane Katrina and by the United States military after the tsunami in the Indian Ocean in 2004.

More than a gooey attitude that life, like love, is a many splendid thing, they knew how to fly helicopters and planes and how to fix broken bones and how to saw through crushed houses and deliver medical services. In additional to having such skills, they had the will and the courage to use them.

Sanctity of Life includes standing up to those that do NOT value or respect life. They will always be there; the bullies, the thugs and tyrants in the home, the school, the community and the world.

Sanctity of Life serves as an overarching ethical narrative that links values and actions and consequences, without which you have only isolated notes that may sound great coming from a wind chime but won't advance moral development. Parents will develop morally resolute children that respect life by teaching them to value life and by helping them acquire the wisdom and courage and skills to act on that principle.

THE SEVEN C'S

CHAPTER 13

CHARACTER

*"Character is the Sum of those qualities of moral excellence
which stimulates a person to do the right thing, which is manifested
through right and proper actions despite internal
or external pressures to the contrary."*

–DEFINITION OF CHARACTER,
THE UNITED STATES AIR FORCE ACADEMY

IS ANYBODY WATCHING?

A BUNCH OF YEARS AGO my family visited Nancy's mom in Hebron, Nebraska. I always looked forward to these visits. I liked the people and I loved the land. I joyfully recall lumbering along with Nancy's brothers, Michael and Jim, on ten to fifteen mile jogs on county roads and being energized by the pungent scents of corn and wheat and milo. Memories of jogging under a shimmering sunset are among my most vivid.

One afternoon I visited my brother-in-law, Steve. We took .22 rifles to a make-shift range on a friend's farm to shoot soda cans and metal plates swinging from cross bars. After an hour or so of having what was referred to in the old days as 'fun,' we drove to my mother-in-law's home to enjoy some of Nebraska's high cuisine, hamburgers covered with melted Velveeta cheese.

Between a bite of hamburger and a sip of light beer, Steve realized he left his rifle at the range. We drove back to the range, looked under the weathered benches, in the parking area and in the bushes. The rifle was gone.

Steve said we would next go to the sheriff's office to see if anyone turned it in. "Are you kidding?" I blurted. "Someone's going to turn in a rifle?" I was not optimistic. Steve shrugged off my cynicism. We entered the sheriff's building. A man in a starched uniform approached. "Bill," Steve asked without emotion, "anyone turn in a rifle?"

"Yeah. Got it right here." Bill walked to the wall by the water cooler and retrieved it. "A guy brought it twenty minutes ago." I was amazed. Steve was unmoved. "People act that way here," he said in exquisite understatement.

Was this a statistical fluke? Was it likely to ever happen again? Who knows, but this unheralded expression of character happened in Hebron, Nebraska and Steve thought it rather routine.

Another story. In the spring of 1983, I and Leonard Davies, a law colleague, traveled to Casablanca, Morocco on business. We hired a private driver, Haj, to take us to Rabat, the capital city, for meetings with Moroccan and U. S. government officials. We stopped for lunch at a picture-perfect restaurant draped in white stucco. We got out of the car and gestured to Haj. "Come on," Leonard said.

Haj shook his head. Drivers were not permitted to be served in that restaurant, he explained. Leonard snapped, "You don't go, we don't go!" Those six words were a towering monument to character. We drove on a few minutes and found a more suitable restaurant, boasting a view of the sun-dappled Atlantic Ocean, crisp white linen and, I bet, better food.

GOT CHARACTER?

It is appropriate that Character is the first of the Seven C's, for Character is the composite of all the virtues. I think of Character as a perfectly crafted veal stock. You might not be able to taste each ingredient individually—the blackened onions and shallots and bones, the carrots, parsley, herbs and spices—but each is critical. Each adds richness and depth and complexity to the stock. Similarly, individual virtues such as will, reason, compassion, courage and competence blend harmoniously when a person acts with moral character.

Character can usefully be described as having three components:

- ethical virtue
- moral reasoning and
- the will to implement virtue and reason

I distinguish reasoning from moral reasoning to show how moral reasoning is a measurement of character. Reasoning is a skill. As a skill, reasoning requires several tools—example, precedent, analogy, selectivity, logic, fact gathering and others. These tools are analogous to a carpenter's tools—saw, miter, ruler, hammer, sander and so forth. These reasoning tools are not inherently moral or ethical. They may or they may not be. Reasoning may be mere logic, where premises are wrong and conclusions are absurd or vile. Many tyrants and doers of evil are skilled at reasoning.

Moral reasoning uses tools—example, selectivity, analogy, etc—to attain virtue. Moral reasoning deals with goals, purposes, consequences, methods, costs and benefits. Moral reasoning is intimately linked to both subject and purpose. It goes to the essence of the function of reason: to achieve virtue and to do 'good.' Moral reasoning is not merely a process; it is a process with a moral purpose. Reasoning, therefore, is an active ethical action.

Reasoning guides us regarding what to do; to understand the ends we want and the means to get there. Moral reasoning, in contrast, leads us to action that will achieve a moral end. Since reasoning can be done ethically or unethically, it is inextricably linked to the morality of one's character.

Through reasoning character is shaped by the examples one uses and by the examples one rejects; by the facts one asserts as well as by the facts one rejects; by the conclusions one reaches and by the conclusions one fails to reach. Moral reasoning becomes a force for and motivation for achieving virtue and becoming a person of moral judgment. Reasoning is different from virtuous reasoning. Our children should be taught the distinction.

Your children probably have a useful understanding of Character. My students generally define character by an application, such as:

- "Like admitting you broke your neighbor's window with a baseball and you wouldn't have gotten caught, and offering to pay for it from your allowance."

- "Your parents go out and they tell you not to watch TV and you obey them."

- "You go out alone and practice soccer kicks because you want to get better."
- "You don't let someone cheat from you because it's not right."
- "You stand up for someone that's being picked on even if she's not your friend."
- "When players on your team yell mean things to the other players and you don't and you tell your teammates to shut up."
- "You stay home and study instead of going to the mall because you want to do well on a test."

Many students define Character as how a person would behave if no one is looking. That standard was a variation of 19th century British historian Thomas B. Macaulay's definition:

> "The measure of a man's character is what he would do if he knew he would never be found out."

Macaulay's standard—character is doing 'good' even when there is no consequence for doing wrong—is fine, as far as it goes. The problem is, it does not go very far. Returning the lost wallet or the forgotten rifle displays character because 'good' was done even though there would have been no price for doing 'wrong.' However, most of our lives are an open display. People see us, people are aware of us and our actions will be discovered.

We are constantly interacting openly and publicly. Therefore, a test of character that is more useful is how a person will behave when someone *is* looking; when someone *will* be found out and when there *will be* a price to pay. I argue that the more important test of character is how a person behaves when the entire world is watching.

I emphasize visible public character when I talk to my classes, the kind of character that shouts to the world: this is what I stand for; this is who I am. My interest lies in learning the nature of a person's character that I can expect or anticipate or rely upon whether or not the world is watching.

Character is your public face to the world. The ability to persuade, to be credible, to be respected and to be viewed as honorable are a function of a person's character. What one believes and what one does not believe are indicators of a person's character. How people treat those who cannot do them any good or do them any harm reveals a lot about their character.

"Your reputation is everything."

–MOTTO, UNITED STATES NAVY SEALS

THE WAY YOU DO THE THINGS YOU DO

Character, then, in its simplest unadorned meaning is about what you do. Consultant Roger Fransecky describes character as the alignment between your internal integrity—the consistency of your values, beliefs and actions—and external moral values. Character means more than being internally consistent. It means being consistently right.

Daniel Goleman, in his insightful book, *Emotional Intelligence*, wrote: "Schooling is not about information. It is about thinking about information. It's about understanding, knowledge and wisdom. And that's all worthless if you don't have character and values."

Information is easily accessible, or relatively so. But data is not sufficient to produce wise actions, as if the technocrat with the most information will produce the best results. Information is not like dough stuffed into a pasta machine and made into perfect linguini when anyone cranks the handle. The best results come from people with the best character. Information acquisition is easy; good character is not.

Gandhi was blunter. One of his Seven Deadly Sins was 'knowledge without character.' Without noble character, (I assume Gandhi was speaking of noble character) knowledge will not lead to virtuous behavior. The informed person lacking moral character will have a mongrelistic morality and make decisions of unpredictable moral content as if they were cannonballs rolling on a ship's pitching deck.

"The most powerful person is he who has himself in his own power."

–SENECA, (5BC-65 AD)

TAKE THE 'CON' OUT OF CONVICTIONS

Jason said that character meant standing up for your convictions. An alarm bell rang in my mind. Is it *always* a virtue to stand up for your convictions? Ask your child that question and see how long it takes to slash through this cliché-driven thinking. Probably not long. I've had many such discussions. Without fail, they began with the students extolling the virtue of standing up for one's convictions.

"Why," I asked? I share the remarks of a typical class.

"It's important to stand up for what you believe in!" the students roared.

"I disagree," I said with a challenging tone. They looked at me with narrowed eyes, like the torch-bearing villagers going after the beast in Beauty and the Beast.

"You're wrong," Samantha retorted. Her words sliced the air like a saber. "You always tell us to stand up for ourselves. You don't even listen to yourself!"

That was the unkindest cut of all!

Softly, as if on the verge of total defeat, I asked "Is it a virtue to stand up for your convictions if you believe people of a certain color should be slaves?"

Silence.

Less softly, is it good to stand up for your convictions if you believed that people should be imprisoned or executed without a trial or without evidence against them? If your convictions demand that you fly jets into office buildings or shove people into gas chambers? Are those examples of noble character?

"Well, what we meant, obviously," Julie harrumphed as if it didn't need to be stated, "was that you should stand up for your convictions if your convictions are good ones. That's what we meant."

Well, good versus bad, that's a rather important distinction, don't you think? The students agreed. Distinguishing between good and bad should be stated again and again. Yet, by George, I think they got it! They learned not to leap to a conclusion based on emotion but to reach conclusions based on reason and facts. This is how we can elevate the moral reasoning of our children.

"Try not to become a man of success,
but rather try to become a man of value."

–ALBERT EINSTEIN

TRADING FACES

I was sitting on the floor, back against the wall, at a local recreation center waiting for my children to finish their gymnastics class. My legs began to get numb so I got up and ambled over to a staff room and read some schedules of future events taped on a wall. Among the papers was this statement by Teddy Roosevelt. I found a pencil and wrote it on a scrap of paper I took from a wastebasket, as excited as if I found a perfect arrowhead on the Colorado plains. This paragraph has become one of my favorite conversation topics.

THE BATTLE OF LIFE
–TEDDY ROOSEVELT

In the battle of life, it is not the critic who counts; not the man who points out how the strong man stumbled or when the doer of a deed could have done better. The credit belongs to the man who is actually in the arena; whose face is marred by dust and sweat and blood; who strives valiantly; who errs and comes short again and again because there is no effort without error and shortcoming; who does actually strive to do the deeds; who knows the great enthusiasms, the great devotion, who spends himself in a worthy cause; who at best knows in the end the triumph of high achievement; and who, at worst, if he fails, at least fails while daring greatly, so that his place shall never be with those cold and timid souls who have tasted neither victory nor defeat.

This motivating statement can lead to hours of vibrant discussions, largely because children identify with so many of the statement's themes. They get engaged. They get excited. They talk to you. Children want to be inspired (Don't we all?) They want to be motivated to excel and to transcend adversity.

Children are attracted to this quotation because they seek out a philosophy that speaks to their dreams as well as to their fears. Teddy Roosevelt was a roughrider, a tough bright guy. He didn't use words in a sloppy or thoughtless way. Each word and phrase is drenched in precise meaning and builds to an over-arching message.

I begin my discussions by asking this general question: What is Roosevelt's message? Students will give responses such as: Don't quit. It's okay to fail. Better to fail than not to try. Be part of life. Don't worry what other people think of you. Some people are jealous when you succeed and some people are happy when you fail. With these generalizations we can grasp Roosevelt's understanding of character.

These are marvelous insights into the quotation that tip toe into larger truths. The next level of discussion is breaking the quotation into bite-sized pieces and dissecting each word and phrase as if you were a lawyer analyzing a contract. I generally begin with the phrase "The credit belongs to the man who is actually in the arena…."The conversation accelerates as if on a Dr. Seuss train ride. This phrase honors participation over result—the person in the arena—a value most of us hold dear.

Maddie, a third grader, gave her interpretation. "What's important is that you're doing something and trying, even if it's difficult, even if there's sweat and blood. Anyone can say someone else messed up. Let's see them do better." She gave a personal example. "I'd rather play on a losing soccer team than sit on the bench of a winning team."

Winning and losing are not as important to children as some parents might think. Playing is important. One child said bluntly, "We just want to play and have fun. The parents should leave us alone."

The phrase "because there is no effort without error and short-coming" is one of the most instructive and one that evokes the strongest responses from the students. Leah said "It means you can't get everything right all the time. If you try to do a lot, you'll make mistakes." Andrew added: "No one is perfect, so you have to make mistakes."

Ethan got the big picture. "If you try, you will fail sometimes. It's part of trying. If you're afraid of making errors, don't even try."

Making an effort showed character. Not making an effort because of fear of error shows lack of character. "You have character if you try your best." "Valiant people fail. They have great character."

Spencer saw the links among character, overcoming fear and achievement. "If you're not afraid of failing, you'll try to do more things and you'll keep going. Then you can win."

Consider the gazillionaire baseball players that have a .300 batting average. That means, Tommy said, "that they don't get a hit most of the time!" On a diabetes sports website I found this motivational quote by superstar basketball player Michael Jordan:

> "I've missed more than 9,000 shots in my life.
> I've lost over 300 games. Thirty-six times I've been trusted
> to take the game winning shot...and missed.
> I have failed over and over again in my life.
> And that is why I succeed."

In his masterful book, *Practicing*, cellist Glenn Kurtz writes that every day he collides with his limits. "It is character that keeps you going past your limits, past your comfort level, past your imagination, past self-defined boundaries."

Roosevelt's most triumphant phrase is: "and who, at worst, if he fails, at least fails while daring greatly, so that his place shall never be with those cold and timid souls who have tasted neither victory nor defeat."

Failure may not be failure at all and even so, some situations are worse than failure. This phrase encourages effort but, more significantly, it judges harshly those that make no effort.

Ponder the power of Roosevelt's rhetoric in the phrase 'cold and timid souls.' He is making searing judgments about the morality and character of those that criticize from the sideline. Use this phrase to help your child perfect the skill of discerning the moral content of words. What does 'cold and timid souls' connote?

"Cold means you have no feelings," Louisa said. "You're dead inside. Nothing matters. That there is nothing that makes you excited or happy that's worth trying." "Timid,' Cassie added, "means you don't care. It means you're afraid of trying and afraid of failing. So you do nothing because you don't have the guts or you're just scared." "It means," Kelsie added, "you have no character. You're nothing."

Move on to the phrase "who have tasted neither victory nor defeat." Timmy said that "victory, like winning, is nice, but defeat isn't really defeat if you're trying hard. But the cold and timid people get nothing at all."

"The people that taste neither victory nor defeat" said Margot, "are the ones that never lose because they never try."

Lilly challenged Margot's statement like a cannon shot, crumbling Margot's reasoning like Feta cheese over a Greek salad. "I disagree," she said assertively. "The person who never tries *does* lose because he never does *anything*! That's losing! That's losing the battle of life."

Many pages of marvelous comments could be written but I will end discussing why Roosevelt describes life as a battle. Roosevelt didn't write 'the challenges of life' or 'the conflicts of life' or 'the character of life.' He used the word battle to convey a specific value. Molly explained, "Because you get hurt in life."

Other students interpreted 'battle' in these ways. "You can never stop trying. It goes on forever." "You can die and people you love can die. It's like a war." "You are always fighting against bad things."

The last comment is closest to the mark. We are always battling the critic and the effete pundit and those who have no accountability for their words. But the battle goes beyond the soccer match or Michael Jordan winning a National Basketball Association championship. Our battles include being diagnosed with lethal diseases, being victims of crime or horrific car accidents, a brutal divorce, a dishonest lawsuit, a financial disaster. Yet, as in any military battle, you have to go on and, as Churchill said, "You may do your worst, but I will do my best."

Roosevelt's statement can help children fight valiantly to bring their dreams to fruition and develop skills to overcome failure and criticism.

I share one poignant moment that illustrates the value of these dialogues. After a third grade class, as I was putting my notes into my briefcase, a student approached me. I heard the voice before I saw him. The voice was familiar.

"Dad," Erik said as he put his arms around me, "I had so many words in my head I couldn't get them out before, but now I know what I was trying to say. Courage is like a fire, and the wood is your character. And if you keep adding wood, the fire gets brighter and brighter."

My eyes moistened, yet again, as I witnessed the delight that comes from learning and recognition. It was a great moment. You can have the same great moments. You will hear the same verbal jewels from your children. The words are inside them. All they need is a conversation with you to coax them out.

CAUSE AND EFFECT

Character is such a powerful force in our lives that as long ago as the fifth century B. C. the Greek philosopher Heraclitus of Ephesus wrote, "Character is destiny . . . . Man's character is his fate." Martin Luther King, Jr. linked a person's value to his character when he said:

> *"I have a dream that my four little children one day*
> *will live in a nation where they will not be judged by*
> *the color of their skin but by the content of their character."*

But let's be honest, character is not the only factor that influences one's fate. Circumstances, bad luck and good luck also influence destiny. But here's the point: character can influence circumstances just as circumstances can influence character.

Circumstances can be beyond your control—a chronic disease, a car accident, skin color, a financial disaster, your home destroyed in a hurricane and so on—but character will dictate the reaction to the circumstances.

In his epic essay, *Politics and the English Language*, George Orwell wrote that a man may be pushed to drink because he sees himself as a failure and then fail all the more because of drinking. Orwell's point was that cause becomes effect but effect becomes cause. This analysis applies to character. Circumstances test character and character influences the impact of the circumstances.

A financial downturn may affect people in different ways. It can inspire a person to be more frugal, to work harder and more creatively or it may cause someone to drink or worse. We have a dear family friend, a young lady now about twenty-five years old. At the age of nine months she was stricken with transverse myelitis, a virus that attacked her spinal cord and rendered her a paraplegic. She is wheelchair bound and, obviously, needs the help of others. But her fate galvanized her extraordinary character. She is now a TV sports producer and writer.

I have never seen her unhappy. I have never heard her lament her fate. I have never seen her express self pity. I have seen only a bright, optimistic young lady determined to transcend her fate. She launches into her battle of life with high megaton force. "You gotta be optimistic, Mike," she always tells me. She humbles as well as motivates me. Tragic circumstances led to the blossoming of her great character, which led to productive and beautiful circumstances.

BUILDING AND DESTROYING CHARACTER

"But, my dear Mrs. Casaubon," said Mr. Farebrother,
smiling gently at her ardor, "character is not cut in marble—
it is not something solid and unalterable. It is something living

and changing, and may become diseased as our bodies do."
"Then it may be rescued and healed," said Dorothea.

–MIDDLEMARCH BY GEORGE ELIOT

The eloquent Yogi Berra, ex-New York Yankee baseball player and manager, said, "When you come to a fork in the road, take it." I'm not sure what the great Yogi had in mind when he shared that pearl of wisdom, but for most of us, when we come to a fork in the road we have to choose which tine on the fork to take. Some choices are better than others, and our choices are determined by our character.

Character is built just like the coral reef, bit by bit, test by test, getting knocked around and weakened by currents and disaster, natural and human caused, and then rebuilt, if one chooses, through discipline and will.

Voids in children's character have had lethal consequences. Day to day, however, children rarely face life or death issues. Challenges to their moral fiber are little, often petty and tedious; telling a small lie, failing to stand up for a besieged classmate, cheating, besmirching people behind their backs.

Character tends to suffer moral diminution by a thousand little pin stabs more than from one or two daunting or apocalyptic confrontations. Peter McLaughlin, consultant and author of *Catchfire*, a book that addresses skills for achieving excellence, writes: "when things start to go wrong, character always goes wrong first."

Parents may impede building character. The dismissal of the stolen item from the store; tolerating the racist remark, the coach that looks the other way when an unethical play is made or, worse, extols it. When someone does something for you and suggests you can't do it for yourself, when you can, your character is degraded, along with your dignity.

Encouraging a child to believe that she is weak and vulnerable and dependent destroys character. Schools that eliminate kick ball and other sports because it is competitive and might hurt the feelings of the losers destroy character as surely as acid corrodes your car battery cable.

If character means anything useful, it means the willingness to confront evil and wrong and injustice. In order to confront and fight, however, one has to be able to distinguish what they are. A person's relationship with 'bad' or evil falls into one of four categories, according to author and lecturer Dennis Prager:

- Those who do evil
- Those who refuse to recognize evil
- Those who see evil and do nothing
- Those who see evil and try to stop it

Most parents work hard to get their children into the fourth category, and that requires developing their children's character based on honor, moral rectitude and the practice of virtue.

> *"Someone who does not know the difference*
> *between good and evil is worth nothing."*
>
> –Miecyslaw Kasprzyk,
> Polish rescuer of Jews during the Holocaust

Distinguishing right from wrong can be difficult sometimes because good people generally don't do bad or evil things, so it's hard for them to imagine or accept that others are doing something bad such as subverting, hurting, lying or demeaning others. There is a powerful tendency to deny it or attenuate its cause. How many of us can fathom that there are super rich people sitting in high priced offices or in their multi-million dollar homes, wearing custom made suits, that spend their days methodically lying to and destroying the lives of thousands of clients and customers?

Who can fathom that there are people that will strap explosives on a Downs Syndrome child and instruct him to walk into a school or market and then detonate the bomb? Yet these things happen, and moral character requires that they be acknowledged for what they are.

For the person that lacks moral character, morality and ethics — all these rules and laws and ethical obligations—become burdens and annoyances. Thus, the seductive appeal to act based on how you feel rather than what is right based on facts. When one lacks the character to do what is right, one has a powerful incentive to tolerate what is wrong.

This reality underlies the statement of 17th century philosopher Benedictus Spinoza: "Peace is not the absence of war, but a virtue based on strength of character." The condition of Liberty itself requires strong moral character and a strong moral code. When liberty is threatened—freedom of speech and the press now leap to mind—the solution, Dennis Prager asserts, is to strengthen character and to instill the willingness to take personal responsibility, not to reduce liberty. Free societies depend on the virtuous character of its people.

Life is full of pain. Raising children is full of pain. Commitment has pain. But a life devoted to avoidance of pain is insular and, in many instances, cowardly. There will always be pain. There will always be tough choices. The measure of one's character is how one behaves when there is pain. When the species is confronted with adversity and stress, the initial fatalities tend to be ethics and character. That's why we have to make our children stronger.

Having been on this planet six decades, I am convinced of one immutable fact: nothing matters more than character. Character matters more than education, intellect, wealth, breeding and culture. Facts and circumstances will change, but character tends to be constant, although character can improve or diminish, of course. I have also more concerned about a person's weaknesses than impressed by his strengths. Minor weaknesses can destroy great strengths.

Character is judged on behavior, not by words or books or speeches. Character, like honor and integrity, can never be taken from you. It can only be surrendered. Tyrants rarely can force free people to their knees. They induce free people to get on their knees voluntarily. Character, like Colorado's stunning mountain wildflowers, is fragile. Once trampled upon, character can take decades to grow back, if at all.

Armand, a fifth grader, distilled into one sentence the process of building and re-building character "Even when you make a mistake, you can build your character by trying to do the right thing. Tomorrow is another day." Lilly summed up one of the finest reasons for developing good character: "It kind of makes you proud."

That's how I try to reach my students: by giving them a solid foundation to make them proud.

CHAPTER 14

CHOICES

*"We who lived in the concentration camps can remember the men
who walked through the huts comforting others, giving away their last
piece of bread. They may have been few in number, but they offer
sufficient proof that everything can be taken from a man but one thing:
the last of his freedoms—to choose one's attitude in any given
set of circumstances, to choose one's own way."*

–VIKTOR FRANKL, *MAN'S SEARCH FOR MEANING*, AUSCHWITZ SURVIVOR

CHOICES, DECISIONS, WHAT'S RIGHT? OH MY!

WELL, YOU CAN'T HAVE EVERYTHING," comedian Steve Wright quips. "Where would you put it?" Wright is right. "You can't always get what you want," wails iconic entertainer Mick Jagger. He's right too. We can't have everything we want not only for lack of space but also because some of the wants conflict irreconcilably with other wants or they conflict with reality. Since we can't have everything we want, we must make choices. "What is not possible," Philosopher Jean Paul Sartre said, "is not to choose."

Making choices can be maddening, unpleasant, painful, humbling, packed with uncertainty and cause turmoil in the soul. We make choices to get things and we make choices to avoid getting things. Every decision or lack of decision is a choice. Choices can be life affirming or life threatening. Choices descend upon us every day like a cascading waterfall. Unrelentingly, life demands that we select one option from among one or more competing ones.

Each option has different risks, rewards, costs and consequences. Some choices have great significance. Some are mundane. Some mundane choices can have profound consequences such as choosing the wrong moment to pass a car on the highway or listening to an iPod while jogging across the street.

Paper or plastic? Coffee, tea or milk? Cheesecake or the fruit plate? Cash, check or charge? Italian, Blue Cheese or Raspberry Balsamic Mango Vinaigrette salad dressing? Take the bus or buy more gas for the car? Have children or not? Stay married or get divorced? Continue your education or get a job? Fire an employee? Fight a war or withdraw? Choices deluge our lives at every level.

This chapter will help parents guide their children through the reefs and shoals of making choices. The better children understand the process, the greater the probability they will make ethical choices that advance their short term and long term interests.

'Choices' is one of my favorite topics because it is about action. All the pondering, the abstractions of the mind, the thinking, the weighing, the worrying and the procrastinating are at last transformed into concrete action. Or maybe inaction. Put up or shut up! Walk the talk. Making choices is where the pedal hits the metal or whatever the cliché is. Choices are not about life's ' couldas, wouldas and shouldas' as memorialized in Shel Silverstein's delightfully instructive poem but are about the 'one little did.' Choices are about what actually gets *done*. Or not done.

IT'S THE ECONOMICS, LITTLE DARLING!

Since we can't have everything, never mind whether we have a place to put it, we choose to give up something to get something else that is presumably more valuable. The best way I have found to teach about choices is to draw upon the discipline of economics.

Economics has been given the unflattering name 'the dismal science' because it is founded on the brutal truth that choices have conflicting costs, consequences and values and that, alas, you cannot have everything. Economics explain the decisions to produce, buy, sell and allocate resources through market systems of competing interests.

Almost every choice involves giving one value precedence over another value: study or play; lose weight or have that seventh piece of rocky road cheesecake, increase safety through intrusive airport security (hopefully) or have more freedom, fight a war and, thus, reduce domestic spending, stand up to bullies or maintain the illusion of peace, report stealing at work or ignore it to avoid negative repercussions? Choices, therefore, like life, are about trade-offs.

I teach this simple description of choices that young children easily understand:

CHOICES

Not What You Want But What Do You Want *More?*

Thinking about choices in terms of what you want *more* rather than just what you want focuses thinking on comparative costs, values, facts, trade-offs and consequences. Thinking about trade-offs deepens children's reasoning capacities and imposes discipline on their choosing process. It forces them to prioritize their values. We all want lots of things, but what and how much are we really willing to pay, fight, sacrifice and tolerate? Our choices disclose the answers.

"One's philosophy is not best expressed in words; it is expressed in the choices one makes. In the long run, we shape our lives and we shape ourselves. The process never ends until we die. And, the choices we make are ultimately our own responsibility."

–ELEANOR ROOSEVELT

You can have a lot of fun talking about choices with your child. I am confident you will be dazzled by their sophisticated insights. Here are a few examples discussed in class of choices and their trade-offs:

- Freedom vs. security
- Automobile fuel efficiency vs. safety
- Greater costs as a machine's precision increases
- Laws requiring bicycle and ski helmets vs. personal freedom
- Nothing tastes as good as being thin feels
- Go to hockey practice or get thrown off the team.
- Go to the mall or do homework
- Save money to buy a bicycle or buy new clothes

- Parents want their children to love them but don't want spoiled brats so they impose standards of conduct and give them addresses of orphanages if the children give them too much grief
- Buy a new car or pay for college

MAKING CHOICES

Making choices is a complex process. Ethical, factual and character issues are involved as well as the need to know the consequence of the choices.

Ask children *how* they make choices and they're likely to shrug and look for the nearest exit and you're likely to think you'd be more useful standing in a cornfield intimidating crows. Don't go wobbly. Teaching children to understand *how* choices are made is one of the most critical skills a parent can impart. Your child will likely answer how he makes choices similarly to these answers:

- I try to do what's right.
- You figure out if what you do makes things better.
- I try to make the best decision for everyone that is involved.
- I try to think about all the things I could do and then choose the best one.
- If you think you can do it, you will try to do it.

From this small collection of answers we can discern several distinct processes in making choices:

- Gather information
- Evaluate information
- Identify options
- Assess the consequences of each option
- Apply ethical values to each of the consequences
- Make moral judgments on each of the options
- Select the best option based on ethics and consequences

OR

- Ignore all of the above and just do what feels good at the moment

You can probably think of other variables for making choices.

Choices involve judgment. Judgment means having the gray matter to know what is right and best. Character is then needed to choose what is right and best. I want my children to use logic and moral reasoning and character to make the choice they believe is the best among the alternatives. I'd be more than a little miffed if my child said something like 'I know this is a dumb or wrong choice but I'm going to choose it anyway.'

When making choices, we look for the best remedy, not the perfect remedy. When we strip away the emotions, the wishing and the hoping and the idealism as if they were a bandage on an old wound, we have to make practical real-world decisions. The mind can deal with great abstractions, but choices have to be concrete. They must deal with reality.

In March, 2001, a parent heard Charles Andrew Williams and others talk about shooting students at Santana High School in Santee, California. The parent did not disclose the information to authorities. He said he thought the students were joking. Of course, every plot, every plan, is just a joke, just a possibility, until it goes off successfully. Then it's a tragedy, and people anguish over how it could have been avoided.

This father thought the students were joking although he had no rational basis to believe that thought, so actually he hoped the students were joking. His choice involved the trade-off between safety and error. The moral choice was to act on the possibility of a threat. He chose to hope rather than to take moral action. Charles Andrew Williams killed two students and wounded thirteen others on March 5, 2001. The father chose hope and got death, although not his own.

Tommy, a fifth grader, described his newly found understanding of the dynamics of choices. "Now, when there is a decision, when there is a moral choice and an immoral choice, I can choose the moral choice."

I asked Tommy how he would do that. He replied: "You think about the consequences and see if it is moral and then, with luck, you make the moral choice."

I tried to read his mind as a photographer reads a light meter. "Is it really luck?" I asked.

He hesitated and then slowly shook his head. "No. I guess it's not luck at all."

He's right.

NOT A DAY FOR A DAY DREAM
NO COST-FREE CHOICES

A category of choices that should be carefully and repeatedly explained to children is the Utopian false choice. This version of the false choice is based on the seductive but illusory idea that a choice can be cost-free. There is no free lunch, so the saying goes, because someone is paying for that lunch, although its cost might be hidden and the person having the lunch might not be paying for it.

It is absolutely true that there are no cost-free choices, at least not choices on important issues: liberty requires vigilance and sacrifice, fighting incurs harm and death, standing up to bullies invites retaliation and requires effort, independence requires knowledge and action, being a skilled physician requires losing leisure time.

The Utopian notion that you can make choices without costs is nonsense. You can't choose to ignore a problem and thereby cause it to go away. Costs can be ignored, denied and covered up but they cannot be wished away. If a school allows a culture of cheating, there will be more cheating, no matter how much a principal wishes otherwise. A parent that permits being targeted by a child's rudeness and vulgarity will not have the respect of the child, no matter how many designer clothes and iPods are showered upon the child.

The parent that permits his young children to do drugs and drink alcohol in the home because 'they're going to do it anyway' engages in Utopian thinking by ignoring the cost of that choice. The youngster that chooses to dress like an impoverished hobo and thinks the world will work valiantly to get beyond appearances and find his inner beauty is a Utopian idealist. More likely the world will despise the youngster's hypocritical dismissal of his relative good fortune.

We may have the freedom to make many choices but making choices alone does not make us free. A person can freely choose to eliminate his freedom. Only making virtuous choices in an environment where others can make virtuous choices makes us free.

Another form of false choice worth discussing is the choice where all the options are not presented or evaluated. For example, telling a child: "Be nice to people or you won't have friends" is a false choice. It fails to include other options, such as, using judgment to be selective concerning to whom you are nice. Similarly, the school administrator that takes no action against bullies and cheaters based on the argument that she can't expel every child accused of bullying or punish every cheater is presenting a false choice. Just expel the ones where the evidence of bullying is strong and punish the cheaters you catch.

SHOCK AND OR

Two sixth graders told me about a choice they made involving a friend. The friend continuously used foul language in school, on the playground, at the movies, in his home and at the boys' homes. The episode has a happy ending and demonstrates that young children can make meaningful choices that result in positive outcomes. In this uplifting case, choosing to stand up to bad behavior reduced bad behavior.

"We really liked him but we didn't like him being mean and nasty to us and to other kids," Erik told me. "We don't talk that way and we don't think it's right. We didn't need that kind of friend." They told the friend they would not spend time with him until he stopped cursing. The friend walked off in a snit, bristling with self-righteous anger. All contact with him ceased. Several months later, the exiled friend approached the boys and said he wouldn't curse any more. And he didn't.

The two sixth graders were willing to make a choice based on a value preference: they liked this friend but they wanted civility more. They were willing to pay a price—the loss of a friend—to gain civility.

"He's really a good friend now. He's changed, and there are no problems. He's really nice. We play a lot together now." Standing up for decency made their friendship stronger.

Sometimes you only have bad choices. A fifth grade girl explained that she would soon have to choose between living with her mother or with her father. Recall the girl with the suicidal friend: either choice could have caused her to lose a friend. The soul shivers from such uninvited choices, but sometimes they cannot be avoided.

The 1984 movie, *Karate Kid*, illustrates an example of a high school student having only bad choices. Daniel LaRusso, the new boy in town, is the outsider targeted for torment and physical assault by John Lawrence and other members of the Cobra Kai karate dojo (school or club). This aggression is encouraged by the sensei (instructor), John Kreese.

Daniel wants to learn karate so he goes to the dojo intending to enroll. Peeking into a class from behind a cloth divider, he sees the sensei strutting with arrogant military bearing, shouting:

- "Fear does not exist in this dojo, does it?"
- "No, sensei!" the students scream reflexively.
- "Pain does not exist in this dojo, does it?"
- "No, sensei!"
- "Defeat does not exist in this dojo, does it?"
- "No, sensei!"
- "What do we learn here?"
- "Strike first, strike hard, no mercy, sir!"

Observing that his attackers are all Cobra Kai students, Daniel unobtrusively leaves the dojo. Mr. Miyagi, an aged handyman who happens to be an advanced karate fighter, tutors Daniel with his of 'wax on, wax off' method and trains him to fight in an up-coming tournament where Daniel will compete against Cobra Kai members. Daniel's enthusiasm for the competition is decidedly mixed.

After months of preparation, the much promoted tournament begins. Daniel is winning his match against Cobra Kai member Bobby Brown. Kreese instructs Brown to 'sweep the leg,' an illegal attack to LaRusso's knee intended to incapacitate him. The sensei hisses "no mercy" as he orders Brown to put Daniel "out of commission." When Brown expresses surprise and a hint of distaste, Kreese challenges, "You have a problem with that?"

Any problem Brown may have had 'with that' was not reflected in his actions. He obeyed Kreese and injured LaRusso. In Hollywood fashion, LaRusso won the tournament championship, improbably defeating the bigger, stronger and, frankly, better looking John Lawrence by employing an exotic one-legged kick technique.

The sugar-coated ending obscures the ethical conflict underlying Brown's behavior. (Although Brown didn't seem too conflicted) It's a great topic to talk about with your children. Discuss Brown's choices and the motivation for each choice.

Your children will certainly acknowledge the real-world consequences of each of Brown's choices. "He had the choice to do the right thing but he'd be thrown off the team," Jonathan said. Sheri added, "The sensei probably would have attacked him. He's a real bad guy."

'Young people generally do what grown-ups tell them to do," Abbie said with a hint of displeasure. She added, "They think the grown-ups know what's best for them." Carla said that Brown didn't want to get into trouble. Andrew saw the matter in terms of the sensei's character. "Brown was afraid of him." Annie offered a dispiriting but probably spot-on explanation. "Most people just like to win. They don't care about being nice or being a good sportsman."

ANGUISH AND EVIL

In the end, education is the ability to make sense of the chaotic present
through the prism of the absolute and eternal truths of the ages.
But if there are no prisms—no absolutes, no eternals, no truths,
no ages past—then the present will appear only as nonsense.

–VICTOR DAVIS HANSON

In the 'only bad choices' department, one of the most gut-wrenching and angering 'only bad choices' experiences I ever confronted occurred on my trip to India. Our tour bus stopped in a city in central Rajasthan—I won't say which one—for lunch and to visit several temples. Immediately we were besieged by dozens of young children. The reality did not compute within the first few minutes after we stopped but, incredibly, almost every child, including very young children, were maimed. These deformed mangled little people approached us using crutches or by propelling themselves on boards with rollers underneath or by just limping to the bus.

The children begged for money, of course. The sight was worse than heart-breaking. It was horrific. Their eyes conveyed unspeakable torment. I send money to charities and I never really know where it ends up; helping discover a new vaccine or feed a hungry child or paying for a Bordeaux wine served at a charity Christmas dinner. Here was a real tangible need that slammed into one's face with the force of a freight train.

We were about to turn on the spigots of cash from our pockets and purses to maximum flow when Sanjay, our guide, sharply urged us not to give any money. The children, he told us, were intentionally maimed and crippled by handlers to generate soul-churning sympathy in tourists so they would give more money. In marketing terms, the handlers had created a successful product line.

Other than my visit to the Dachau concentration camp outside of Munich, Germany years before, this was my most intense visual interaction with pure evil, and at Dachau I only saw photographs.

Sanjay was credible. If he said this was true, I believed him. Also, it seemed improbable that so many crippled children of such a young age would otherwise congregate in this one location.

Anguish mutated to white-hot hatred. But this was the real world, not Utopia. No wishing away pernicious behavior and hoping people would just get along and be nice. Some people do really bad things to children—far worse than this, actually.

To give or not to give? We had only bad choices. But, upon cold detached analysis, one choice was better—or less horrible—than the other. According to the Devil's economics, giving money rewarded the torturers of children and created economic incentives to torture and maim more children. We chose not to give money.

One lesson from this vile behavior that deserves emphasis is that making a choice carries the moral obligation to know the consequences of that choice. When you make a choice, you are choosing the consequences of that choice and you are morally accountable for that consequence. I impress that point in class like a jackhammer. It cannot be taught often enough.

When the squishy principal caved in to the bullying mom of the cheater, he chose the consequences of more cheating just as surely as giving money to the maimed children guaranteed that more children would be maimed. Dennis Prager argues out that when you are decent to the cruel, you end up being cruel to those that are decent, and, in this case, cruel to the innocent.

This is the real world. It is very dangerous to throw reality up like a toss of the coin and choose to be blissfully ignorant of or deny the consequences of your choices.

I don't discuss this maiming event in class. Young children need to be protected from too much reality. But I choose to share this experience with you to burnish two points:

- A person is morally accountable for the consequences of his choices and

- Even between two terrible choices, in almost all instances one choice is better than the other

Making choices can be tough. Anyone that tells a child otherwise is selling snake oil. Children should be taught that they will have to struggle. They should be taught that some decisions are painful. The right or better decision in some instances may be unclear. Teaching this reality is both affirming and comforting. It reinforces the requirement of hard work and reminds children that they are not alone in the battle of right against wrong. Others are also struggling to make moral choices.

ESCAPE TO THE FUTURE

And you cannot go on indefinitely being just an ordinary, decent egg.
We must be hatched or go bad.

–C. S. LEWIS

Most of the time we make choices to avoid more difficult choices in the future. I take antibiotics now each time I go to the dentist so that I won't need a heart transplant later. We fight small battles now so we won't have to fight larger, more deadly battles later. We work in school to become more competitive in the job market and enjoy a better life in the future. We don't get into a car driven by a drunk driver because, once the car is moving, our options to protect ourselves are severely reduced. We don't smoke cigarettes so we may reduce the odds that we will be ravaged by cancer. We must think long term, but life is lived in the short term. The soon will be gone tomorrow, so what counts is what we do NOW.

TO BE OR NOT TO BE
IT'S YOUR CHOICE

Destiny is not a matter of chance. It is a matter of choice.

–SIR ERIC TILGNER

In perhaps the best known soliloquy in English literature, Hamlet muses:

To be or not to be, that is the question.

Whether 'tis nobler in the mind to suffer the slings and arrows
of outrageous fortune,

Or to take arms against a sea of troubles, and by opposing end them?

Hamlet was talking about choices. The profound truth is that choosing is the essence of your 'being.' The morality of your choices is the fullest expression of the morality of your being. Nothing reveals your character or mind or 'being' as accurately as the decisions you make. You have the power to choose to be moral, to be honorable, to be responsible, to be informed, to be educated, even, for the most part, to be happy. It is up to you.

Making choices is an expression of your autonomy. You choose your peers and thereby choose your peer group pressure. You can choose to be a member of a murderous gang or to be a volunteer at a hospital. It's your choice and it is a testament to the character of your being. In the chapter on Autonomy, I wrote about respecting others. I wrote that the highest acknowledgment of respect for another person is holding that person accountable for his choices. We are not billiard balls on a table that respond predictably—deterministically—when struck by another ball. We choose.

The belief that you are responsible for your own actions is essential to self-respect. Being responsible for choices confers dignity as well as accountability. These concepts teach our children how 'to be' and how to avoid 'not being.'

The thinkers I most admire are the ones that see connections in events that may initially appear unconnected. Frankl's statement quoted at the beginning of this chapter prompts me to think of Todd Beamer, one of the passengers on United flight 93 that was attacked by Islamic murderers on September 11, 2001. Faced with certain death, he said to other brave souls, "Are you guys ready? Let's roll."

His heroic action, along with others, caused the jet to crash into a field in Shanksville, Pennsylvania rather than into its intended target, thereby likely saving many lives. Even though they were his last moments of life, Todd Beamer chose 'to be.' He refused to allow anyone to take away his humanity. He chose to define himself. He was noble with his last crust of bread.

Most parents don't want their children drowning in life's oceans of alternatives. Most want to give their children life rafts, buoys and ropes to survive, which are the skills and structures for making proper moral choices.

Grant, a spunky fifth grader, said to me after class, "You make bad choices and you just keep feeling worse and worse and worse about yourself." Think about that comment and then note how Matt's comment in Chapter 5, re-stated here, explains a child's need for guidance to make virtuous choices. "I want to know whether I can be proud of what I decide."

I hope to teach my children and my students to make choices that make them proud. Mastering the process for making ethical choices helps our children 'to be' in the fullest and most honorable sense. It also makes the world a better place.

CHAPTER 15

COMPASSION

"No one could make a greater mistake than he who did nothing because he could do only a little."

—EDMUND BURKE

I WANTED TO HELP

I HAD BEEN AT the Cherry Hills Village Elementary School only a few months when I did this experiment in Elise's first grade class. Teacher Sandy Pratt instructed the children to stay in their seats while she and I went to the principal's office. Outside the classroom I slammed a nearby door, which reverberated thunderously, and yelled 'help' several times. Within moments half the students had scurried into the hallway to see what had happened. Unpersuasively, I am sure, I told the students that I slipped and fell against the door. Moments later we returned to the classroom.

Stacey was one of the first students that ran into the hallway. I asked the students if Stacey was 'good' since she had disobeyed Ms. Pratt's instruction.

"Stacey was both good and bad," Katie answered. Her seemingly contradictory and ambivalent answer actually showed complex thinking. "She was bad when she disobeyed and got out of her seat but good when she tried to help you."

Kelly elaborated using a high level of thinking. She expressed a preference for one value over another. "Helping is more important than disobeying about sitting in a seat." Stacey made a defense of her disobedience that sounded sarcastic but was actually an astute dispassionate observation. "If you're dead you can't come back to life." This youngster affirmed that she valued life over obedience by pointing out that the cost of obedience could be high and possibly irreversible.

Often the imagination of these youngsters can be delightfully uplifting and downright funny. Joan held her chair to her bottom and awkwardly maneuvered herself to the door and then opened it to see if help was required! Technically, she didn't get out of her chair and, thus, technically, she did not disobey Ms. Pratt. Joan crafted an ingenious resolution to the moral conflict. Marvelous! Remember, these are first graders!

Other students justified their disobedience based on feelings, empathy, mercy and the desire to reciprocate for those times they had been helped. "I'd want someone to help me." "We cared about the person." "I'd feel bad if I didn't help the person." "I am happy when people helped me when I needed it so I wanted to help you."

Incrementally, like a snail cautiously sticking its head out of its shell, these little ones explained that they were motivated to help me because they identified with another person's suffering. Note that the students feelings—empathy and a desire to aid someone — motivated their actions to such a degree that most were willing to disobey the teacher's instructions.

The children were experiencing and expressing the moral virtue Compassion. Compassion is a much-idealized virtue. Posters extolling its virtue hang reverentially on school walls like paintings in a museum. Its laudable qualities have been sown into the fabric of our culture with threads as strong as Kevlar. Accusing someone of lacking compassion is akin to accusing the person of spreading the Black Plague or text messaging during a funeral service. Lack of compassion means you don't care. It means you're not nice. It means you are not a good person.

Compassion is born of Latin roots defining sympathy and suffering. Its meaning has evolved to have two components: a feeling of deep sympathy and sorrow for another person stricken by misfortune coupled with a strong desire to alleviate the suffering or remove its cause. Compassion, then, requires both empathy and a desire to act on that empathy. To be compassionate, you can't have one without the other.

Compassion is a precursor to the ethical principal, Beneficence, which I previously defined as the moral duty or command to help others. Compassion is the fertile soil in which the motivation for Beneficence blossoms. But what is the value of those wonderful feelings and empathies and desires to help? Ask your little ones that question and quite early in the conversation they will express the insight that compassion is realized and measured by action. Behavior is compassion's life blood.

I always ask my students to share personal experiences of compassion. Their hundreds of examples give wings to words of hope, comfort and respect. McKenna and her brother, for example, were on a hike and found an injured cat. They took it home, nursed it to health, and found a home for it. Their noble actions were drenched in compassion.

Lauren, a fifth grader, spoke with pride about how she earned money doing chores around the house and donated $20.00 each month to animal shelters. Nefi's mom offered to buy a panhandler breakfast. Gabriela, another fifth grader, captured compassion's essential fusion of intention and action when she described the process of tutoring younger children. "Well, you just can't tell them to read. They need help!"

Giving blood, donating to charity, collecting clothes for homeless shelters, helping someone in a car crash and tutoring are among the dozens of expressions of the children's compassion. Note that I used the phrase, "expressions of compassion." They *did* something to improve a situation or benefit another person. They gave tangible expression to their inclinations.

As a virtue, compassion is unique, and its particular uniqueness can turn it into a troublesome and abused concept. Consider compassion's two components: sympathy and a desire to alleviate sorrow. If we want to get technical, and I always do, compassion can be achieved by merely experiencing feelings. Technically, one doesn't have to *do* anything to be compassionate. That's a nifty cost-free way to be moral! Recall Aristotle's words, "It's easy to be moral in your sleep." The danger of such a strict interpretation of this limited meaning is that it is easy for this noble virtue to lose its integrity and moral power, like a battery losing its charge.

If you helped a homeless person, you had compassion. If you felt pity for the homeless person and really wanted to help but did nothing but bite your nails, technically, you had compassion. However, your compassion didn't amount to a hill of beans, as the expression goes, since you took no action to alleviate the condition.

Compassion's feelings-based definition can enable this virtue to slip and slide into becoming disingenuous and rather phony. I can smugly feel a ton of compassion for victims of injustice or hurricanes or whatever while tying my shoes or eating pizza. No one is helped, of course, but as James Brown wailed, "I feel good!"

ALL YOU NEED IS LOVE . . . NOT!

One crisp autumn morning a most intriguing and enlightening discussion arose unexpectedly, as so many wonderful discussions do. We were talking about friendship in a third grade class. We got onto the subject of caring and its relationship to doing something. Some students said that caring about friends was the same as helping them. My eyebrows arched. How could that be?

Julie explained. "Because, with both, you are doing something good and you feel better." Ponder Julie's logic: caring is good and doing is good, therefore, *caring* is equal to *doing*. Significantly, one good is no better than the other good. This is the logic of moral equivalence, and, frankly, it's not logical. As a bonus—the metaphoric moral icing on the cake—each experience makes you feel better. Feelings are becoming an increasingly legitimate factor for making decisions. This development, which diminishes the value of logic and moral reasoning, can be dangerous.

However, I suppose, in the abstract, Julie is correct that caring is doing something that is good. Certainly caring is better than not caring, although, as we shall see, they may have identical results. Assuredly Julie is correct that caring makes folks feel better. Even so, Julie's conclusion is not logical. That two things are good does not make them equally good. Caring is not equal to doing, just as reading a book about lifesaving is not equivalent to saving a drowning person.

Julie's moral equivalence between caring and doing prompted me to create a class exercise. I asked the class to think about an unfortunate situation they would like to make better. The topic of homeless children was chosen. I told the students to close their eyes and concentrate for fifteen seconds on caring about homeless children and improving their lives. Imagine giving them books and clothing and shelter, I instructed.

They then opened their eyes. I asked if they had any evidence that the lives of the homeless children had been improved. Nothing. Zero. Zip. Perhaps they weren't caring enough, I suggested. I tripled the caring time to forty-five seconds and told them to *really* care this time. "Don't hold back," I commanded. Enthusiasm abounded. Some students cared so much they clenched their fists. The over achievers bit their lower lips. The allotted time elapsed and all eyes opened.

Any change for the better? Nope. The children conceded that their caring was ineffective. "It takes no work to care," Jordan blurted. Indeed! Unlike Peter Pan, you don't get to fly just by thinking lovely thoughts.

The class exercise led to productive conversations, however. Samantha shared that she was a volunteer at a homeless shelter. She brought clothing for children and tutored them. I asked the students to compare Samantha's work with the caring done in the class experiment. "I see," Morgan exclaimed, her eyes twinkling like diamonds. "They're not equal at all! Doing is better"

Elena, emitting a little screech like a phonograph needle hitting a scratch on a record, spoke one of the most profound truths stated in all my classes. "It's easy to care about things when you don't have to do anything."

Such a simple exercise can quickly lead to wisdom through deeper levels of thinking. With new-found clarity as if struck from a bell, the students acknowledged that feelings have a value different from and far less useful than doing. Intensity of feeling is meaningless except to the extent that it motivates action. I felt rewarded. Parents can easily see how such a dialogue gently guides children toward perfecting moral reasoning skills.

Since action is the practical real-world measure of compassion, in order to appreciate all of its components it is useful to discuss compassion in the context of an event requiring compassion. I was writing the final draft of this chapter at about the time the horrific hurricanes struck Haiti in January 2010. Volunteers and money flooded into the impoverished country, and although much of the world shed tears and rhetoric over the disaster, most of the aid and sophisticated medical care came from the United States and Israel.

Many decent people wanted to help, of course, and those that acted did so primarily by sending money. As the much needed money and supplies arrived, the people who actually *saved* the lives and *alleviated* the suffering were the ones that knew how to *do* things—people that knew how to fly planes to reach all of the vast destroyed areas, operate bulldozers to uncover buried living people, saw bones and stop the bleeding, give blood transfusions and perform surgeries under squalid conditions, purify water and deliver assistance while under assault from marauding thieves and feral thugs and on and on. You get the point.

Decent compassionate people had to fight political corruption and bureaucratic resistance and crime that fed on the aid supplies and money like vultures on carrion. Meaningful compassion in Haiti required skill, talent, knowledge, courage, motivation and moral virtue. Feelings and empathy and wanting favorable outcomes were motivational, of course, but work and sacrifice saved lives and made lives better.

Absent people with those characteristics, all the money and supplies in the world would have been as useful as rubble or a United Nations resolution expressing deep concern. Talk with your children about what was needed to enable compassionate people to benefit the people in Haiti. Their thoughtful and heart-felt answers will deepen their realization that compassion is achieved through virtuous action.

Caring and compassion are fine, and I prefer that folks care than not care, but they are, at best, just precursors and initiators. Compassion is not an end. It is the beginning. Compassion for homeless children is not as effective as sending a check. In fact, sending a check even if you *don't* have compassion is better than compassion alone.

"Some cause happiness wherever they go;
others, whenever they go."

−OSCAR WILDE

GIT 'R DONE!

Because compassion is defined by feelings but measured by action, a plan or strategy is needed to convert compassion's motivation into behavior. Attitudes are not substitutes for policies. You might have compassion for any of the plights listed below, but what are you going to do about them?

- You think the world stinks? You're not the first to think so. What's your solution for making it better?

- You want to eliminate poverty? What specific acts will you take to eliminate it?

- Wealth is unevenly distributed? What's the problem, what's your solution and how does your solution makes things better?

- All you need is love? How, precisely, will your love make the world better?

Brandishing your compassion but having no plan of action to alleviate the suffering makes you no more than a whine connoisseur. One gets to be a bore, cutting off invitations to the livelier cocktail parties. Serena, a fifth grader, adroitly hit the old beaten nail on the head once again. "If you're not going to do anything about your beliefs, you might as well not have them." Although their words may be inelegant, the moral reasoning of young children can rapidly become quite sophisticated.

To say 'I feel your pain,' and then do nothing to alleviate it is cynical manipulative rhetoric. It's bad enough I have to feel my pain! If you are inclined to say you feel it also but are not inclined to alleviate it, at least have the decency to shut up!

I see automobile bumper stickers promoting *ad nauseum* compassion and virtuous beliefs. When I think about them—which I assume the author never intends anyone to actually do or is so morally self-righteous he doesn't grasp the implications of his words—I realize these little ditties often contain messages that, in fact, contradict their moral posing.

I see a lot of "Free Tibet" bumper stickers on Colorado cars, which, I note, are conveniently driven far from Tibet. I'll bet there are not a lot of those lofty injunctions pasted onto Chinese cars. The acid-pen writer Mark Steyn makes the point that a lot more people favor a free Tibet than are willing to free Tibet. It's easy to be supportive when you have no intention of being helpful.

I see lots of "End Racism" bumper stickers or bumper stickers that show the word "Racism" in a circle with a downward angled line going through it. Well and good. Ending racism is a laudable sentiment but what's your plan? What are you willing to do to advance the cause? Civil rights marchers wanted to end racism also, but they changed this nation's racial landscape by marching and sitting and picketing and being jailed and shot and slammed to the ground by water cannons and attacked by politically incorrect dogs. Compassion, for them, meant action and courage and personal risk. Even death.

> *"It's not what you feel inside that counts.*
> *It's what you do that defines you."*
>
> –RACHEL DAWES
> TO A SOGGY BRUCE WAYNE (BATMAN)

My point is fundamental: the 'imagine great caring' dialogue illustrates how compassion can be manipulative or even counter productive if virtuous feelings and thoughts are permitted to become substitutes, whether unaware or intentionally, for virtuous action. Think of the problem this way: if you are already compassionate, why work up a sweat doing anything? If we teach our children that they can be compassionate just by experiencing uplifting feelings, we are teaching our children to be self-indulgent passive do-nothings. That would be a sham and a shame.

MORAL JUDGMENT

"Tenderness is greater proof of love than the most passionate vows."

–MARLENE DIETRICH, GERMAN-BORN AMERICAN FILM ACTRESS

Meaningful compassion, then, requires qualities in addition to 'compassion.' As mentioned above, the compassionate person needs a strategy for action. To analyze the morality of situations and to act compassionately, moral judgment is required. Compassion is a necessary component of human interaction but it is not the most important of human existence. Unrestrained by other virtues, compassion can lead to catastrophe. Think about appeasing bullies, whether a child or an organization or a nation. Compassion, if it is to be moral, must be discriminating.

For example, compassion is a necessary part of justice, but it should not trump justice. Let's say you were on a jury in a criminal case and you felt sympathy for the defendant—his or her background, race, religion, hard life, world view, personal struggles, whatever—but you knew that the prosecution proved the defendant guilty beyond a reasonable doubt. Thus you have a moral and legal duty to find the defendant guilty. Allowing compassion to nullify moral and legal obligations would be injustice.

Because compassion is based on feelings—sympathy and desire—it is easy for it to degrade or deteriorate into other feelings or beliefs that may be contrary to moral reasoning and which may conflict with moral action. The concept of tolerance, which I mentioned earlier, is an example of compassion's deterioration. Empathy for or identification with or acceptance of a person or of a behavior not grounded in morality becomes immoral, just as the tolerance of injustice is injustice.

Lenient judges and squishy prosecutors that continuously give 'breaks' to law breakers aren't necessarily expressing compassion, although, no doubt, many believe they are. There is always a trade-off between compassion for the victim and compassion for the aggressor. Compassion for the guilty at the expense of the victim may lead to the suffering of future innocent victims as well as express disrespect for the victim.

Thus, we see a paradox: compassion for the cruel becomes cruelty to the innocent. The compassionate policeman that allows the drunk driver to drive the few blocks to the drunk's home becomes legally and morally responsible for the deaths and injuries to the innocent people caused by the drunk driver.

"Tolerance becomes a crime when applied to evil."

–THOMAS MANN

TEACHING COMPASSION
A Fish Story

We now have an understanding of what compassion is and what it is not. The soul of compassion is *identifying* with the suffering of another. For those inclined toward compassion, this identification produces a desire to remedy or alleviate the suffering. Together, both should lead to moral action. Any behavior or discussion that promotes in children the moral identification with another person will strengthen a child's capacity for compassion. Helping as a volunteer, for example, in any of the many ways needed by society enhances a child's capacity for compassion.

In her superb book, *Building Moral Intelligence*, Michele Borba explains how helping your child empathize with the feelings and thoughts of others—the victim of unkind words or taunting—will teach the causal relationship between acts and words and their consequences. Understanding this relationship between acts and consequences will, we hope, encourage children to act to avoid undesirable consequences. Compassion, thus, can be seen also as the motivation for *not* acting; not saying hurtful words or doing hurtful deeds.

Every year I talk about the starfish lady. It is one of the most effective stories for nurturing compassion. I've spoken about her so many times it seems I know her. In my mind's eye I see a middle aged or older woman wearing clothing that is disdainful to fashion, possessing a confident authoritative bearing and whose face shows she doesn't suffer fools lightly. She reminds me of my mom, to tell you the truth.

The starfish lady story is uncomplicated. A lady is walking on the beach when a ferocious storm suddenly erupts, whipping the waves like egg whites for a soufflé. Hundreds of starfish are washed ashore. Methodically and tediously the lady picks up handful after handful of starfish and walks to the ocean's edge and casts them into the sea.

A jogger lopes by, stops and in a belittling tone, questions the woman. "Why do you bother picking up the starfish? There are so many and you can only get a few into the water before they die. You won't make a difference."

"It will make a difference to the ones I save," the woman replied tersely. My mom might have added a phrase or two.

This is a powerful engaging story that will not fail to draw your child into a vibrant dialogue. Ask your children if saving only a few starfish matters? Ask your children to describe the starfish lady's values. Discuss the dilemma of what should be done when only a little can be done.

Most likely your child's responses will be similar to those of my students. "I respect the starfish lady. She cared and she did something." "The lady showed courage. She didn't let the stupid jogger stop her." "She did what she thought was right, and she *was* right." "You do what you can when it's right."

Compassion for the dying starfish motivated the lady to alleviate the suffering of as many starfish as she could. The students, without exception, condemned the jogger's values. "Saving one is better than saving none." Indeed, Jordan accurately sized up the jogger's character, saying acidly, "The jogger had no values." Erik, my son, drew upon on Roosevelt's "The Battle of Life" philosophy that I discussed in the Courage chapter, to critique the jogger's character. "The jogger was a cold and timid soul. He did nothing except criticize."

Brittany posed a brilliant rhetorical question that effectively launched the jogger's argument into the trash can. "Should a fireman not try to save anyone in a fire just because he can't save everyone?" I know I have successfully impacted the children when they see links between a story and their own experiences and with real world situations.

According to the jogger's logic, the fireman's rescue effort should not be attempted. This reasoning can be extended endlessly. Don't tutor children because you can't tutor them all. Don't give money to charity because you can't save the world. Don't try to compete because it is unlikely you will be the best. The message is repulsive: hide your head in a tortoise shell of indifference and inaction.

In its most benign form, such repugnant reasoning illustrates the classic fallacy of allowing perfection to be the enemy of the good. In its most malignant form, the inability to attain perfection becomes an excuse to do nothing. The jogger is the poster boy for this philosophy. "He knew better," Andrew yelled. "He's just lazy and selfish." I found it hard to argue with that conclusion.

I talked about examples of compassionate behavior that I had discussed in previous classes. When I mentioned the Zaborek family and their heroic adoption, an insight exploded within Andrew like fireworks. He saw their refusal to abandon the child in the new context of the starfish lady metaphor. "Now I get it," Andrew said as if striking gold. "That kid is like the starfish! The Zaboreks couldn't save all the kids but they saved him. It mattered to him! Now he will have a great family."

Allison then added an eloquent soul-churning grace note that did moisten the aging eyes. "I guess sometimes we're all starfish." How's that for empathy? And from a third grader!

I am ceaselessly dazzled by the insight and eloquence of young children. I am humbled by their words. I cautiously permit myself to be re-energized with hope for the future of our species. Take a moment to talk with your child about things like the starfish lady and these wonderful conversations will be yours and then you can use up all your Kleenex.

If you want to have a dialogue with your child that touches their heart, the starfish lady story is a fine beginning. Ask your child questions such as these (you will quickly think of better ones):

- Which person do you admire, the lady or the jogger?
- Which person would the starfish prefer?
- What qualities did the lady have and what qualities did the jogger have?
- Which person makes the world a better place?
- Should you not try to accomplish anything just because you can't accomplish everything?

I remember this next moment with great clarity because it was one of the most impacting in almost two decades in the classroom. I had been talking about the starfish lady. The bell rang signaling the end of the class. A student approached me as I placed my papers into my briefcase.

In a voice a decibel above a whisper, the little fellow said, "I guess I was a starfish." I asked what he meant. He explained he had bone cancer years before. He was not expected to survive. He underwent a bone marrow transplant. "I'm lucky they didn't give up on me. They kinda threw me back and I lived." Can you see in your mind's eye that little child sharing such an intimate revelation? Your children will say essentially the same words to you.

For him, the starfish story was not an allegory. This little fellow *was* the starfish. He was the allegory. Now had a deeper understanding of the meaning of the morality of compassion. He survived because someone's compassion for a dying child led to action, just as Rex saved the life of my friend's son.

As my years speed by at an accelerating rate, I realize that acting with love is the ultimate expression of compassion. Love is also a virtuous energizing motivation for action. As with compassion, love is measured by doing, not by feeling.

I have written this book based on the belief that the readers' compassion and love will motivate them to talk with their children about serious things; honor, sacrifice, character and those great principles required living a virtuous life. We can never talk about every important matter, of course. We will rarely have a perfect life-transforming conversation, but should that prevent us from talking? Think of the little boy who realized he was a starfish and you will know the answer.

CHAPTER 16

COMPETENCE

BRAINS, BODY AND BELIEFS

"Nothing splendid has been achieved except by those who dared to believe that something inside them was superior to circumstances."

—BRUCE BARTON

I WANTED A MECHANIC, NOT A PHILOSOPHER, to slice out my infected aortic valve and stitch in the prosthetic valve. I wanted someone competent. Highly competent. As for caring about me, the best way Doctor Dan could care about me was by being well-rested, sober, versed in the latest medical data, prepared in the operating room and not be distracted by personal concerns.

This chapter is about Competence. I describe the virtue's several components, show how competence can motivate moral behavior and share some ideas about how we can nurture competence in our children.

A few days after the Columbine High School killings I met Bill Pessemier, then Chief of the Littleton Fire Department, at a community meeting. In an atmosphere pervaded by confoundment, hundreds of parents tried to extract useful lessons from the horrific event. Of the several matters the chief and I talked about, one was how to instill ethical character in children. Shortly thereafter, over a period of five or six weeks, I had the privilege of speaking to over one hundred members of the department about moral reasoning skills and how they could be added to existing school programs.

During dozens of hours of discussion, these extraordinary men and women described how they train to achieve excellence under daunting and life threatening situations. They study the construction and design of buildings in order to most effectively evacuate people. Some practice driving at high speeds. They learn first aid. They run and lift weights to enhance their physical conditioning.

The better their conditioning, the more capably they can perform under more challenging circumstances.

They described their criteria for attaining the highest level of excellence in competence. "You have to be able to leave your personal problems outside the fire house." "You have to control your fear and go on kind of automatic pilot." "You can't think too much about what's happening because you might develop doubts, and that causes hesitation, and that can lose lives." "Your environment demands total trust." "You have to focus on the task confronting you." "You need to know how to handle all the equipment and how to use it in each kind of fire or injury." "We have to know when to enter a building and when to abandon it."

> *"You gotta be prepared inside to meet*
> *what's coming at you from the outside."*

–DAVID BIBBER, CHIEF, DOVER FIRE DEPARTMENT, DOVER, NEW HAMPSHIRE

Parents need a smorgasbord of competencies. Indeed, we need all of the above and arguably more. The complexity of our lives is measured by the number of bills we receive; the passing of our lives is measured by the velocity of their arrival. Accompanying my tax returns each year, my accountant, Coach Sam, sends a cover letter that advises: "These records should be kept forever." That's a long time. Organizing and filing are not among my greatest competencies.

Parents must fight valiantly every day just to keep up with the mail, which descends like an unceasing avalanche. We must separate the unrequested junk from those missives that will, if we don't take prompt action or make a payment in the next seven minutes, ruin our credit scores, subject us to rapacious interest charges and catapult us into every circle of Dante's Hell.

We have to coordinate doctors' appointments, school meetings, jobs, charitable activities, sports practice and games, trips to the supermarkets, maintenance of cars and vacuum cleaners and dishwashers and our own numerous personal obligations, all of which, in my case, are precisely recorded in my personal organizer, which I often can't find. As I sprint to my house door, briefcase dragging like an anchor, a spine chilling question erupts like a mummified hand in a horror movie: "Where are my keys?"

We hustle and bustle and drive and run. Then our carefully-crafted schedules and plans are tossed asunder: a child contracts an intractable disease; one of our parents is dying or has become incapacitated; a child is injured or worse in a car crash; we have become victims of an illness or are suffering financial distress. We have to cope, somehow. Often, we have to be absolutely unemotional. We must exercise flawless judgment. Constantly.

THE ELEMENTS OF COMPETENCE

Ask your child what qualities are needed to become better students or athletes or friends or musicians or to be successful later in life, however you define success. Most likely you will get answers similar to the ones I've heard in my classes: "study hard," "set goals," "have discipline," "have good values," "make good choices," "be organized," "have good time management skills," "learn your limits," "learn the rules," "be aware, listen and pay attention," "learn how to read and write," "use the right utensils and tools."

Soccer players do ball juggling to increase eye-body coordination. One little fellow described how he practices dribbling two basketballs at a time to develop coordination and a 'feel' for the location of the ball. Cynthia explained the grunt work of practicing scales on her violin. But doing all that juggling and practicing and dribbling requires additional skills and virtues: pride, honor, dedication, focus and others previously mentioned.

A child with dyslexia explained that he forced himself to read and re-read sections of his books in order to understand the material. Forcing himself to read and re-read is a compelling personal competence. Asking for directions is a personal competence. I could drive the course at the Indy 500 and I'd have to stop and ask for directions to the finish line.

Let's study the comments made by the fire fighters and the children and review the skills parents need to raise children. Analyzing these examples and descriptions, we discern two primary components or categories of competence:

- Technical Competence and

- Personal Competence

Qualities that belong in the Technical Competence category for fire fighters, for example, are:

- Driving skills

- Administering first aid

- Knowing the construction of buildings

- Knowing how to operate relevant machinery

- Having the strength to perform certain tasks

Some of the traits that belong in the Personal Competence category for fire fighters and for the rest of us may seem obvious. Others may require analysis and thought but once the thinking has occurred, most likely the reader will conclude something like,

- "Of course, I should have known that!"

- Self discipline

- Calm and poise

- Earn the trust of your colleagues

- Focus

- Leave personal problems at home

- Pride in doing excellent work

- The ability to be self critical

- The ability to be self correcting

The competent person seamlessly combines personal and technical qualities, just as the molecules of hydrogen and oxygen combine, extraordinarily, to create life-sustaining water. Regarding life sustaining, I certainly wanted my doctors and nurses to possess all the personal and technical competence qualities relevant to treating my heart condition. I was fortunate. They all had them.

A STUDY OF EXTRAORDINARY PERSONAL COMPETENCE

Is That a Gun in Your Playground?

I share a few class topics to illustrate the dominant aspects of competence. These discussions are delightfully thought provoking as well as energizing. I think of them as finger painting for the mind. I am confident that readers will derive equal joy and reward talking about these subjects with their children.

I write, unabashedly, that the facts of this first dialogue are among the most extraordinary I have ever discussed. A bunch of years ago I read in the local papers about Lorenzo Hernandez, a third grader in a Denver elementary school. He was with a few classmates in the school playground when he found a pistol. He believed he should give the pistol to his principal. Lorenzo was taunted by his peers and subjected to their anger for not giving the weapon to them. Some argued it wasn't a real gun. Others said it wasn't loaded. Some classmates urged him to sell it.

Overcoming their berating and derision, Lorenzo delivered the pistol to his principal. It turned out to be a loaded operable firearm. I knew I had struck gold in this story.

My class discussions about Lorenzo are confined to competence. The quality of Lorenzo's technical competence was substantially less than his personal competence, which is one reason the story is so compelling. Lorenzo didn't know if the gun was real. He didn't know if was capable of firing. He didn't know if it was loaded. He had little technical competence beyond knowing the object was a gun and not a horseradish. He knew guns are dangerous. He knew little children shouldn't be playing with them.

His personal competencies, however, were diverse, deeply rooted, moral and extraordinary. He had an overarching value system that gave him strength: he was morally compelled to protect life. He knew that this gun might hurt or kill people.

Prominent among his personal competencies was an intuitive sense of knowing his limitations. This remarkable youngster knew what he didn't know—whether the gun was real, loaded or operable. He knew that uncertainty should not be an excuse for failing to act. He knew the right action to take. Lorenzo was also aware of possible consequences of those limitations. He new failing to act morally could be devastating.

Discuss Lorenzo's personal competencies with your child and you will likely hear comments similar to the ones made in my classes. "He was strong." "He had courage." "He valued life." Some students astutely remarked that Lorenzo valued the other kids' lives more than they valued their own.

"He was able to stand up to his friends." Maria elaborated: "He didn't let them push him around because he knew he was right."

The moral person must be able to evaluate a particular situation, recognize it for what it is and evaluate different responses. Such analytical skills, the ability to "size up" a particular event, come from experience, habit, and education. But it is unlikely that Lorenzo had much experience, habit and education in situations like this one. In this remarkable instance, personal competence triumphed over the absence of technical competence.

However, I'd go a step further: it wouldn't make any difference if Lorenzo had technical competence. The result should be the same whether the gun was a toy or was unloaded or real but inoperable. But that's another discussion.

Talking about alternative hypothetical outcomes with your children has value because you can discuss what could have happened if Lorenzo had not demonstrated such unassailable character and competence: children might have been injured and/or killed.

A morally weak child whose behavior led to the death or injury of another child might seek refuge in arguments like: "I thought it was a toy." or "I didn't think it was loaded" or some such nonsense. This unethical thinking must be bluntly confronted and discredited.

Under these facts, classmates had no basis to believe that the gun was a toy or was unloaded or was not operable. What those children thought didn't matter. The only element that mattered was that an error in judgment created a great a risk of harm. As it turned out, the gun was real and loaded.

In wrapping up the discussion in one class, I asked if Lorenzo had qualities not yet mentioned. Karla's answered astonished me. "Lorenzo would have had to trust his principal." I confess the matter of trust had not occurred to me but once verbalized, the truth of her insight was obvious.

Yet again the students saw things that escaped me. Lorenzo trusted that his principal would accept his version of the event. That entailed taking a risk. Catching the wind of Karla's comment, Jimmy added, "He probably wouldn't have turned in the pistol if he knew he would get into trouble." This important theme will be revisited in the Consequences chapter.

Karla's comment reminded me of a statement by a cardiac surgical nurse about trust and competence. "You have to demonstrate that you can be trusted and trust is based on proving your skills. Without skill and trust within the team, you can't perform at the highest level, and that means the outcomes are more likely to be jeopardized."

The relationship between the students and Lorenzo's principal can rightly be viewed as that of a team. The principal evidently cultivated the student's trust. Had there been no trust on that team, students might have died.

The matter of turning in a pistol found in a schoolyard, then, is not simply a matter of 'doing good' or 'doing what's right.' As I wrote earlier, doing 'good' is not easy. Lorenzo's behavior was the consequence of powerful personal competence traits, including possessing an unshakeable moral value system. (Perhaps, too, a bit of a miracle.)

Talk to your little ones about Lorenzo. Discuss if they would have had the strength of character and the personal competence to turn the gun into the principal. If your children are unsure, review the competencies involved and the devastating consequences that might have occurred if those competencies did not exist. This dialogue is unsurpassed for developing your child's moral competence.

"I don't know the key to success,
but the key to failure is trying to please everybody."

–BILL COSBY

THE WAY YOU DO THE THINGS YOU DO

"If everyone knew how to work, everyone would be a genius!"

–WANDA LANDOWSKA, HARPSICHORDIST

My second topic analyzes a brief statement on achievement by Alexander Hamilton. Hamilton's skills and accomplishments were of extraordinary breadth. One of the Founding Fathers of the United States, he signed the Declaration of Independence, helped draft the Constitution and served as the first Secretary of the Treasury. Under the pseudonym "Publius," he and John Jay and James Madison authored the Federalist Papers, the brilliant collection of essays written to support the ratification of the Constitution.

We analyzed this statement by Hamilton:

"When I have a subject at hand, I study it profoundly.
Day and night it is before me. My mind becomes pervaded with it.
Then the effort which I have made is what people are pleased to call
the 'fruit of genius.' It is the fruit of labor and thought."

I go over this statement word by word, just as I did with Roosevelt's statement, 'The Battle of Life.' Unless someone knows it, I ask a child to find the definition of 'pervaded' in a dictionary. It means 'to spread throughout,' 'to saturate.' When presented with issues or subjects, Hamilton works ceaselessly, day and night. That part is rather straightforward. Robert referred to the well-worn phrase: Genius is 2% inspiration and 98% perspiration. Your children can give you examples of when they worked very hard to achieve a goal and, no doubt, when they chose not to.

This intriguing sentence prompts animated dialogues:

"Then the effort which I have made is what people are pleased to call the 'fruit of genius.'

What's Hamilton's point? "It's like, they're saying that it's easy for him and that it didn't take much work," James remarked.

Correct, but why did Hamilton believe that people are "pleased to call..." What's there about genius that makes the non-geniuses pleased? That's the second of Hamilton's two key points. The children quickly grasped Hamilton's meaning.

"They're pleased to call it genius because it takes away from Hamilton's hard work." "It makes his hard work mean nothing." "It makes people feel better when they do nothing because they won't work as hard." Alex said sharply: "It's a compliment to be told you did well, but it's an insult to be told it's the fruit of genius when you work so hard."

"People are pleased to call it genius," Julie said, "because it becomes an excuse for those people that don't accomplish the same things." "It's an excuse for not trying," Nora added. "They think, well, he's a genius so there's no point in me trying to do anything," Andrew concluded.

In a flash of brilliance, Emily saw the link between the people that say 'fruit of genius' and the critics in Roosevelt's 'Battle of Life.' They diminish and trivialize hard work, as do those who refer to an athlete as 'gifted' or as a 'natural' even when the athlete trains endlessly. They are the cold and timid souls.

Most of us can identify with Hamilton's lament. I am familiar with the legal profession more than I am with others. I know that far more than brilliance, the lonely studying in the library or on the computer late into the night and the unglamorous tedious review of documents, motivated by pride and dedication, lead to the dramatic moments in the courtroom and to favorable outcomes.

Of course, some lawyers are brighter than others, but the brightest lawyers I know are also the hardest workers. Where the first quality tip toes into the other I'll never know. But it doesn't matter. Both are needed.

"The reason a lot of people do not recognize opportunity is because it usually goes around wearing overalls looking like hard work."

–THOMAS EDISON

A few years after I discovered the Hamilton quote, I heard an interview on the Dennis Prager radio show about research on praising children done by Carol S. Dweck, a Stanford University psychologist and professor. Her riveting work examines not only how praise influences personal competence but also gives insight into the limitations—and perhaps the fears—of the kinds of people who are 'pleased to call' the work of great achievers like Hamilton the 'fruit of genius.'

Dweck found that praise would influence motivation positively and negatively. Praising a child's intellect was likely to stifle achievement. Praising a child's work ethic and tenacity encouraged risk taking, reduced the fear of failure and motivated achievement. The most motivated and resilient students, her research showed, were those that had the highest sense of competence and who believed that their competence could be enhanced by work, learning and effort. Those who thought their achievement was a primarily a function of their innate intelligence were more restrained and self-limiting. They gave up sooner.

Students who believed they were bright tended to believe that their intellect, their 'brightness,' was finite. These youngsters were more likely to avoid challenges than those students who believed that achievement is the result of work. Effort is not only relatively limitless—Hamilton's 'pervaded' and 'night and day'—but emphasizing effort gives a child a variable that can be controlled. You can choose the work harder.

Interviewed in a New York Magazine article, Dweck said, "When you praise kids' intelligence and then they fail, they think they're not smart anymore, and they lose interest in their work. In contrast, kids praised for effort show no impairment and often are energized in the face of difficulty."

I promptly began discussing this provocative research in my classes. Max, one of my go-to guys at Ebert Polaris Elementary School when I introduce a new topic, said simply, "What she says makes sense."

Latisha captured the core of Dweck's concepts: "Smart has limits. Trying doesn't."

The 'fruit of genius' explanation focuses on being bright. It is a demoralizer, not a motivator. The 'fruit of labor and thought' concept energizes and empowers. That's what we want for our children.

So many times I've heard comments such as this one: "I know I'm not a good athlete (or whatever), but I felt good when my dad (or mom) told me he was proud of me for trying. So I tried harder." Another oft-repeated comment goes something like this: "When people tell me I can't do something, I try harder to prove them wrong."

Trying harder may well be the quintessential personal competence. Stated bluntly, there is a difference between being aware of your limitations and submitting to them. The first inspires overcoming and achievement; the second means giving up.

MORALITY, COMPETENCE AND DUTY

"There is a tide in the affairs of men
Which, taken at the flood, leads on to fortune;
Omitted, all the voyage of their life
Is bound in shallows and in miseries.
On such a full sea are we now afloat;
And we must take the current when it serves,
Or lose our ventures."

–JULIUS CAESAR, WILLIAM SHAKESPEARE

I got a flat tire three days before completing the tenth draft of this chapter. I drove back to the Discount Tire location where I bought the tire just two months before. Rei, the manager, said he would repair it. I walked across the street to get a sandwich and returned a few minutes later. Rei told me that driving the car on the totally flat tire as I had for several miles at high speed had compromised the tire's structural integrity. It could not be safely repaired. Since it was a new tire, Rei replaced it without cost.

Rei could have taken the cheap way out and repaired the tire. I never would have known it was unsafe—until, perhaps, after a cataclysmic crash, and then only if I survived. I relied on his judgment and competence. I was fortunate. Rei was not only competent; he was moral. But, and I emphasize this, he was doing his job. He had a moral duty to be competent. People could have died or been injured if he gave me a defective tire.

Here's another example. A few years ago I hired Greg, a plumber, to install a new water heater in my home. Greg was superb; sawing and soldering copper pipes into a maze that looked like shiny linguini. As he was leaving, Greg mentioned, as casually as someone changing their salad dressing order from Ranch to Blue Cheese, that he had checked the carbon monoxide levels in the furnace room and found it to be high. He investigated, found the leak and repaired it. Carbon monoxide leaks kill people.

Once again, a person was both competent and moral. Once again, Greg, too, like Rei, was doing his job by fulfilling their moral obligation to be competent.

Consider the worker in the grease-stained non-designer shirt that tightens the lugs on your tire after rotating them or the mechanic that checks the de-icing system on aircraft or the nurse that disinfects your arm before drawing blood or the police officer trained to use firearms or the local butcher tasked with throwing away food that has spoiled. The list goes on and on. They have a duty to be competent. We all do.

Lives were saved during hurricanes Katrina and Ike because helicopter pilots had the skill to stabilize their aircraft in high winds and retrieve beleaguered survivors from buildings and cars. The United States military was able to save lives after the horrific tsunami in the India Ocean in December, 2004 because soldiers had the skill and the equipment to fly food to isolated populations and to evacuate them. They didn't just value life. They had the competence to implement their values. They also fulfilled their moral duty to be competent.

Talk to your children about the numerous day-to-day instances where they rely, perhaps unthinkingly, on the competence of their fellow citizens. Such a discussion is valuable because it prompts children to think about the importance of doing things competently and of the intimate relationship between competence and morality. Indeed, this relationship prompts many theorists to opine that ninety-five percent of ethics is competence. Ethical behavior is based on the duty of competence.

COMPETENCE AND MOTIVATION

"There is no sin except stupidity."

—OSCAR WILDE

Competence, however, is not enough to ensure moral action. Ability is not the same as willingness. A person must be motivated to act morally. Dr. Dan knew where to find the heart when he cut me open. The fire fighters could accurately assess the risk of entering a specific burning building. Their knowledge became useful, however, when they were motivated to do their duty. The human can *know* and the human can *will* but they are not the same.

Think about the link between competence and motivation. The person skilled in life saving techniques is more likely to try to save a drowning person than an unskilled person. If, on an airplane flight, a passenger appears to suffer a life-threatening episode—a heart attack, a stroke, choking—a medically trained person would likely be highly motivated to offer assistance. A person skilled in self defense or the martial arts would likely be motivated to intervene in an assault on an innocent victim. Lacking competence, a person is likely to choose to be uninvolved. With competence as with compassion, you cannot give what you do not have.

My students talk about how they respond when their competence increases. "The more you try, the better you get, and the more you want to do," Maggie said. Regarding his efforts to learn math, Charles said: "You get more confidence, so you try harder, and when you see that you're improving, so you feel better about yourself." Competence means being motivated to fight the fight within you to do what is right.

Studying the comments made by the students and the fire fighters and learning the lessons from Lorenzo and Hamilton and

Dweck, among others, we learn that motivation is influenced, if not determined, by:

- Competence
- Values and
- Expectations of consequences

Think of Lorenzo's values. Think of his expectation that he would be trusted by the principal. Think of the fire fighters' values and their expectations that training will save lives. I offer this formula to define the source of motivation: I didn't create this formula but I don't recall where I read it.

$$M = C_{P+T} + V + E$$

where

M = motivation

C_{P+T} = Personal and Technical Competence

V = values and

E = Expectations

The morally competent person, therefore, is more motivated to act morally. Note I use the phrase 'morally competent.' The competence of intellect or skill is not sufficient to motivate moral action. The 9/11 terrorists had skill and motivation but no morality. Hitler was skilled and competent. The Columbine High School murderers were competent killers. A lawyer can be highly skilled and competent and quite successful yet be thoroughly immoral.

Talk to your children about competence and motivation. They will share many experiences proving the relationship. Ask them what they expect when they choose to do something good. Ask them about their values. Ask them why some values are better than others. They will tell you that the better they become as athletes, as an example, the greater their willingness to attempt difficult moves or exercises. The same will be true regarding their musical training, math skills, reading, studying, even in selecting friends.

This general rule applies to parenting. Parents have told me that as they became more competent, they acted more confidently and authoritatively yet also with greater compassion and understanding. Their strength allowed them to be more flexible.

SHTICKS AND STONES
A Worm Story

"To prepare a face to meet the faces that you meet."

–T. S. ELIOT, *THE LOVE SONG OF J. ALFRED PRUFROCK*

Here is a deliciously humorous anecdote that has profound lessons for teaching competence. I was speaking about bullying to a fifth grade class at CHVE. At one point the discussion took a jaunt to the issue of why people—in this case, children—are so mean about matters that are so trivial.

In my class were children, among most economically privileged on the planet, describing how they are picked on and humiliated about clothing, of all things. "Your label says Polio, not Polo!" "Your clothes are from dumpster designers." "Those look like hand-me-down from a wino!" We've heard worse, of course, but this is mean stuff. And it's just plain stupid.

Perplexed, I bluntly asked why there is so much meanness about things that are so meaningless. "We don't do what we know is right." Lexa replied.

Reade offered his insight: "People who tease others about their clothes don't feel good about themselves. They need to hurt people to feel better."

Maybe so.

I suggested the students learn to strike back at those tiny haber-dasher aggressors. Mean people tend to hurt others because they derive pleasure from inflicting pain or discomfort. Perhaps we could create a skill that would de-fang that pleasure, if that is something one can do to pleasure, and reduce the incidents of meanness. I started to think of an argument. I paced in front of the chalkboard. I gestured with my hands. My eyes darted to the windows, to the floor, to the ceiling.

"How about saying something like this….." I paused as I impro-vised. "You pathetic little worm. What an empty sad life you lead, that you need to find meaning by hurting others as you crawl from under the rocks of prejudice and pettiness that litter your life in a desert of denial and despair! How sad. How pathetic and profoundly sad!"

It's not *King Lear quality* but it was late in the afternoon. I stopped and turned toward the children. My jaw dropped. Almost every child was furiously scribbling my words into their notebooks or on scraps of paper.

"Can you start again after the part about the 'desert'?" Samantha asked.

"Also repeat the part about the rocks," Jack added.

"No, say the whole thing again," Suzy implored.

I repeated the statement as best as I could remember.

Reade asked, "Are you adding new stuff this time?"

"Sure! I made it up once. I'll do it again."

Megan yelled out, "I'm going to use that!"

With a twinkle in his eyes, John Mollicone, the fifth grade teacher said, "You're on to something. That's what they need."

I had given them a script, a template, a formula, a tool to deflect the attacks on them. I helped them construct a defense. In an admittedly small way, I had made them more competent.

About half a year later I asked the class whether any of the discussions had caused anyone to act differently in any situation. With evident enthusiasm, Alexa answered promptly, "Yes!" Someone had criticized her jeans, she explained. "So I gave them the 'worm speech.' They were awed by what I said." A smile blossomed. "Your sad pathetic little worm speech worked out quite well for me, thank you!"

That the children were so responsive to the 'worm speech' shows that they are looking for guidance, searching for help to become more competent youngsters. Lauren said, "You have to be strong and not let them get to you."

Morgan stunningly affirmed that children need competence to elevate their self confidence. "It's not that we need to learn how to be strong. We are already strong. We just don't think we are."

Many children—and quite a few parents—have expressed this sentiment: "I know I'm right. I just don't know how to say it." Children know they must become competent. Telling them to be strong or to stand up for themselves without providing the tools to do so makes as much sense as using a Stairmaster in an elevator.

I view the 'worm speech' as a metaphor for this book. It is my hope that my dialogues and topics, refined over two decades, will make it easier for parents to talk with their children about serious things, thereby enabling them to become stronger and more competent.

I share a personal story that supports this point. It is not atypical. I bought a typing software program for Erik when he was in the fourth or fifth grade, which he received with the enthusiasm of washing the dishes. We worked on the program one evening. Erik typed slowly as I dictated words from the manual. After a few moments I took some liberties with the manual's text and dictated my own lines, which Erik dutifully typed:

"Erik has a mean Dad that makes him type even though Erik really doesn't want to type anything at all and would rather be . . . ."

I stopped speaking. Erik kept typing. These words appeared on the computer monitor as if by their own will:

". . . and Erik loves him for it."

Wow!

Your efforts to make your child more competent will lead to similar responses.

THE ALLURE OF INCOMPETENCE

It is worth a moment to mention the phenomenon of giving up one's competence; the willingness to present one's self as incompetent, a dullard, a dependent, a hapless victim. This abdication has consequences.

Thanks to my legal profession, we see such intergalactic wisdom on labels such as warning not to iron clothes when wearing them; on large hook-studded fishing lures warning they are harmful if swallowed; warnings not to place ladders on unstable surfaces; a warning to remove the baby from the stroller before folding it and warnings not to place pets in microwave ovens.

Giving up our competence not only leads to higher social costs. It leads to being treated as dismal infants irrespective of our ages. The individual is destroyed. Destroyed individuals destroy the culture. Yet, in our degraded society, incompetence can lead to riches; a courtroom victory—the label didn't warn me.

We relate to the world through our competence. We are defined by our competence or by our lack of it. To be morally competent, we parents and our children must be humble, truthful, persistent and informed.

A parent's most important role is raising morally competent children—children capable of dealing with the real world rather than a world as we wish it to be. If we can teach these competence skills, and there is no reason why we cannot, then our children will transcend competence. They will have a most extraordinary power: control of themselves.

Children will make mistakes, of course, but the competent child will develop the ability to repair its mistakes. They will be honorable children and more likely to grow to be adults of achievement and virtue. But first, they need our help, and we know that competent parents are the greatest forces for creating competent children.

CHAPTER 17

CONSCIENCE

"Having a conscience is like having your parents in your head."

–LAUREN, FIRST GRADE

I BEGIN WITH AN ANECDOTE about an experience I had in court. It's not earth shaking; nothing near the level of an O. J. Dream Team story, but it jarred me to my bones. It influenced my career.

About thirty years ago and only a few years after I received my law degree, I represented a man charged with multiple counts of aggravated robbery, meaning he used a dangerous weapon—a gun in this case—while robbing several fast food restaurants. The several cases were consolidated and tried together in one trial.

Early in the trial the prosecutor asked the second victim, a young woman of about twenty, if the person that robbed her was in the courtroom. Before she could answer, per proper procedure, I objected to her making what we called an in-court identification. I requested a hearing in the judge's chambers to determine if her anticipated identification would be consistent with required procedures.

The judge granted my request for the hearing. The jury was excused from the courtroom. I, the defendant, the prosecutor, the victim and the judge went into the judge's chambers. At the narrow conference table my client sat to my right, directly across from the young lady, close enough to feel each other's breath. My client stared menacingly at her. She avoided his glare.

The prosecutor had the burden to prove that the identification of the defendant met constitutional standards, meaning that it was not the result of coercion or bias. The victim was the prosecutor's only witness. He began his direct examination of her. He inquired how she identified my client's photograph from the array of photographs shown to her at the police station and which he produced and placed on the table. He asked questions to demonstrate her memory and credibility.

The young lady haltingly described how the defendant aimed a handgun at her head, demanded money and threatened to shoot her. The questions were formulaic. "Were you working that day at the XYZ hamburger restaurant?" "Did the robber point a gun at you?" "Did you see the man's face?" "Did he speak to you?" "Did you pick him out of this photo lineup one day later?" "Did anyone suggest which photo you should select?" "Is the person that robbed you across the table from you?"

She whispered her answers but she was confident. My client had robbed her.

She had precisely described to the police my client's hair color, his fireplug compact size, his weight, his slack jaw and sloping forehead and thick neck. My task was to undermine her credibility, no matter how truthful her testimony. My approach, as I began my cross examination of her, was typical of defense lawyers.

"He only talked to you for a few seconds?" "What color was the weapon?" "Was it a revolver or a pistol?'" "You focused on the gun?" "You looked at the gun more than at the man's face?" "You looked at his face for just a few seconds?" "You were frightened?" "You agree that fear can distort your memory?"

I wouldn't have earned a guest appearance on Boston Legal. She was holding up fine.

Then I asked her, "In which hand did the man hold the gun?"

"The right hand," she said softly.

My client's left elbow slammed into my right shoulder like a jackhammer. "She's lying! She's lying!" he hissed into my ear.

My body tensed. I leaned toward him, our faces almost touching. "What are you talking about? You weren't there?"

"It was the left hand! It was the left hand!" He spit his words as a cobra spits venom. I recoiled with disbelief. He saw himself as the victim of her lie! That he had pointed a loaded revolver at this woman's face and threatened to kill her was of no significance. That he or she might have been mistaken about the hand that held the pistol was irrelevant to him. He was victimized!

No doubt you've seen or read about such people, exquisitely sensitive to the slightest injury to themselves or to their rights yet completely oblivious to or unconcerned about the harm they inflict on others.

My eyes turned to the woman. She was undergoing therapy and working two jobs to help her single mother raise her family. I looked at my client. He was a thug. He had no conscience. In suggesting I attack the woman over which hand held the gun, he hoped that I had no conscience either. I vowed I would never again use my skills, no matter how modest, for such a purpose.

THE CONSCIENCE
A Moral Compass

The word conscience is used in many contexts: a 'good' conscience, a 'bad' conscience, a 'clear' conscience, a 'guilty' conscience, having a 'crisis of conscience' and having no conscience. Perhaps you can think of other examples.

Most parents want to cultivate a strong moral conscience in their children. In this chapter I discuss the parents' role in forming their children's conscience and how to build a moral conscience.

Black's Law Dictionary defines the human conscience as a:

> "moral sense; the faculty of judging the moral qualities of actions, or of discriminating between right and wrong; particularly applied to one's perception and judgment of the moral qualities of his own conduct, but in a wider sense, denoting a similar application of the standards of morality to the acts of others."

Black's definition perceives the conscience as a mechanism for identifying and judging what is moral. This perspective harkens back more than two thousand years. Plato and Aristotle viewed the conscience as an internal guidance system residing within a virtuous soul. The soul pursued what was good and struggled to repress what was bad in the on-going effort to develop a moral *ethos*, character, and to attain *eudaimonia*, happiness based on virtuous action and fulfillment.

Since virtue is based on action, and action required thought, the conscience was viewed as an impervious moral vault extending from the soul to the mind, designed to protect ethical values against outside assaults and subversion. A soul that deviated from the moral conscience led the body's actions towards 'chaos,' that is, toward destruction and immoral behavior.

The conscience should tell what is right and what is wrong, as most students said. Jenny, a third grader, described the conscience this way: "It's like that annoying beeping bell that tells you to fasten your car seatbelt." I found intriguing that this fine comment analogized conscience to an alarm system.

But if it only distinguished right from wrong, the conscience would be little more than a nature book distinguishing, for example, edible mushrooms from poisonous ones. That's good, of course, particularly if you are inclined to make mushroom and cheese omelets, but to be ethical, more is required than knowing the difference between right and wrong.

More than distinguishing right from wrong, the conscience commands that right and good *should be done*. Conscience is the force that compels moral action. Ryan creatively analogized conscience to a railroad switch track where "there are tracks you can switch to to make good choices."

When does the conscience begin to work? "As soon as you have to make a choice," Tommy answered, insightfully linking the conscience to action.

Obligation and moral judgment constitute the core of conscience. Morality and intellectual judgment are woven into one fabric. Obeying your conscience, however, is a matter of character and will. Good character builds good conscience and vice versa.

BUILDING A CONSCIENCE
The Coral Reef Metaphor

I used to scuba dive. I'm not supposed to scuba dive now because I take anticoagulants. Evidently, micro capillaries rupture naturally even at minor depths and, given the anticoagulants, would not heal sufficiently quickly, resulting in dangerous internal bleeding.

Too bad. I loved the sport even though I rarely did it. I found solace and relaxation in the rhythm of the water and the ocean's crackling sound. And, to be honest, I relished the tingling sense of possible danger although, admittedly, I was always in safe water.

Even so, stupidity can always arise, as it did when I fed a piece of fish dangling from my mouth to a huge Moray eel partially emerged from its cave. And then there was the time an intergalactic moron in my dive group tied a lasso around the tail of an eight-foot nurse shark napping tranquilly on the ocean floor and then violently pulled the rope. The shark launched at us like a stinger missile and, being closer to its path than I should have been, I feared I would soon take my last breath.

Studying large coral formations and reefs enchanted me. The coral reef is a complex ecosystem, formed from a massive collection of tiny carbonaceous invertebrate polyps, minute animals with calcium carbonate skeletons. Over many years these tiny skeletons accumulate and are cemented together by sponges, coral, algae and other living organisms. Millimeter by millimeter, these deposits create monumental structures of rich and vast biodiversity that provide food, shelter and safety to innumerable creatures.

The coral reef is an elegant metaphor for the incremental development of the conscience. Like the reef, the conscience is built particle by particle, event by event, adding knowledge, wisdom, success, failure and judgment to what was built before.

TALK ABOUT IT . . . TALK ABOUT IT

Dialogues about moral decisions are an effective method for building a child's conscience. You can begin by simply asking, "If you do this today (whatever this is) will you be proud of yourself tomorrow?" The question raises the relationships among choices, behavior, values and consequences, all components for building the conscience.

An example of the subject poked its way into my class due to a mailing error during the 2008 Christmas Holiday season. Someone knocked on the front door of my home. By the time I got to the door the person had left but a package had been placed on the stoop. It was from Caboose Hobbies, the largest model train store in the United States, conveniently (often too conveniently) located on South Broadway in Denver, a few miles north of my home.

I'd been a customer for almost forty years but I hadn't bought anything lately and wasn't expecting any deliveries. I was perplexed. Inside the box was an 'O' scale diesel locomotive with the gorgeous Santa Fe 'War Bonnet' paint scheme. A receipt showed that this expensive model had been paid in full by what seemed to be an out-of-state buyer.

Obviously the model train stork made a mistake. I called Jay, the store's sales manager. He had no explanation for the error. I drove to the store and returned the model.

As a reward for my honesty, Jay offered me a $25.00 gift certificate. I refused. I would not take a gift for doing what was right. Jay persuaded me to keep the certificate and raffle it off in my class at Ebert Polaris. Excellent resolution. That's what I did.

In the next class I asked my fifth graders what they would have done with the model train.

One student said she would return the model because she didn't like trains.

"So," I challenged, "you would have kept the train if you had liked it?"

"Well, I'm not saying that."

"But you are saying that," I retorted playfully.

"Okay, I am saying that," she conceded with a self-conscious giggle.

Only fifteen seconds were needed to clarify the morality of that student's thinking. She hadn't thought through the implications of her words.

Keeping the little choo choo had consequences. To build their consciences, the consequences had to be identified and the morality of the consequences had to be evaluated. We thought of some of the consequences. Your child will figure out a few also.

The real purchaser would demand that Caboose Hobbies send another model or refund the payment. In either instance the store would lose money. People would be embarrassed. An employee might be fired or charged for the error. An injustice would result. The error might be tracked to me, disclosing my dishonesty. I would be disgraced in the eyes of my friends. My bad, or something like that.

Rationalizations for doing wrong always exist. Charles said "I know someone who thought it was okay to steal an ashtray from a restaurant because the food was expensive and it was just a little thing." Studies show this is a common justification for pilfering.

"Hardly a moral argument," I replied.

"I'm just saying...." Charles' argument receded. Then, like a fighter rising from the mat before being counted out, he said energetically, "I love to argue! Both my parents are lawyers," he boasted. "It's in the blood."

"Well, given your argument," I quipped, "I'd say you're a quart low!" Charles laughed.

Amman approached me after the class. He's a bright youngster with a sheepish smile and is generally quiet. "You made it clear for me. The class changed my attitude," he said softly. "Before the class, I might have kept the train but now I know returning it is the right thing to do."

I was elated, of course, but Amman's realization was not the result of my brilliance. The development of his conscience was the result of a ten-minute dialogue that dealt forthrightly and logically with the topic.

By the way, I confide that writing these exchanges is joyful. In my mind's eye I see the children's faces and their furrowed brows as they pound their ideas like pizza dough, trying to get them into shape. A smile unfurls, no matter the hour, because they were wonderful moments.

CRIME AND PUNISHMENT
Guilt is Good!

Conscience doesn't develop in a vacuum. It develops in an environment. Reason and emotion shape environments. Guilt and shame, consequences of moral reasoning, can contribute to building a moral conscience. Self-esteem fetishists assert that guilt is an out-dated and unhealthy emotion. I disagree. Guilt is fundamental to conscience building. Guilt, like shame, links emotion to behavior and links both to moral judgment and accountability. Guilt acknowledges the failure of responsibility and the cost of consequences.

Children have no difficulty recognizing the value of guilt. One child admitted stealing shoes from a store but said she didn't like feeling guilty, as if guilt were an unfair burden. It made her uncomfortable.

Jasmine lashed out, "You're supposed to feel guilty! You are guilty! You did something wrong!" Jasmine trashed the impulse to allow sentiment to trump moral responsibility.

A solution seemed obvious. "If you don't like feeling guilty, don't steal," I suggested.

I chuckle when someone says, referring to people that did something wrong, "They must have a guilty conscience. I don't know how they can sleep at night!" To each his own, I guess, but I've represented a lot of people who had done lots of bad things and they all looked well rested when they arrived at court in the morning.

Punishment can be an effective force for creating a moral conscience. It can also be a force that subverts conscience building. We know that a conscience requires the internalization of moral values. The desire to avoid shame and guilt can influence moral behavior only if a person has an internal moral compass. Any process or philosophy that undermines this internalization will corrupt conscience building.

When avoiding punishment is the motivation to do 'good,' it is likely to be dropped like a hot potato when punishment is unlikely, remote or trivial.

The kinds of 'bad' things my students admit they have done to deserve punishment are, in the greater scheme of things, minimal. None has robbed, slit throats, been a drug kingpin, engineered ponzi schemes, falsely testified before congressional committees, sold worthless stock or committed vehicular homicide. Nevertheless, even at that minor level, punishment may have a negative effect on developing their conscience.

Students have made comments such as: "Yeah, I got grounded for a week and then it's over." "I couldn't go to a party so I stayed in my room and watched DVDs." Children become adept score keepers, calculating the punishment versus the offense and deciding whether the offense is worth doing again. Right versus wrong are ignored.

I am not saying punishment should not be imposed. I am saying to build a child's conscience, deeper levels of understanding must also occur. Rudeness, for example, is, in part, the result of a breakdown of conscience. Recall the discussion about rudeness in the Autonomy chapter. The notion that a person should feel entitled to hurt another because his feelings are hurt or because he is unhappy or angry or undisciplined indicates a lack of conscience.

Another topic of reasoning that influences conscience building is embedded deeply in our so-called criminal justice system. I address it because it has parallels to teaching conscience-building in children. I'm referring to the belief or ideology that a criminal has 'paid his debt to society' upon completing his punishment. I am convinced this belief undermines the development of the actor's conscience.

The general meaning of paying your debt is that your agreed-upon obligation has been fulfilled; you are finished with the debt and the debtor and the creditor are equal. Your car is paid for; the plumber is fully paid, your college loan is paid and so on. Now you start anew, as if receiving a shiny new credit card.

The notion that a criminal becomes paid up or equalizes a bargain with its victim or with society after serving time in a tax-payer funded environment or under its control impresses me as morally perverse. The belief encourages an unrepentant mindset that diminishes introspection and personal accountability for the consequences of the criminal behavior. More troublesome, it allows the perpetrator to cloak itself with the cloth of victim status if the allegedly paid-up perpetrator is not treated 'fairly' in someone's opinion.

If one is paid up, there is no need to consider the past, which now may be forgotten like last year's bout with the flu. Indeed, even bringing up the past crime may be viewed as an unjustified annoyance. It's time to move on, even though one may have learned and done nothing to morally justify the onward travel.

Perhaps the most significant flaw—moral and intellectual—with the 'paid my debt to society' philosophy is the belief that society is the victim, that society has been injured by the crime. By and large, this is nonsense and to the extent it is true, it is mostly trivial. This 'society has been injured' premise subverts conscience building.

It's a bait and switch moral scam, substituting a meaningless abstraction—society—for flesh and blood hurting victims. Society is not hurt. Individuals are hurt. Moms and dads and children are hurt. They bleed, they cry, they suffer, they bury their dead. Not society. Society keeps chugging along. Obviously a lot of bad actions collectively can hurt society. They can ruin it and turn it into something hellish, but that is the consequence of hurting people.

Any rational parent knows this is true. If your child was shot during a robbery or mangled in a car crash caused by a drunk driver, it is unlikely that you would wail, "What an injury society has suffered!"

The "paid my debt" belief is platitudinous nonsense. No matter how many payments the criminal makes, the dead child does not arise from the grave, the mom crippled in the car crash never walks again, the scarred mind and body from an assault are never healed and the life's savings lost by financial fraud are never recovered.

Although the debt is never paid, the philosophy bestows upon the aggressor society's legitimacy to claim that it is so. The offense becomes impersonal, abstract, unemotional and detached. The aggressor can ignore—indeed, reject—any impulse or imploring for empathy because the aggressor and society have become equal. When all is equal, no motivation exists to revisit past actions.

I suggest an alternative philosophy: the aggressor's debt is to the victim and it can never be paid in most situations. Such a belief is far more likely to develop a conscience in the perpetrator. The removal of the phony equality would nurture a sense of responsibility for hurting another person that could not be erased.

A possible benefit of my suggested philosophy would be that the violator might develop a moral obligation to do good in the future as a rehabilitative effort to offset the unfulfilled debt to the previous victim. It may be a long shot but my philosophy is more likely to cause this sense of duty and a conscience than would the belief that a debt has been fully paid. Empathy and self-betterment are more likely to be advanced.

PARENTS R CONSCIENCE

"An emotion, as such, tells you nothing about reality beyond the fact that something makes you feel something."

–AYN RAND, PHILOSOPHICAL DETECTION

I read about this event a few years ago. A small child, five or six years old, attacked a smaller child at a playground. The aggressor's mother ran to her child and said, "Honey, what's troubling you?"

The mother didn't reprimand her little moppet for beating the child. She didn't say her child's behavior was wrong. She did not impose a punishment. The mother only valued self-centered feelings. Her message to her child was that feelings justify anything, even an attack on a helpless child. She subverted conscience building.

A parent desiring to raise a child with a conscience would have reacted differently. "You did something terribly wrong. Apologize to the child and don't ever do that again! If you do, you will be punished." A moral conscience acknowledges good and demands that 'good' or virtue should constrain human action.

Ponder the following words of these three students and the reader will gain insights into how they may develop their child's conscience.

"I feel the worst when my parents tell me I've disappointed them when I do something wrong," Ashley said.

Candace said, "It hurts the most when my mom says she doesn't trust me anymore,"

"I don't like being grounded and not going to a party," Arda said, "but it's worse when my dad tells me that I hurt him, like when I took money from his wallet."

Parents *are* conscience. Children internalize their values from their parents. Recall the comment: "You learn from parents what is right."

That's what Lauren meant when she said "Having a conscience is like having your parents in your head."

The singular importance of parents in building the consciences of their children cannot be overemphasized. In every class students vigorously say that parents are the source for learning 'good.' Parents are respected above all other groups of people. They are, thus, in a unique position to shape their child's conscience.

Creating excuses for and covering for bad behavior does not build a conscience. Recall the mom that excused her son's cheating and the mom with the child at the playground. The first subverted the development of a conscience not only her child but also of the other students; the second impaired her own child's conscience. If there is no accountability, why go through the anguishing process of choosing right over wrong? In such situations, a conscience just gets in the way.

In her book *The Magic Years*, Selma H. Fraiberg describes 'the education of conscience' as crafting a system of built-in controls that go beyond shame and what parents will reward or punish. Conscience requires an internal value system. Ashley, Candace and Arda had it; the mother in the playground didn't.

Parents can nurture a child's conscience by recoiling at racist comments, by making the child return the stolen gum, by making the child apologize for a hurtful word or action and by demonstrating that they value virtue.

The qualities that matter most to your children—trust, approval, love, avoiding harming those they love—are the same that form the foundation for building a conscience. These concepts should be infused into your discussions about right and wrong.

Let's say your child took money from your wallet or purse. You might say something like: "Taking money from my purse was wrong, but your dishonesty was worse. Your dishonesty and disrespect for my property show you didn't care how your actions affected me. Would you want your child to behave as you did?"

These words appeal to your child's honor and decency. They are uplifting and they are about virtue. They, and a caress on the face, will have a greater impact on developing a conscience than a swat on the behind, not going out a few weekends or banishing the child to the woods to forage for berries and chew on tree bark. Such words develop a conscience because they develop empathy and show that you value morality and your child. Also, they offer a path for your child to regain your trust.

Don't be afraid to talk about these topics—hurt feelings, dismay, displeasure, loss of trust and so forth. You may fear your child will greet your words like a third rate Las Vegas lounge act. Not to worry. My students confide that when they talk about serious things, content trumps style.

The book *Crucial Conversations* shows how skills for high stakes conversations can be learned. One skill is getting "all relevant information out into the open." Putting everything on the table, as the cliché goes, allows meaning to flow freely through a dialogue because truth and honesty are not withheld.

Parents should be comforted that dialogues are never finished. Dialogues are organic. They are connected. They are constantly being refined. You can always say something like, "Remember what I said a few weeks ago? Well, I want to clarify one point...." or "Remember that talk about punishment? Well, I changed my mind." Changing one's mind is not an admission of weakness or obtuseness or being dumber than a pile of rocks. It's the confident expression of having the wisdom to re-evaluate your thoughts and having the courage to admit it.

Do not force arguments or analogies. A conversation is more like casting a fly into the current's seam. Give it some line and see where it floats. With your encouragement, your child will be thoughtful and candid, creating an experience as rich as gold tapestry.

IT'S NOT CRICKET!

Every time I begin a conversation about conscience, children exuberantly yell, "Always let your conscience be your guide," quoting Jiminy Cricket, the little insect in the family Gryllidae featured in the movie 'Pinocchio.'

I always ask, "Is that good advice?"

Ask your child if a person should always let its conscience be its guide?

Jenna, a second grader, immediately grasped the moral issue. "It's okay if your conscience is good. Otherwise, you shouldn't follow it."

This subject is a variation of the issue of following one's heart. In short, it depends on your heart. How about acting with a clear or good conscience? Many people tend to think that a clear conscience is a reliable guideline for moral behavior. Fugeddaboutit! It's not.

We all know of evil so vile done with a clear conscience it eludes being captured in words. Blaise Pascal, the French philosopher, observed "Evil is never done so thoroughly or so well as when it is done with a good conscience." Voltaire expressed a similar idea this way: "If we believe absurdities, we will commit atrocities."

A clear conscience is not a useful or reliable measure of moral behavior. The unsentimental reality is that a clear conscience is morally meaningless.

When the little cricket chirps merrily about being guided by one's conscience, your child should be sufficiently schooled to respond, "Well, maybe."

Paige, a fifth grader, understood the significance of measurements for gauging moral behavior, when she said, poetically, "A conscience is like a thermometer. It helps you see right and wrong …and then you know how good or bad you are."

A conscience should be a measuring guide such as a thermometer when it is based on morality and virtue. We determine the morality and virtue of the conscience the same way we determine the morality of an opinion or of an action or of a judgment: we view a conscience through the lens of the Moral Measures.

Will the conscience advance the four Ethical Principles and the The Seven C's? In a moral conscience, these principles and virtues blend together like the bands of a rainbow.

Thomas Jefferson devised a test for the morality of the conscience when he instructed his nephew, Peter Carr, "How would you act if all the world was watching."

Lilly, a fifth grader, offered an equally elegant test: "You have to understand that whatever you do, you are affecting other people and that what they do can affect you."

Children should be encouraged to reach out beyond the self and not be like self-sealing inner tubes that are impervious to punctures from reason, logic or evidence. The Moral Measures offer standards for guiding the conscience. Without them, the risk is that the conscience will be guided by whim, caprice, bias, emotion and selfishness. Such a conscience can then justify anything, bringing to reality the full horror of Pascal's and Voltaire's observations. Conscience either gives license to immorality or it restricts and prohibits it.

FATAL ABSTRACTION

"Labor to keep alive in your breast
that little celestial fire called conscience."

–GEORGE WASHINGTON, *110 RULES OF CIVILITY & DECENT BEHAVIOR* #110

I won't sugarcoat the issue. The undeodorized truth is that a moral conscience does not make life easier. That's the paradox. It can make life more difficult. A conscience demands you live up to ethical standards. A conscience demands that you take a stand against immorality.

If you view yourself as moral, then you have to act that way. If your conscience obligates you to act and you don't, you may fail to live up to your own standards. That's unpleasant. One is motivated to avoid that, and the easiest way to avoid failing to live up to your standards is to have no standards. It is much easier to have a weak or flexible conscience.

Such folks may become Roosevelt's 'cold and timid souls' that stand for nothing virtuous. Their lives may be relatively empty, but they will be easier in some respects. Think of the students in the school cheating example. The children with a conscience had the tough challenge, not the cheaters.

> *"A mind incapable of revolt and indignation*
> *is a mind without value."*
>
> –ANDRE GIDE

Raising a child with a moral conscience is a daunting responsibility. It does not develop quickly and, significantly, it is not self-sustaining. One must work—labor—to nurture it and keep it alive. Living with a strong conscience makes life richer and more honorable but it does not make life easier.

A parent does its child no favors by convincing it otherwise. That's why I wrote it is better that a parent help its child become stronger than try to make its life easier. Yet, if the world were full of strong moral people of conscience, life would be easier. Certainly it would be more peaceful.

To His Conscience

–ROBERT HERRICK

Can I not sin, but thou wilt be
My private protonotary?
Can I not woo thee to pass by
A short and sweet iniquity?
I'll cast a mist and cloud upon
My delicate transgression,
So utter dark as that no eye
Shall see the hugged impiety.
Gifts blind the wise, and bribes do please,
And wind all other witnesses;
And wilt not thou with gold be tied
To lay thy pen and ink aside,
That in the murk and tongueless night
Wanton I may, and thou not write?
It will not be; and therefore now,
For times to come I'll make this vow,
From aberrations to live free,
So I'll not fear the judge, or thee.

CHAPTER 18

CONSEQUENCES

"What is done cannot be undone.
But one can prevent it happening again."

–ANNE FRANK, AGE 14, BELSEN CONCENTRATION CAMP,
THE DAY OF HER DEATH, SUNDAY, MAY 7, 1944

BACK TO THE FUTURE

DOCTOR FULKERSON WAS MY DENTIST many years ago. His office was in the Republic building on 16th Street, downtown Denver. The floors were marble; the elevators boasted brass fixtures burnished to a shimmering gold patina and ornate molding bordered the ceilings. The landmark building evoked a sense of timeless elegance rarely found in modern structures. In one of his procedure rooms was a plaque with this inscription. It always caused a chuckle.

You don't have to floss all your teeth.
Just the ones you want to keep.

Since I was indecisive about which teeth I wanted to keep, I flossed all of them—when I flossed, which was not frequently. The inscription conveyed two messages. One was fact-specific: floss or you will lose your teeth. The other was general: action—and inaction—have consequences.

The concept of consequences is one of the most vital a child—indeed, any person—should master. Consequences are the result or effect or outcome of something occurring earlier. As Jonathan, a first grader, described it, "One darn thing leads to another." One thing causes another thing to happen. Life is not a process of unconnected present moments, like a single leaf floating on a stream and then disappearing. Nothing occurs in isolation. Consequences demand we ask the question, "What's next?"

Consequences illustrate causation. If you study, you will likely do well on your test. If you don't clean your room, you can't go to the party. If you drive recklessly, you are more likely to crash. If you read diverse materials, you will likely become a better thinker. If you don't stand up to bullies, you're likely to get more bullies.

Consequences are future oriented yet they are influenced by past events and behavior. Thus, they can be predicted based on past events and behavior. Marshall McLuhan accurately captures this forward-backward dynamic: "We drive into the future using our rearview mirror." By examining consequences we place the lens on the past to bring the present into focus in order to foresee the probable future.

> "Mr. President, it is natural to man to indulge in the illusions of hope. We are apt to shut our eyes against a painful truth, and listen to the song of that siren till she transforms us into beasts. Is this the part of wise men, engaged in a great and arduous struggle for liberty? Are we disposed to be of the number of those who, having eyes, see not, and, having ears, hear not, the things which so nearly concern their temporal salvation: For my part, whatever anguish of spirit it may cost, I am willing to know the whole truth; to know the worst, and to provide for it. . . . I have but one lamp by which my feet are guided, and that is the lamp of experience. I know of no way of judging the future but by the past."
>
> –PATRICK HENRY, MARCH 23, 1775, GIVE ME LIBERTY OR GIVE ME DEATH

Although we may wish, hope, intend or deny otherwise, consequences are inescapably aligned with unrelenting reality. Consequences result from predictable laws and forces and human nature. Therefore, reasoning skills and imagination enable us to anticipate consequences. Moral judgment enables us to make comparative moral assessments of what will probably occur. Moral character will compel action that is most likely to lead to moral consequences. A person may then act, if motivated, based on the analysis of those consequences.

IT'S NO SECRET, VICTORIA!

*"It's tough to make predictions,
especially about the future."*

–YOGI BERRA

At the end of my first year teaching fifth grade at the Ebert Polaris School the students invited me to give the continuation address. I was honored. It meant those little folks valued what I said. Geoffrey introduced me. He told the audience that I taught how to know right from wrong, about Socrates and about Victoria's Secret lingerie. Eyebrows rose.

I began my remarks, "I must explain that comment." Here's the explanation.

In the latter part of September 2000, Melissa Todd and James Gipson committed several kidnappings and sexual assaults in the Denver area. According to media reporting, Todd lured women from Denver's 16th Street Mall and other locations under the pretense of offering free lingerie—Victoria's Secret products were mentioned—and the opportunity to attend a lingerie party. Each woman accepting Todd's offer was taken to an isolated location and sexually assaulted by Gipson.

This adult version of the old 'don't take candy from strangers' theme blends actions, consequences and personal responsibility into an understandable narrative. Of all my conversations, few generated such angry and searing opinions. I divide this discussion into two parts.

- Evaluating the wisdom of the choices the women made and

- Analyzing a social worker's opinion that the victimized women were not responsible for what happened to them.

Using current events as teaching material, we see, once again, that the world is a textbook. If the brutal facts are softened, the topic is appropriate for children as young as kindergarten.

I begin my class by asking if the women were reasonable when they went along with Todd. Answers require a careful analysis of the facts and drawing logical inferences from them. The students thought the women were unreasonable.

"These ladies were stupid to believe her," Carolina asserted with the crispness of a starched shirt. "It just doesn't make sense to go off with someone who stopped you on the street to give you free clothing." "If you're the only one being asked to go, something is wrong." The fact that Todd wanted the ladies to go with her immediately raised the children's suspicions. "That should make them realize the deal was phony," Isabella said dryly.

If it were a real party with real gifts for a legitimate purpose, students suggested that Todd would have invited them to an event to be held in the near future, which would give more women the opportunity to participate. "If it seems too good to be true it probably is," Lawrence said, resorting to a cliché that has proved its worth. "They made foolish choices." "The women who said 'no' were smarter."

My students were critical of the women's motives that accepted Todd's offer. "They were greedy." "They were flattered so they went along." "They just wanted free stuff." "They thought they were pretty enough to be models but that's a dumb way to find out." "What really disgusts me," fifth grader Emily said in a contemptuous tone, "is that the women didn't need these things." They took a significant risk for something trivial.

It's probably impossible to know how many women turned down Todd's offer and why. Regarding those that accepted, logic and reason were not used to dispassionately weigh the risks of negative consequences.

Ask your child if he or she would have gone along with a person under similar circumstances if something were offered that the child liked. No doubt your child will answer with an emphatic 'no!' He knows the correct answer. Even so, a detailed discussion about facts and their inferences will sharpen analytical skills and strengthen character, enhancing a child's ability to say 'no.' Similar to cooking a roast, there's no need to rush.

YOU BETTER THINK!

Think About What They're Trying To Do To Me!

The second part of the discussion raises issues of greater complexity: the origins and consequences of personal responsibility.

After the arrests of Todd and Gipson, a social worker said of the victims: "It wasn't their fault. The man was very purposeful. He was shrewd."

When I shared this statement in class, the students reacted with disbelief. They yelled their disagreement: "Of course it was their fault. They made the decision!" Words flew like sparks from a blade against a sharpening stone. "They could have walked away." "No one made them go."

Saying someone is not at fault means the person is not responsible for the outcome. A driver involved in a car crash that is not at fault means that the driver did nothing to cause the crash. A mechanic that fails to tighten lug nuts on a replaced tire which then falls off causing the car to crash is at fault for causing the crash. A tort lawyer would phrase it this way: the mechanic's negligence—or willful omission— in failing to tighten the lug nuts was the or a proximate cause of the car crash.

Tort law identifies another principle of fault called 'foreseeability.' If an action—or an omission or failure to act—can be reasonably expected or foreseen to result in a certain consequence, then that action or omission is considered the cause of the consequence. It doesn't have to be the *only* cause. It can be *a* cause of the consequence. The person that did—or failed to do—the act is then at fault, meaning legally responsible or liable for the consequences.

A person setting off firecrackers while pumping gas into a car is at fault for injuries resulting from a gas tank explosion because it is foreseeable that flaming fireworks could ignite a gas tank and cause an explosion. The foreseeable consequence of pampering spoiled rude children is more rude and bratty behavior. Thus, the pampering person is at fault for the behavior, although the pampering might not be the only cause of the behavior. The point is that if the consequence is reasonably foreseeable, then the person causing it is at fault or is considered responsible for it.

Predicting consequences requires understanding these two concepts:

- Foreseeability'

- Causation

Think about the school principal and the cheating student. The foreseeable results of the principal's caving into the cheater's mom were that good teachers would no longer enforce moral codes and that more kids would cheat.

The principal can yap all day… I didn't mean it, I didn't intend it, I didn't expect it, how dare you accuse me of such a thing…. blah blah blah, deny, deny, deny, but he was responsible for those consequences. They were his fault.

"The fault, dear Brutus, lies not in the stars but in ourselves."

–JULIUS CAESAR, WILLIAM SHAKESPEARE

The social worker's opinion merits analysis because it deals with arguably the most important component for the development of moral character: the relationship between personal responsibility and ethical consequences.

Word by word and carefully considering the facts, let's examine the social worker's comment, "It wasn't their fault" and see if any useful lessons about consequences can be learned. Castigating the social worker's comment is like picking low hanging fruit. That's easy. That is not my goal. I want to teach thinking skills that will lead to more moral future decisions.

The journey to identify the consequences of the social worker's opinion begins with the reasoning skill, 'What's your opinion?/What are your facts?

We know the social worker's opinion: "It wasn't their fault." Do any facts support her opinion?

We know:

- The women were approached in a public area by a stranger, Melissa Todd

- Todd offered them free stuff as an incentive to go to a party
- The party was at an undisclosed location
- Todd did not threaten or intimidate the women
- The women were asked to go with Todd immediately

The women's behavior was voluntary. "They did what they wanted to do." "Some ladies didn't want to go so they didn't." "They made their own choices." The women accepting Todd's offer acted freely and voluntarily. They were responsible—at fault—for going along with Todd. No evidence suggests otherwise. But wait! The social worker offered two 'facts' to support her not-at-fault opinion:

- He was purposeful and
- He was shrewd

Really?

Perhaps the reader remembers the old TV commercial for some fast food joint where actress Clara Pell yelled, "Where's the beef?" to express her displeasure with the small wimpy hamburgers sold to her. I asked the students, and you might ask your child, where's the evidence that anyone (Gipson or Todd) was purposeful and/or shrewd?

Let's start with 'purposeful.' Where's the beef? Putting butter on toast is purposeful. Flossing teeth is purposeful. Let's say Todd was purposeful—she put on her shoes; she approached the women. So what? This kind of purposefulness is thoroughly meaningless. There is no evidence that this purposefulness trumped the women's voluntary exercise of free will.

This purposefulness does not negate the women's personal responsibility. If a drunk driver purposefully asks you to get into his car and you do, it would be illogical—indeed, absurd—to say that the driver's purposefulness eliminated your free will and that getting into the car was not your fault.

The women's freely willed *response* to the purposeful (if any) actions led to the terrible consequences. Todd didn't have the power to hurt the women. Only the women had the power to put themselves in danger. They could have just as well walked away, got a triple soy latte and read about the Denver Broncos.

As for being shrewd, little Julie offered an intriguing insight. Todd must have been a good judge of character to pick out the weak women. It's possible Todd had that quality, but no evidence supports it. We don't know how many people rejected Todd's overtures.

We may concede that the Gipson/Todd team understood human nature to the degree that they correctly intuited that some women, compelled by vanity and the desire to get something for nothing, would be foolish and irresponsible. But is that shrewd? Not very.

The dialogue skill is to continuously ask your child about the significance of each fact—why each fact matters. So, for example, if there was any shrewdness, so what? What did it cause? Consider Gipson. By the time the women were brought to him, he had no need to be shrewd. There is no evidence that shrewdness—which I do not believe existed—negated fault. Shrewdness did not cause the women to go along with Todd. Their misfortune was their fault.

Remember Aristotle's teaching that the character and credibility of an argument is based not only on the facts that are used but also on the facts that are excluded. It is important to note that the social worker ignored the inconvenient truth that the purposefulness and shrewdness, such as it existed, were selectively influential. The women that rejected Todd's offer did not succumb to those qualities. The social worker offers no explanation why some women overcame the purposeful/shrewd duet and rejected Todd's offer.

Note that the social worker gives no credit to any quality—intellect, judgment, will, suspicion, character, cynicism—that motivated some women to reject Todd's siren song. Her argument for freedom from fault is more akin to protective stupidity.

Why bother with all this? Because it is critical that children realize the social worker's belief creates a false moral equivalence between the prudent women that walked away and the irresponsible women that accepted Todd's offer. By denying fault, there is no moral or intellectual distinction between those that accepted and those that rejected Todd's offer. Morality and judgment are irrelevant. The conclusion, then, is that it was just bad luck for the victims.

At this point the reader might think, Listen up, you narcissistic lawyer! Before you go manipulating the minds of helpless little children, hold on for a moment! The social worker was saying it wasn't their fault for being *assaulted!*'

Maybe, but if that was what she social worker meant, she didn't say it. She didn't say that the women should not have gone with Todd. If she meant that they were not at fault for the assault, why did she throw into her opinion stew the 'purposeful' and 'shrewd' ingredients? Those qualities had nothing to do with being at fault for a criminal assault that occurred after the women were captive.

What is perplexing, and potentially dangerous, is that for whatever reason or need, the social worker was so committed to absolving these women of all responsibility that she abandoned reason and logic and fabricated shrewdness and purposefulness as fantasy excuses to let them off the hook.

But here's where critical thinking must be employed. We may correctly place the blame for the assault on Gipson but that doesn't resolve all aspects of fault. That would be like looking through a porthole and thinking you're seeing the whole ocean. That's not the big picture.

By the way, the no-fault-for-the-assault argument is routinely made in each class. The children get it. For example, in one class, a week after we talked about the topic, Elena said she discussed the social worker's comment with her parents. They also thought the women were at fault for getting into the dangerous situation but were not at fault for the assaults.

Elena's comment delighted me for two reasons. First, the moral and intellectual integrity of her parent's comment added clarity to the discussion and elevated our thinking. Second, my remarks had inspired a quality conversation among a student and her parents. No better way exists to influence the moral development of a child.

"Behavior is molded by consequences."

–B. F. SKINNER

I hope the reader does not criticize me for being overly tedious in this presentation. The social worker had free speech, but speech is never free from consequences. I spend a lot of time on the social worker's statement to show how her belief may lead to unethical consequences.

Just as you can get hurt jumping on a trampoline, you can get hurt jumping to conclusions. The social worker's opinion reduces or eliminates incentives to learn from experience. If the foolish person is viewed as no different from the intelligent person, if the person lacking judgment is treated as equal to the person that exercises sound judgment, then no reality test can be imposed on measuring the wisdom of actions.

Nicole, a fifth grader who tends to speak with measured words and clenched fists, linked personal responsibility and behavior incentives. "If she didn't think it was her fault, then there is no lesson to learn. You won't learn from your mistakes." That's an insightful fifth grader! With gentle questioning, your children will reach similarly astute conclusions. Without accountability, there is no incentive to analyze, to ponder or to think introspectively about actions, choices and consequences.

Learning from mistakes first requires acknowledging that mistakes were made. By denying the causality between acts and consequences, the social worker undercuts any incentive to do the hard work of distinguishing between right and wrong, smart or dumb, innocent or guilty.

According to the social worker, all any victim has to do is accuse an aggressor of being shrewd or purposeful (even if it's not true) and then, boom, like the rabbit returned to the magician's hat, all personal responsibility disappears. This is the philosophy of irresponsibility. This is the language of an infant, not an adult of free spirit and mind. The gap between the social worker and the morally responsible person is unbridgeable.

By the way, the shrewd and purposeful folks are precisely those that I want my children to recognize and defend against. I'm not too worried about the armed robber who asks my child to hold his gun while he adjusts his mask. I want my children to understand that the clever, insidious, smooth talking hustler can be as great a threat as the obviously violent thug. Most readers want the same for their children.

Without accountability determined by fault, the actor is absolved of all responsibility for anything that happens. Thus, they may indulge in the dangerous comfort of thinking of themselves as victims rather than seeing themselves honestly as accomplices in their fate.

Taking responsibility builds character. Subverting responsibility destroys character. One of the greatest character building exercises is the refusal to accept excuses.

Perhaps you've seen those nihilistic automobile bumper stickers that pronounce: S _ _ _ Happens! Well, yes, it's true, it happens. But that's not a particularly useful observation. It inspires passivity, fatalism and, ultimately indifference that turns into rancid complicity.

Even so, the statement is incomplete. The s _ _ _ happens for a reason. I want my children and students to understand the reason. Then, perhaps, we can prevent it from happening again, which was the lofty ideal expressed by little Anne Frank the day she was murdered in Belsen.

GUNS AND BUTTER

"Perhaps the scariest aspect of our times is how many people think in talking points rather than in terms of real world consequences."

–THOMAS SOWELL, ECONOMIST

I search and ponder and anguish about how to teach meaningful lessons with clarity and force. One successful method is to take two different events, switch the facts and then discuss whether it is likely that the outcome would have been the same as in the original event. Many of us engage in this kind of fact shifting, particularly in political analysis to see if bias or prejudice or hypocrisy is present.

A politician from one party says something and we ponder whether the public reaction would have been the same if a politician from another party had made the same comment. Or a statement is made about one religion and we ponder whether the public reaction would have been the same if the statement were made about a different religion.

Substituting facts is a powerful technique for clarifying values, policies and expected consequences. I applied this technique to two events at two different schools. I asked the students to speculate if the facts were substituted, would the outcomes likely have been the same as those that actually occurred.

The first event for comparison occurred about fifteen years ago. A little girl, a seventh grader, as I recall, attended a public school in northern Colorado. On the fateful day, she opened her lunchbox and realized she had mistakenly brought her mother's lunchbox to school. Inside, tossed among the sandwich and drink and cookie or whatever, was a butter knife. An honors student, and by all accounts a terrific upstanding young lady, she promptly gave the knife to her teacher. She knew students were prohibited from bringing knives to school.

She explained and apologized for the mistake.

In response to the child's noble demonstration of character, the teacher took the girl to the principal and presented her as a violator. The child was suspended immediately.

The school had implemented what is known as a 'zero tolerance' policy. Pervasive in school districts, it prohibits—will not tolerate—students bringing weapons to school. Punishment is inflicted without discretion or exception. That's the 'zero' part of the tolerance and, according to educators, therein lies the policy's virtue—consistency.

The child's logical and exculpatory explanation meant nothing. They were outside the policy's box mentality. Intelligence, honesty, morality and justice were vandalized by bureaucratic demagogues. I concede that policies have a proper place in the governance of society, including schools, but they can rarely, if ever, be a substitute for adjudication of specific events in a moral context.

Should any readers be unfamiliar with these 'zero tolerance' policies in schools, a Google search will yield in 0.22 seconds about a gazillion disgraceful examples of the lemming-like implementation of this pernicious policy by educators entrusted to shape the minds of our children.

The irony of these zero tolerance policies is almost too exquisite for words. By trading on an imagined virtue of consistent enforcement of inflexible rules, these so-called educators show zero judgment, zero brains, zero morality and, relevant to this chapter, zero concern for consequences.

I compared this sorry tale to the uplifting extraordinary story of Lorenzo Hernandez described in the Competence chapter. Re-read the challenges Lorenzo faced. Recall, particularly, the students' brilliant insight that Lorenzo's decisions to admit finding the pistol and to give it to the principal must have been motivated by his trust in the principal's integrity and morality.

To expand the breadth of their reasoning skills and, in this instance, to demonstrate how virtuous reasoning can predict consequences, I presented the students with this hypothetical fact pattern: What would have been the likely consequence if Lorenzo had attended the same school as the butter knife girl *and* if he found the pistol in the playground *after* the girl was suspended for violating the zero tolerance policy?

The students' answers were confident and immediate. Likely, your children's answers would be also.

"Lorenzo never would have turned in the gun."

"The principal would throw him out of school, so he would just keep the pistol."

"It wouldn't even matter if the principal believed he found it. He still had it, so he'd get suspended anyway."

"He'd be stupid to turn in the pistol."

Good so far, but the most morally significant question is what would be the likely consequences of not turning in the gun? These previous comments considered the likely *immediate* consequences. Sam was the first to grasp the likely consequence—a consequence of a consequence—that would follow. "Kids would probably die." Sam grasped brutal reality.

Let's think this through. Lorenzo would likely have given the gun to someone else because he wouldn't want to be punished. Predictably, one or more children would play with the loaded gun. Likely none of them knew how to determine if the gun was loaded and, if it were, how to unload it. A likely consequence would be—of course, we can't be certain—that one or more children would have been injured or killed.

It is a human characteristic, sometimes regrettable, to seek comfort and virtue by merging one's self into an abstraction, no matter how foolish. In this instance, it was 'zero tolerance.' But, occasionally one has to look at the results of these purported brilliant abstract theories. If Lorenzo had been subjected to the beliefs of the butter knife principal, his motivation to act morally would have been subverted.

As a likely consequence, moms and dads might be attending funerals or perhaps visiting their child at the Craig Rehabilitation Hospital up the block from my home. They'd be crying, "How could this happen? Why would a child give the gun to other children? How could a child be so irresponsible?"

Now you know. Unethical consequences encourage irresponsible behavior. This scenario explains not only *how* such tragedy could happen but *why* it would be *likely* to happen. There are few mysteries here. Ideas have consequences. Stupid ideas yield ugly consequences.

The hypothetical consequences that might have arisen if Lorenzo had been in the butter knife school follow a broad economic principle: that which is rewarded will be repeated and that which is penalized or taxed will be reduced. The honor student's moral behavior of turning in the knife was penalized. Thus, future moral behavior in the school will be reduced.

If we want to motivate moral behavior, we would do well to be guided by Thomas Sowell's profound advice: "Always take an economic perspective, looking not at proclaimed goals as much as incentives that are created."

In the Competence chapter I pointed out that consequences were one of three factors that motivate behavior. The others were competence and values. When we drill a little deeper we see that:

- Incentives influence behavior and, therefore,
- Incentives influence consequences

Stated simply, consequences change behavior, and incentives change consequences.

To deepen their understanding of consequences, I also introduce to my classes the principle of moral hazards, another factor that influences consequences. The moral hazards concept is a subset of the broader economic principle I mentioned above. It is based on the economic theory that rewarding bad behavior will lead to more bad behavior.

"Sins repeated seem permitted."

–THE TALMUD

We see the application of the moral hazard principle every day. The principal rewarding the cheater and the social worker refusing to hold the Victoria Secret victims accountable for their behavior are two examples, but examples are universal. Promoting people that threaten lawsuits leads to more threatening lawsuits; dumbing down tests leads to dumbed-down students; appeasing aggressors leads to more aggression and paying ransoms to pirates leads to more piracy.

I see the moral hazard principle applied in my field of trust administration, almost always with unhappy consequences. A mom or dad wants to 'protect' or 'take care of' the alcoholic or drug addled child or provide for the child that just can't seem to hold a job or live within her means. Money flows to or on behalf of those that are imprudent. The responsible child receive less or nothing.

As a consequence, imprudent and irresponsible behavior tends to flourish—just can't seem to find the right job or just need a little more therapy and money to beat the alcohol or drug addiction or need only a little more money to avoid getting my car repossessed—and responsible behavior is ignored, goes unrewarded and, relatively, is punished.

*"The greatest incentive for future immoral action is moral weakness
by those who failed to stand up to past immorality."*

—Melanie Phillips, British Author

Many people make a big deal about people's good intentions as
if good intentions are ends in themselves. They are not. Let me be
clear: good intentions tell us *nothing* about real consequences. Good
intentions do *not* determine good consequences. Many policies born
of good (presumably) intentions to reduce crime or illiteracy or
inequality or poverty or sexual harassment or terrorism or cheating
or whatever have had disastrous consequences. Noble ideas do *not*
make people noble. Only people that create noble consequences are
noble.

Good intentions divorced from predictable consequences are
self-indulgent and can be destructive, although they might not be
destructive to the person implementing the intentions. The mis-
guided social worker counseling crime victims may ruin the lives of
her clients but likely will keep her job and prosper.

Many people have spouted grand words and paid no price for
the catastrophic consequences of their words. We parents are not so
fortunate. We—and our children—will pay a price when the consequences of our words and actions are bad, no matter our intent.
Rather than words and intentions, act based upon real world consequences.

SURPRISE!

Since we hear about it so often, particularly in the world of politics,
another concept worth addressing is the category of Unintended
Consequences. In simplest terms, an unintended consequence
is...drum roll...a consequence that was not intended. It is a consequence that was undesired, unwanted, wished it didn't happen,
can't explain it, who'd a thunk it and so forth.

You have the noble goal to raise education standards so the government legislates holding back students that don't pass the stan-
dardized tests. Bammo, teachers give the tests to students in

advance so they won't fail and they falsely grade the exams by inflating the grades and parents sue the school districts to prevent enforcement of the law. The laudable goal had detrimental unintended consequences.

The category of unintended consequences contains complex and often naïve or downright dishonest characteristics, so it merits attention. Earlier I wrote that consequences can be anticipated by studying history and economic theory, by factual analysis, assessing probabilities and by studying human nature. You'd think that if a policy or action were analyzed thoroughly, the likelihood of an unintended consequence would be close to zero. Yet, indeed, as shown above, sometimes they occur.

An unintended consequence, or what some try to pass off as an unintended consequence, is the result of one or more situations. I have identified several of them. I may have missed one or two, but I am confident the reader will get the drift of what I mean.

Unintended consequences can be the result of:

- Something occurred that was by reason, logic, history and morality, not reasonably foreseeable

- The consequences were foreseeable but were not thought through and were unintended

- The actor was indifferent to the consequence and was being disingenuous or dishonest about them being unintended

- People misjudged the risk of a consequence resulting from an action

- The consequence was predictable and the actor didn't want it but the actor thought the consequence was a price worth paying to attain the goal. In this situation, it is disingenuous to say that the consequence was unintended.

- The consequence was undesired but fully predictable and occurred because of a lack of moral will and courage. In this instance, describing the consequence as unintended is deceitful.

A valuable characteristic of consequences is that they punish recklessness, including reckless thinking, just as the loss part of the profit and loss system serves to punish reckless and sloppy economic activity. Human nature compels one to avoid punishment or accountability for error and thus, people tend to declare a bad consequence as unintended. Here's the argument: one cannot be responsible for what was unintended and unexpected. Recall the discussion about foreseeability.

It is important to use reason, logic and moral analysis to judge whether a claim of unintended consequences is valid. It is fundamentally dishonest, for example, to claim you did not intend something when that 'something' is certain or almost certain to occur.

Revisiting the principal and the cheater, I hope the principal did not *intend* that his decision would lead to increased cheating and to a fine teacher refusing to enforce moral codes. But it will. Even a pet rock knows it. Whether this was intended is perhaps a question more appropriate for a metaphysician or for a government grant, but logic and morality require the principal to be held accountable for the consequences because they were predictable costs of his decision.

Another consequence worth mentioning seen in the often-referred cheating incident is not unique to it. I opined that the principal's behavior would lead to more cheating. I don't assert, however, that every student would cheat. Some students will have sufficient ethical backbone to transcend the principal's unethical standard.

The non-cheaters will not be immune to the more cheating consequences, although their consequences will be of a dramatically different kind. The honest ethical students will believe, as some of my students have said, that honesty is dumb. Nevertheless, they will adhere to the higher moral standard due to their character and honor. But they will become more cynical of those in authority and they will resent and have contempt for the school because justice and honor were crushed and because being moral places them at a disadvantage.

TAKING IT HOME

Consequences are predictive, not determinative. Consequences can only shape and influence our choices. They do not determine them. They do not necessarily force them. Understanding consequences and acting in anticipation of them require the many skills I've mentioned earlier, including the willingness to think, to examine, to compare and to muster the courage to do what will yield the most moral outcome.

Understanding consequences is the beginning of making moral choices. The bottom line is that words matter little. The morality of words, speeches, promises of hope, of change, of reform to enhance equality and justice is determined by only one measurement: the morality of the consequences of actions that might occur or that did occur. Nothing else matters. Nothing. Consequences determine morality.

Parents will often deal with consequences on very personal levels. Alexa told me that when she asks her parents for help and gets ignored repeatedly, "you kind of stop asking after a while." A teenage friend of one of my children confided to her parents that she had once tried marijuana. She told them she would not do so again. Her parents were savage in their condemnation of her, calling her names and making accusations with no basis in fact. The daughter to my child, "I'll never tell my parents anything again."

One dad had to bond his son out of jail. He was charged with drunk driving. "I've got to learn to interact with my son," he told me. "It's pretty tough to look at the face of your seventeen-year-old who's so drunk he can't stand," he confided, "but that's a lot easier than looking at his face at the funeral home. Sure, I want to wring his neck, but I want my son more. I have to find a way, even if it means being really tough."

In the final analysis, we parents deal with the consequences of our children's actions, whether joyous or hurtful. It is deliciously easy for others to give opinions and advice about handling our children when they don't have to pay the price of their consequences.

We parents do. We are the ones with the heartbreak, the medical bills and the legal bills. We're the ones that remain the longest at the hospitals and cemeteries.

So we parents better get it right, at least most of the time, and at least with the major things in our children's lives. Part of that process involves teaching our children to take the long view; to realize that consequences can be stretched over decades or even a lifetime. We can experience infinite joy with our children, but there can be very unpleasant consequences when we forget that there are consequences for not teaching our children about consequences.

CHAPTER 19

COURAGE

*"I know we're all going to die.
There's three of us who are going to do something about it.
I love you, honey."*

—THOMAS BURNETT, IN A PHONE CALL TO HIS WIFE, DEENA, REGARDING THE
TERRORIST HIGHJACKERS OF UNITED AIRLINES FLIGHT 93, MOMENTS BEFORE
CRASHING IN SHANKSVILLE, PENNSYLVANIA, SEPTEMBER 11, 2001

T HE AFTERNOON DRIVE TO PICK UP ANNIE AND ELISE at
school on November 12, 1997 began unremarkably. I traveled east on Hampden Avenue, across the Interstate 25
overpass and drove about a quarter mile or so when I heard shriek-
ing sirens and saw police cars—lots of police cars—some blocking
northbound Monaco Boulevard. I punched radio station buttons
hoping to learn what was happening in this placid well-manicured
part of southeast Denver.

Over the next few days I learned that a so-called skinhead,
Matthaeus Jaehnig, and his female partner, Lisa Aulman, had com-
mitted several burglaries about thirty miles west of Denver. They
had been chased to an apartment complex in the vicinity of the
Hampden and Monaco intersection. That's where I saw most of the
police cars. I learned that Jaehnig fired a fully automatic rifle at
Denver police officers trying to apprehend him. He killed Officer
Bruce VanderJagt.

I learned that Officer VanderJagt, an eleven-year veteran with
the Denver Police Department, had twice been awarded the
Distinguished Service Cross—once for disarming a gunman threatening employees of Porter Memorial Hospital, where I had my heart
operation, and once for running into a burning building to help
save the occupants. I learned also that Denver Special Weapons and
Tactics (SWAT) officers tried to rescue VanderJagt even as Jaehnig
fired an automatic rifle at them.

At the time, I hosted a children's radio show, Radio Aahs! Each Sunday afternoon half dozen or so youngsters, including my three children, their friends and children from my class joined me in the studio. We'd chat with young callers about character and moral issues. Lines were always jammed. We must have filled a need.

Awed by the courage and heroism of these SWAT officers, I knew their story would be uplifting for my radio audience. I called the Denver SWAT headquarters, explained my purpose and asked to speak to one of the team. Mark Haney returned my call.

Mark and I met at a restaurant. He was paradoxical: soft spoken, almost shy, he modestly brushed away any praise of his heroism as if it were an annoying cobweb. Yet he was intense, physically strong and manifestly mentally tough.

A few minutes into the conversation, I asked about the source of his extraordinary courage. He answered awkwardly. "I was trying to save someone's life." He spoke slowly as if he were learning something about himself. "My parents taught me to help if I could."

In my next class I spoke about this part of my conversation with Mark. Mark's words resonated with Jeffery, a fourth grader. Jeffery's words offer lessons to every thoughtful parent. "I think everything you learn you learn at home. Except school stuff."

David's follow-up comment is representative of these youngsters' capacity for introspection and unalloyed honesty. It also provides a glimpse into their aspirations; their sense of how they *want* to be. With measured words, David said, "I'm not sure I could do that. I know it's right but I don't know if I could. Officer Haney must have really cared about that police officer."

Mark has become good friend. I know he cared about Bruce VanderJagt. I know he cared about Officer VanderJagt's wife, Anna, and his toddler daughter, Haley. Mark cared enough about them and public safety to risk his life. That's courage.

> *"Courage is rightly esteemed the first of human qualities,*
> *because it is the quality that guarantees all others"*
>
> –Sir Winston S. Churchill

The Latin root of Courage is *cor*, which means heart, and we know from the musical *Damn Yankees* that you gotta have it if you want to accomplish anything worth accomplishing. Courage is associated with bravery, with the willingness to risk one's self interest or life for a noble cause; to face danger, difficulty or pain.

There is moral courage in addition to physical courage.

Moral courage requires the will to act in accordance with the demands of virtue, often despite criticism or being outnumbered. A physical threat may not exist if one exercises moral courage but other threats may; ostracism, loss of employment, loss of friends and worse, not being invited to A-list cocktail parties.

"Courage," English author C. S. Lewis, wrote, "is not simply one of the virtues but the form of every virtue at the testing point, which means at the point of highest reality." Courage may rightly be viewed as the actualization of all the virtues.

Your children can quickly give many examples of courage. You may be delightfully surprised that they consider as courageous something you did. Don't hesitate to ask. Some examples of courage likely to be mentioned by your child are spectacularly dramatic and well-known. Others may be quite personal. Since 9/11, most children immediately cite the courageous folks that went *into* the burning Twin Towers to save others.

There is the courage of Chesley "Sully" Sullenberger, the pilot of US Airways flight 1549 that struck a flock of birds during takeoff from LaGuardia Airport and made a crash landing in the frigid Hudson River. Assisting the passengers and flight personnel, Sully didn't leave the aircraft until every person was rescued.

Daily we learn of courageous folks that save people from burning homes and cars, that rescue swimmers being attacked by sharks and that thwart muggers and would-be murderers. In rare instances, as with Thomas Burnett, people exhibit extraordinary courage to the end, knowing they are not likely to survive. Yet they act courageously to reduce the deaths and injuries of others.

We also see courage on a more micro scale, a little closer to home: the boy that told his classmates not to throw rocks at the snake, the girl that got help for her suicidal friend, the student that stood up to bullies, the youngster that stood up to the pressure of his peers and gave the pistol to his principal. One student spoke of his dad breaking up a fight at a restaurant. Another child saw courage when his father helped a stranger change a tire in the middle of the night.

On an airplane flight several years ago I sat next to a blind skier who had just participated in a competition in Winter Park, Colorado for handicapped skiers. I told him I admired his courage. He tersely replied, "I'd rather risk dying than sit and do nothing."

He didn't see himself as courageous, only doing what he needed to do to bring meaning to his life. He didn't persuade me. He had courage.

Courage is not the absence of fear. Anyone present at ground zero on 9/11 would have to have been brain dead not to be fearful. Courage is the decision to transcend fear. Courage is the ability to enlist other virtues when you are afraid. Courage is the willingness to act virtuously when undesirable consequences are possible or probable.

One student's question required me to distinguish between courage and foolishness. Taking a risk is not an indicator of courage. It depends on the facts. Recall the 'saving a drowning person' discussion. Running in the path of a moving car to save a child is courageous. Running in the path of a moving car to retrieve a baseball is not. Third-grader Robbie challenged me. "But what if it's a baseball signed by Mickey Mantle or Hank Aaron?"

"Well," I replied, "there are always exceptions."

A PROFILE IN COURAGE

"To make a nation truly great, a handful of heroes capable of great deeds at a supreme moment is not enough. Heroes are not always available, and one can often do without them!
But it is essential to have thousands of reliable people—honest citizens—who steadfastly place the public interest before their own."

–PASQUALE VILLANI

In the spring of 2000 some chemicals and unusual components were delivered to a Denver-area high school student's home. The father learned about the contents of the package and asked his son why he had ordered that material. The son said they were for a school project. The father was skeptical. He contacted school officials and learned the materials weren't required for any project. The father reported his son to the police.

An investigation disclosed that the boy had taken substantial steps toward utilizing the materials to create a bomb to be detonated in his school.

Few topics are inherently as volcanic or as uncomfortable as one where a parent appears to subvert or undermine its child. Recall the conversations about little Jessica and the airplane. This topic packs a lot of emotion but it also presents issues of trust, reason and duty that require dispassionate analysis but have the potential for yielding profound lessons. As we progress through the dialogue, note the eloquence, compassion and morality expressed by these youngsters as they grapple with this conflict-plagued topic.

Asked to characterize the father's behavior, courage was the first quality mentioned. Henry's comment represented the thinking of most students. "It took a lot of courage for the dad to call the police. The dad knew the son would be angry, but the dad knew there were more important things than an angry son."

Justin said, "When he learned his son lied, he had to do something. The father was courageous because he did something he didn't really want to do. He cared about his son and he cared about the other people."

Ellie said, "The father was courageous because he risked learning the painful truth that his son lied to him and that his own son would hurt people."

Morgan said, "Turning in his son showed that he cared about his son and sometimes you have to be strong to do what's right."

"But," Tulley added, "even though it's his son, he's just like any other person."

The students admired the father. Abbie observed: "He stood up for himself and his family and the community and also for his son."

The students viewed the father turning in his son as protecting him.

All the students talked about the likelihood that the son would be angry with the father. None of them gave the son's anger any weight. All were dismissive of the son's feelings. Julie blurted, "So what? He's wrong!" The students rejected the proposition that the father should be concerned about angering a person that was preparing to kill people.

Recall Aristotle's admonition about anger: "Anybody can become angry; but to be angry with the right person, and to the right degree, and at the right time, and for the right purpose, and in the right way, that is not within everybody's power; that is not easy."

Idimar noted both the similarity and the difference in outcomes if the father did not call the police. He judged one outcome was worse than the other. "If the kid did make a bomb, he'd go to jail anyhow but there would be more people hurt by not calling the police." Calling the police was not only the most virtuous behavior; it was also the most practical option.

One of the finer discussion points addressed the sequence of the father's actions. The father did not act out of rage or emotion. His actions were methodical, incremental and logically sequential. My son, Erik, said, "The order of what the father did was important: If he called the police first before checking with the school to learn if there were a science project, and there was, then the son would hate him for not trusting him and being arrested would ruin his school record."

The students praised the father for offering the son several opportunities to be truthful. By being truthful the son could have demonstrated he was worthy of his father's trust. The father went to the school because he did not find his son's explanation to be credible. Neither did my students.

Note the youngsters' capacity for applying logical reasoning to facts. "If it was a real project, the son would be proud to talk to his parents about it," Karen asserted.

Morgan saw the issue as a risk analysis. "It meant that the father couldn't take a chance that his son was doing something wrong." Perhaps the father was less inclined to take risks because memories of the recent Columbine slaughter were seared into his mind. When informed that the son's story was false, the trust was lost and the father had to take additional action.

Consider how elegantly Lilly, a fifth grader, explored and evaluated the dimensions of trust in the context of time and evidence. "It didn't mean that the father never trusted the son. It meant that the father didn't trust the son once the father learned all the facts. After he lied, he forfeited being trusted."

Think back to the lessons that changing facts change the morality of a situation and that duties to act change as facts change. Recall the 'what do we know, what do we need to know' exercise. When the father's doubt dissolved into concrete truth, a moral duty arose to take action calibrated to the seriousness of the possible consequences. Once again we see that truth is not an end in itself but is a force to compel virtuous action.

RISKS AND CONSEQUENCES

"The hottest places in Hell are reserved for those who, in times of great moral crisis, maintain their neutrality."

–DANTE ALIGHIERI

The father was reasonable not to take at face value his son's explanation for possessing the chemical components. Moreover, as Sheryl pointed out, "We don't know how truthful the son was in the past." Maybe there was a history of the son's dishonesty. Maybe, based on that history, the father had cause to be cynical and not to give his son the benefit of a doubt. Alternatively, even if the son had never been dishonest, the father erred on the side of caution by checking out the son's story at school.

Levi leveled a restrained criticism at the father. The father's actions were not based on a certainty that the son was acting improperly. "The dad couldn't be sure the son was doing something wrong."

The class trampled that comment as if it were grass under fighting elephants. "Well, you never can be totally certain," Amanda retorted sharply. "Better safe than sorry," many children said. "Better to do this and be wrong than to do nothing and have the kid make a bomb," Armand added.

Imagine if the father had done nothing and students were killed!

Just a few months later a situation presenting similar moral issues arose in Santee, San Diego. The results were tragically different because, in this instance, adults did nothing. High school student Charles Andrew Williams threatened to shoot students at Santana High School.

Charles Reynolds, the father of one of Williams' friends, failed to notify authorities when he learned of the threats. On March 5, 2001, Charles Andrew Williams killed Bryan Zuckor and Randy Gordon and wounded thirteen other students.

"Everybody can't believe that he actually did it," Reynolds said. "Williams said he was just joking."

Mr. Reynolds said, "I do regret that I didn't do something because I should've stepped up even if it wasn't true and stuff to take that precaution. If someone did die over there and stuff, that's going to be haunting me for a long time, that's going to be with me for a long time. It just hurts because I could've maybe done something about it."

Returning to the topic of the dad and the chemicals, the dad had options. He could have not called the police and destroyed the chemicals or he could have done nothing, as in the Charles Andrew Williams case.

The students considered these options also. Their comments illustrate their capacity for sophisticated thinking. For example, many students saw benefits resulting from the son's involvement with the police. Consider Jack's exquisite reasoning: "We know the kid already lied. If the dad alone dealt with the son, he would not have had as much impact on the child for teaching lessons for acting in the future. The police made it more serious. The police made it more likely that the kid would learn. Without the police, the kid might learn that he could fool his dad all the time."

This is stunning reasoning by anyone, let alone a fifth grader.

You don't have to be the greatest wit since Socrates to draw brilliant words from your children. Just ask a question such as: "What was the father thinking about?" My students' answers offered insight infused with compassion.

Anna said "Maybe the dad was worried he wasn't a good father. Maybe he didn't raise his son right but now he could do the right thing."

To give yet another example of how profound and poignant your children's remarks can be, I share Stacey's stunning comment that weaves a long term perspective with soul-churning empathy. "Turning in the son may have been the lowest point in his life as a parent, but it may be the highest point when he looks back on it." Can you believe the wisdom of these little folks?

As Joni Mitchell's song about paving paradise says, "Well, you don't know what you've got till it's gone." This dad didn't want to wait around for his son to be gone so he could know what he had. The dad knew what he had—a son that he loved—and he wanted to keep him. He knew that in many instances, hesitation, inaction and/or cowardice lead to death. The father displayed courage.

Students raised an intriguing perspective—what would the son learn about his father? I present Allister's comment last because it distills the primary theme of this book and poignantly answered this question with crystalline clarity. "The son will learn that his father was tough. He will learn that his father will do what is right even if it is unpopular and causes someone in the family to be unhappy. The son will learn that his father will act on his values."

All I can write is wow! Those are the kinds of statements that, as some might say, make my day. Wouldn't all caring parents want to be thought of in that way by their children? I do!

For whatever it's worth, I confide that I am not certain I would have turned my child into the police, even in the heated post-Columbine environment. But I might have been wrong. I might not have had the courage. I just don't know, reminding me once again that it is easier to give advice than to follow it.

I've learned a few overarching lessons from these classes that are as important in directing our behavior as a lighthouse in a storm. Students did not view the father's behavior as a betrayal of his child. They saw it as acts of caring and love toward a person that was doing something very wrong. That's how children measure love: taking responsibility to protect those you care about. The money quote here is that children want their parents to take responsibility.

I share a brief exchange with my daughter, Alexandra, to support this conclusion. She was about thirteen and the subject of contention was trivial. She asked me if she could go out with friends that night. "You didn't clean your room," I said. It had become indistinguishable from the county landfill near Denver International Airport. I consider myself a gracious chap, with the milk of human kindness by the quart in every vein, as Henry Higgins sung in 'My Fair Lady.' I asked, "You didn't obey me. Should I punish you and make you stay at home?"

"I don't know," Alexandra snapped like an animal trainer's whip. "You're the parent! You decide." She has not mellowed over time.

It is unlikely, of course, that the son with the chemicals would tell the dad something like, "Thanks for turning me in, pops! It was the right thing to do." But in the long term, the son might interpret the father's actions as beneficial. Stacey beautifully expressed this point. "Some day the son would admit the dad was right. The dad would help his son build his character."

"The phone calls to friends and family from those who knew that they were about to die did not express fear or hate but love and courage."

—NEWS COMMENTATOR, SPEAKING OF THE ATTACK ON THE
WORLD TRADE CENTER, SEPTEMBER 11, 2001

TEACHING COURAGE

"A man or a nation is not placed upon this earth to do merely what is pleasant and what is profitable. It is often called upon to carry out what is both unpleasant and unprofitable, but if it is obviously right it is mere shirking not to undertake it."

–SIR ARTHUR CONAN DOYLE, THE TRAGEDY OF THE KOROSKO

We can discern that courage has several qualities. It is not limited in amount. Like smiles and hugs, courage is limitless. Courage is fluid. One may lack it today in one situation but be courageously triumphant tomorrow in the same or similar situation.

Courage is not something in a vacuum. It's not like a medal pinned on the lion in the Wizard of Oz, bright and shiny and glistening in the sun for all to see and say, "Take a look!" Courage is complex. It is often gritty, anguishing, filled with doubt and exercised without congratulations or praise.

Courage often requires confrontation. Thus the person of weak character will not act courageously because of the desire to avoid confrontation and conflict. It is so much easier—and safer—to demand that others have the courage of your convictions.

Courage is the consequence of many qualities such as character and competence. Recall Erik's comment in the chapter on Character. "Courage is like a fire, and the wood is your character. And if you keep adding wood, the fire gets brighter and brighter."

Courage, then, is linked inextricably to personal morality. Being smart is not enough; having a high IQ is not enough; knowing right from wrong is not enough. These characteristics are like matchsticks in a box—they represent potential but they light nothing. They guarantee nothing.

Courage, then, is the consequence of character, competence and will. When Todd Beamer yelled "Let's roll!" on United Flight 93 and attacked the terrorists, he acted morally, competently and strategically as a person of free independent will, thereby preventing greater slaughter.

Courage can be taught. The first step is to explain that it is the distillate of many qualities. It's not in its own lockbox, unconnected to other virtues. Through discussion, rhetorical devices such as analogy and example and, of course, by your own actions, courage can be cultivated, motivated and strengthened.

Courage can also be taught by teaching children to think strategically: what do I have to do to get the result I want? How do I have to behave to be the kind of person I want to be? What risks must be taken and what sacrifices must be made to achieve a virtuous result in a particular situation?

Strategic thinking clarifies moral reasoning by identifying and evaluating the moral qualities of available choices of behavior. The cost of courage versus the cost of cowardice can be measured, evaluated and can serve as motivation for virtuous behavior. Reinforcing competence and ethical values increases the motivation to act courageously.

Courage can be taught in many ways. Dialogues on topics in this book can be effective teaching tools if the morality and the competence and the strategies for courageous behavior are identified and analyzed.

Peter McLaughlin shared a story. An inquisitive engaging mom asked her seven-year-old son what he thought were his best qualities. The little fellow answered, "Bravery." Intrigued, the mom asked the not-too-complicated question, "Why bravery?"

The child described his standing up to a bully in school that was harassing a little girl. "Isn't that bravery, mom?" he asked. That little interaction opened up a world of discussions at the dinner table. Dissecting the meaning of courage had the beneficial consequence of increasing the competence and confidence of the youngster and also gave the mom an opportunity to define and reinforce her own moral values.

Courage must be analyzed in particular fact situations. It cannot be usefully understood in the abstract. Pick a moment when your little angel is messing up the carpet with her growing carbon footprint and pop the question whether she has courage. Ask if she would have defied the sensei John Kreese's order to sweep Daniel's leg? If he's seen the movie Jaws, ask what he thought of the coroner giving in to the mayor's pressure to falsify the death report so it would not indicate that the woman was killed by a shark?

Ask how she would have behaved if she had found the pistol in the school playground? The Lorenzo Hernandez story dramatically illustrates that courage is difficult, complicated and can have costs, whether or not courage is exercised. It's not a Lion King Hakuna Matata no-worry problem-free philosophy. Courage is tough. Presenting courage any other way does a disservice to a child.

Only recently have I considered another technique for teaching courage. The method borrows heavily from skills used to enhance achievement in all kinds of disciplines, from athletic performance to musicians to surgeons and others. The technique is learning how to strengthen your weaknesses. Almost every successful person focuses as much or more on his weaknesses as on his strengths.

If your child thinks he is too shy, tell him to close his eyes and visualize getting out of his shell and speaking up. That's what great athletes do: they visualize the results they want to achieve. A great golfer will play every course in his mind—several times—before every competition. A basketball player will shoot a thousand foul shots in his or her mind. A tennis player plays complete matches in her mind. Trial lawyers and athletes pay a lot of money for this coaching.

Tell your child to see in her mind's eye that she is ignoring the classmates trying to take the pistol she found. Tell her to hear herself rejecting their criticism and taunts and entreaties. Tell her to see herself marching confidently into the principal's office with the firearm. Tell her to see it clearly. Have her imagine acknowledging to herself that her courage saved lives; that friends are not dead because of her actions.

So, let's say your child doesn't have confidence in verbally responding to people. Have her visualize an argument. Recall the 'worm under the rock' example. Tell her to hear her words as she responds to the other person. Keep visualizing the conversation until the words flow smoothly and effectively. Visualize scenes and words. Have your child imagine standing up to friends, to bullies or to a coach. (Perhaps anyone but you! Don't get carried away!) See it, hear it, believe it and then do it.

Values are clarified when comparisons are made between who one stands up to and who one does not. Think about courage in terms of who gets offended and who gets rewarded. The school principal didn't have the courage to stand up to the mom of the cheater but he insolently trivialized the teacher. The mom could hurt the principal although she was wrong. The teacher couldn't hurt him although the teacher was right. Courage and its absence thus become selective and convenient.

"Should one point out that from ancient times a decline in courage has been considered the beginning of the end?"

–ALEXANDER SOLZHENITSYN

Good character and courage are contagious. Judge John Kane noted, "The habitual demonstration of rectitude makes it easier for others to be courageous." Set a virtuous example and more people will behave more virtuously.

An advertisement recently seen on television comes to mind when I think of parents instilling courage in their children. The advertisement pushes cell phone service contracts by boasting 'just sign up, no money down, no length of contract and no commitment.' Maybe those values are a sign of the times—no length of commitment; indeed, no commitment at all! Advertisers are pretty good at identifying and exploiting society's values, the virtuous as well as the ethically deficient.

The values and criteria in that cell phone advertisement should not be accepted by good parents. As seen with the dad and the chemicals, we parents have made commitments to our children as strong as titanium bands and the length of our contract with them is considerable, certainly a life time, sometimes more. The price of defaulting can be high.

The Greek historian Thucydides wrote, "The secret to happiness is freedom, and the secret to freedom is courage."

If courage is not cultivated and rewarded, then indifference and selfishness will flourish like kudzu. We might lose our children and our family. We might lose our friends and neighbors. If we lose our courage we may also lose our society; for they are interconnected as sunlight is connected to warmth. But even more, if we lose our courage, we lose our soul.

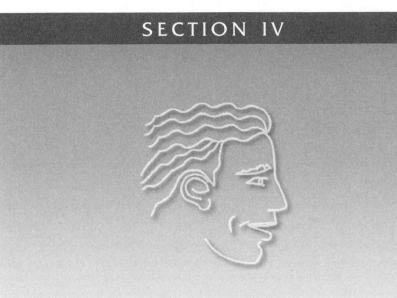

SECTION IV

THREE STORIES
& ALL ROADS
LEAD TO HOME

CHAPTER 20

THE DEATH OF KITTY GENOVESE

"Please do not forget us."

–ANONYMOUS. SCRATCHED ON A WALL INSIDE A GAS CHAMBER AT TREBLINKA.

A WAVE OF THE HAND

I COULD NOT HAVE PREDICTED how this seemingly trivial interaction would influence my ethics classes that began about eight years later. In December 1982 Nancy and I drove from Denver to Hebron, Nebraska to meet her family. The itinerary was unfamiliar; Denver to Interstate 25 North to Interstate 70 East, exit at Byers, Colorado on Highway 36 East, stay on 36 almost four hundred miles, exit at Belleville, Kansas and go north on Highway 81 to Hebron. We traveled through dozens of farming and ranching towns, some prospering and some facing extinction, all a great swath of America I'd never seen.

A mile or so east of Byers I experienced something new: drivers—strangers—in approaching trucks and cars made a gesture, lifting a hand off the steering wheel. I seemed to be the gesture's target. Oncoming drivers looked at me; tried to make eye contact with me. Some even smiled. I was befuddled.

"Nancy, did you see that gesture? There's another! What's that about?"

"They're waving. It's being neighborly. We do that in the Midwest."

Some motions were not true 'waves' of a freely moving hand but a minimalist raising of the palm while the heel of the hand maintained contact with the steering wheel, a kind of 'green' energy saving variation. Sometimes the hand movement was more minimalist yet, raising one finger off the wheel, a gesture I did not accurately interpret until Nancy pointed out that the forefinger was raised.

I consider myself multicultural in the best sense of the word and, not being a shy sort, began waving back. At first I was shy and awkward, making ambiguous half-waving motions in the event the driver of the on-coming vehicle didn't initiate a wave or didn't wave back, which made me feel unappreciated. I alternated waving styles through four hundred miles of verdant Colorado, Kansas and Nebraska farm country.

The drive seemed unending but I found it entertaining sometimes. Every fifty miles or so I'd see a sign advertising something such as Bill's Fine Dining, Tires and Plumbing. I'd chuckle at the combination of services and hope Bill didn't commingle parts from his product lines. Maybe a steak could be used to repair a car's radiator. The most humorous sign was on the west bound side of Highway 36 in Mankato, Kansas. The words "Sanitary Landfill" were in big block letters and the arrow-shaped sign pointed across the highway directly at the Jewell County cemetery. A testament to clean living, I guess.

I've made that drive perhaps a hundred times. I waved through the majestic fruited plains of wheat, soybeans and corn, acrid smelling livestock yards and dozens of small towns. I have become a more confident aggressive waver and I no longer feel an existential rejection when someone doesn't wave back. Tell you the truth, it's pretty neat.

ONLY A CALL AWAY

*"Our lives begin to end the day we become silent
about things that matter."*

—MARTIN LUTHER KING, JR.

I interpreted the waving as an indicator of community, an acknowledgment of the other person and of a marvelous inclusiveness. I shared with every class my Nebraska driving experience and wove those themes into as many discussions as my brain could conjure. Of all the discussions, none was as appropriate as the topic of the murder of Kitty Genovese.

I remember my anguished reaction when I learned of her death. I was a few days short of my seventeenth birthday. I wailed, "It could not be true!"

My understanding of the facts is based on what I remember from news coverage at the time and from my research over the years preparing for classes. You can do a Google search to get more details but I am confident I have accurately presented the main facts. The facts are as gruesome as they are incredible.

If you discuss this incident with your child, it may be wise to soften some of the facts. In one sixth grade class my presentation was evidently too graphic. A parent notified the principal that her daughter had nightmares. I was cautioned to be less descriptive.

Kitty Genovese finished working at a restaurant at about two o'clock in the morning on March 13, 1964, and walked to her apartment, one of several within the complex in Kew Gardens, a section of Queens in New York City. Almost getting to her apartment door, Kitty was savagely attacked and stabbed in an open area within the complex.

She screamed for help. Several people put on the lights in their apartments. Several people went to their windows and watched the assailant, later arrested and identified as Winston Mosely, repeatedly stab the twenty-three year old woman about fifty feet from some of them. No one came to her aid. No one called the police. Someone yelled. Mosely ran away.

Kitty continued to scream for help as she crawled toward her apartment. No one helped. No one called the police. Moments later, Mosely returned and continued his attack. Kitty's screaming continued. More lights went on. Mosely fled again.

Mosely returned a third time and continued his attack. Someone called the police. They arrived within two minutes. Mosely was gone. Kitty Genovese was dead. The assaults lasted about half an hour.

Thirty-eight people admitted observing some or all of the assaults. They gave several reasons for not helping. Some bluntly said they didn't want to get involved. Some said it was none of their business. One or more said they didn't help because they thought it was a lover's quarrel, implying it was a private matter properly insulated from intrusion. One or more said they were too tired and wanted to go back to bed. One person physically moved his chair to the window, opened the curtains and ghoulishly watched the assaults, amusing himself with death as if it were a perverse reality show.

The country was, of course, outraged . . . for a while. Explanations for such lethal indifference proliferated. Pundits, sociologists, psychiatrists and other educated folks placed blame on the nature of modern society—that it was impersonal, disaffecting and alienating. People no longer felt connected to each other, the argument went. The term 'bystander syndrome' became popular, referring to people who watch human evil and do nothing to deter it.

A few other theories attempted to explain the on-lookers' disinterest in helping Kitty. One was called the 'diffusion of responsibility.' This proposition held that a person tended to avoid acting because he assumed other people would or were likely to help. Therefore, the on-looker wasn't certain his assistance was needed. In a sense, the responsibility was diffused.

Another theory held that a person did not help because he assumed that if other people weren't helping, it was because they had better information which justified their decision not to help.

Talk about these two theories with your child and see if you can discern their morality. Ask, "Do you think it is moral not to help someone because someone else might help?" Or ask, "Do you think it is moral not to help someone because no one else was helping?"

Most likely you and your children will quickly note the deficiencies of the 'diffused responsibility' theory and the 'maybe everyone else knows more than I so I'll do nothing' theory. Your children will probably point out that moral character and moral duty were not incorporated into these two theories. They might say something like, "Who cares what other people are doing? You should still help if you can!" These theories impress me as the love children of Houdini and his blindfold and are lame to the tenth power.

WHETHER PIGS HAVE WINGS

Kitty Genovese was one of the earliest discussions in Elise's first grade class. I didn't delve into whether society was disaffecting, impersonal, alienating or otherwise. I limited my discussions to thinking skills, character and competence. If those qualities were enhanced, I figured society would become a little less alienating, disaffected and impersonal.

Your children will likely describe the bystanders' behavior as my students did:

- The people were horrible.
- They had no feelings.
- How would they like it if they were lying on the ground dying and no one helped?
- What if it was their mother or wife down there?
- They didn't have compassion.
- They were immoral.
- They were cowards.

I won't quibble with any of these statements, but a dialogue about this horrific event is useful only to the extent it teaches lessons that will reduce the likelihood it will happen again. It is not ethically or intellectually useful or satisfying to disparage the thirty-eight bystanders and harp on their immorality. That belabors the obvious. It's a waste of time. My approach was to give these youngsters the skills to do better if they faced a similar situation. That was the best way I could honor Kitty Genovese.

Moral behavior is a function of character, facts and consequences. I wrote that morality changes as facts change. To distill the lessons of the Kitty Genovese murder, I challenged the class to interpret the facts using the Moral Measures. I discussed each of the bystanders' excuses through the lenses of these criteria. Each excuse is worthy of an independent conversation.

1. I Didn't Want to Get Involved.

With this excuse, the bystander expressed no doubt or confusion about the facts. The speaker is not concerned about what other people are doing. Right and wrong, good and evil and the suffering of another human being are irrelevant. Justice, Beneficence and Sanctity of Life curdle into irrelevance like an overheated Hollandaise sauce. No diffusion of responsibility or ambiguity worms its way through this decaying excuse. The excuse rages with selfish indifference.

We can judge the bystanders' behavior as immoral. However there is another more complex issue that deserves analysis. Jonathan yelled, "But wait, There could be a danger to the person that gets involved!" He was familiar with the criminal prosecution process. The bystander's name and address could become known to the assailant. The assailant or someone on his behalf might threaten or injure the witness.

Elena rejected Jonathan's concern. "You can't make the excuse that you're scared," she said. "You could call without telling your name."

Both students made good points. The witness' self preservation conflicted with duties based on justice and respect for life. We can only speculate about the risk from disclosing information to the assailant. But we don't need to be stuck on that point. Alternative actions were available.

Discuss the many ways the bystanders could have helped Kitty without giving up their personal information. The police could have been called with total anonymity. "Just tell the police that a lady is getting killed and give them the address. That should get the police to go there," Jenna said forcefully.

People could have yelled from their windows, thrown plates and shoes at the attacker and threatened to confront him directly. None of those actions would have jeopardized the anonymity or the safety of the on-lookers.

Someone in the apartment building could have fired a gun to scare him off. "You don't need to kill him, just make him leave,"

Emilee said. Apartment residents could have contacted each other and yelled, essentially, 'Let's roll!' and gone out as a group to rescue Kitty. And let's not forget, they could have rescued Kitty during those times that Mosely fled. Again, anonymity would have been assured.

"Even if you don't catch the stabber," Jamie said, "at least the girl is saved." There's a youngster with proper priorities!

Since there were many ways a person could have helped without personal risk, the duty to help trumped the right to protect one's self. Jonathan's discredited point had prompted a valuable discussion.

But let's say that a helper's anonymity could *not* be maintained? Let's say there was some risk to someone helping Kitty. What are the moral implications of the argument that no one should have helped her because there was a risk? Would Rex have donated bone marrow? Would anyone try to save a drowning person? Would any fire fighter go into a burning building? The entire criminal justice system would collapse. The human spirit would be reduced to something akin to the sludge at the bottom of a car's transmission.

My daughter, Elise, pointed out, "Just because something might happen to you doesn't mean you shouldn't help someone." The classes always conclude that the small risk that something *might* happen does not excuse failing to help a person dying within a few feet of your door.

2. It Was None of my Business.

This excuse is different from the first. This excuse makes a value judgment. The 'I didn't want to get involved' excuse did not. This excuse says there is no duty to help because it's not my business. In a way, this excuse is more perverse than the first one. It's more calculating. It is more bloodless. It is more inhuman.

This excuse says that a person attacked a few feet away is not your business. You are not connected in any way to the victim. Connor eloquently rejected this argument by appealing to broad moral principles. "Beneficence means that it is our business!"

Maddie drew upon another ethical principle, showing how these little folks can grasp big themes. "Sanctity of Life means it is their business to care about other people and to try to save them."

Andrew emphasized the notion of reciprocity that links us to each other. "What if it was happening to them? They wouldn't want someone to just sit there! So it is their business!" One of the most brilliant insights came, not surprisingly, from fifth grader Tulley. She saw the moral relationship between the ability to help and personal accountability for the consequences. "They kind of allowed Kitty to die, so it was their business." Moral responsibility made it their business.

3. A Lover's Quarrel

Think about this excuse—that there was no duty to help Kitty because she might have been romantically involved with the man killing her. Go figure! This excuse was so far out the children needed the Hubble telescope to see it.

There are two elements to this excuse: whether it was a lover's quarrel and, if so, so what? Discuss this excuse with your children. See how their words compare with my students' comments. Stacey exclaimed, "What was going on here?" Stacey was in my first class with Mrs. Pratt. In my mind's eye I see her fiery red hair and intense eyes as vividly as if the class had been this morning. Stacey continued. "She was screaming for help! She had been stabbed! She was outside yelling. A man kept coming back to hurt her. That's not a lover's quarrel!"

"And what kind of boyfriend hurts the girl like that?" Karen challenged. "I wouldn't want a boyfriend like that. That's not real love. It's just being mean."

Irina, a nine-year-old, offered a comprehensive evaluation of facts and conclusions. "How could it be a lover's quarrel? I'm sure all these adults know about violence and could tell from the tone of the voice that the lady is in trouble. They just didn't want to do anything. It's an excuse. They were lazy and didn't care and now they have to cover it up." And if it were a lover's quarrel, as Sam acutely commented, "So what? You have no right to hurt people, whether or not you love them."

Love is not an asbestos suit that insulates one from responsibility for harming another. Such an argument would immunize people from punishment for beating spouses and children. Who believes that? What contempt for humanity to argue one person can slaughter another because of an emotion generally considered a virtue!

4. I Was Tired. I Went Back to Bed.

What is there to say about this excuse? Close your eyes and see the scene in your mind. I don't need to repeat the horrid description. Try to fathom the bystander seeing and hearing what has been described. Imagine the bystander contemplating the many ways he could help Kitty, then methodically rejecting each one and returning to his protective sheets and blankets. This excuse represents a thorough rejection of morality and humanity.

> *"Yo soy yo y mi circumstancia.*
> *I am I and my circumstances."*
>
> —ORTEGA Y GASSET

The bystanders tried to excuse that which cannot be excused. By their inaction, Kitty Genovese's neighbors were morally complicit in her murder. When the situation was manageable, it was ignored. When it was lost, one or two people tried to manage it. Then it was too late.

We see how youngsters enthusiastically grappled with important subjects in a serious way. With words infused with pride, they tried to speak with moral and intellectual integrity. Observing this process year after year provided the same joy as when seeing a rainbow. You can experience equal joy.

I'M NOT SURE!

> *"To see what is in front of one's own nose needs constant struggle."*
>
> —GEORGE ORWELL

A variation on the theme of the bystanders' behavior that led to the death of Kitty Genovese is analyzing how people act in ambiguous situations. First, the ambiguity of the situation has to be credible. Katie said, "Maybe the lady was screaming just to get attention."

"Yeah, right," Sarah blasted. "You could see her crawling on the ground. Get real!"

Several ambiguous scenarios have already been presented, such as little Lorenzo not knowing whether he found an operating loaded pistol; the dad whose child received a box of chemicals; and how some people responded to the braggadocio of Charles Andrew Williams' threat to shoot school classmates.

People can 'what if' something to death, figuratively and literally. At some point, there is what the CIA types call actionable intelligence, when what you have is enough, and a duty to act arises.

> "Nothing will ever be attempted if all possible objections
> must first be overcome."
>
> –DR. JOHNSON, 1759

How can we teach our children to act morally in ambiguous situations? Research demonstrates that people will hesitate to do what they know is right if they believe they don't understand the situation. People fear making mistakes generally. They fear negative consequences if they act and were wrong about the situation. Students confide they often don't do something to avoid embarrassment or feeling foolish or stupid.

Research also suggests that children are unlikely to do what they know is right unless they have definite reasons to believe that they will not incur disapproval.

Here is a delightful student exchange that confronts head on the ambiguity/embarrassment dilemma that was raised indirectly in the Kitty Genovese situation.

Brenda, an articulate fifth grader, made one of the most powerful statements ever spoken in my classes. "Now, let's wake up here! This woman was screaming for help. Who could sit there and let that happen? I would be embarrassed if I didn't do anything."

I asked what would likely have happened where someone did try to help and there had been no attack. Friends in the police have shared many situations where people scream and cry but were not in danger.

Sarah admitted she might feel silly. Here is the key part of the exchange and it contains the moral core of the issue of ambiguity.

Patrick disagreed with Sarah. "I wouldn't feel embarrassed. At least I tried."

Stacey's comment expressed a moral judgment about negative feelings. "So you feel silly. So what?"

Somin offered a mature cost-benefit analysis of feeling foolish. "I'd rather be laughed at than have someone die."

These delightful and affirming comments should not be permitted to create an unrealistic comfort level that our children will always overcome these negative feelings and act morally. These factors are powerful and run deep in the human psyche. The best way I know to reduce the power of these negative forces is to talk about them openly and honestly and repeatedly. Admit that they exist and expose them wherever they are seen.

The teaching strategy for parents is to loop moral analysis into each discussion. Through dialogue parents can de-fang the fear of being wrong and take the sting out of embarrassment by showing that the benefit of acting when you are correct is far greater than the embarrassment from acting when you are wrong. This looping should be done continuously, mindful of Aristotle's admonition that excellence is not an act but a habit. Practice! Practice! Practice! This is how we make our children stronger.

Here's an example of a looping type of discussion. Lauren said that maybe the bystanders thought that someone else was calling the police. Okay, some may have thought that, but so what? If *you* are not calling the police, the possibility that no one else is calling the police should percolate in your noggin. Call them! What's the downside? The police receive another call.

But here's the more profound point to loop in this example: the person that does not act because he thinks someone else will act or did act has transferred his moral power to others. He has made himself morally meaningless. That person has become a bystander in his own life. He is no longer a free-thinking individual. He has become a backboard.

AMBIGUITY AS AN EXCUSE

If you really don't know what's going on—the situation is ambiguous—it might be understandable that you don't know the right thing to do. If you lived, for example, in a college dorm that had a history of prank false fire alarms and an alarm went off at four in the morning, it is understandable that you might not flee the dorm.

Such was the case in Boland Hall dormitory at Seton Hall University in South Orange, New Jersey on January 19, 2000. Except this time two students set the hall on fire. Three students died and many more were injured.

The prudent action is to get out of the building. The downside of remaining inside and there is a fire is worse than the annoyance of leaving the building and learning the alarm was yet another prank.

However, ambiguity has a morally poisonous aspect. Ambiguity can serve as an excuse to justify passivity and the evasion of moral responsibility. The lover's quarrel excuse—if one were to believe it at all –is an example. You can 'maybe this . . . maybe that' to absurdities in the attempt to justify doing nothing. Ambiguity can become a cover for immoral action.

Those who are not inclined to act ethically have powerful incentives to justify their immorality by creating ambiguity or by overemphasizing trivial ambiguities. The coward and the indifferent are heavily invested in finding confusion in what is obvious, such as believing a woman being stabbed is having a lover's quarrel.

A paralysis of analysis can be seductively comforting but it can be unethical. David E. Purpel, in his provocative book, *The Moral & Spiritual Crisis in Education*, crafted a magnificent phrase that captures the moral element of dealing with ambiguity: "The avowal of skepticism without moral commitment, at best, amounts to incompleteness and evasion and, at worst, to irresponsibility and cowardice." It's one of the most morally lucid statements I've read. I give copies to every student.

Mr. Reynolds was skeptical about Charles Andrew Williams' declarations about shooting students but made no effort to learn the truth or to reduce the risk to students in the event that Williams was serious. Lorenzo was skeptical about the pistol but acted heroically despite the ambiguity. Recall the high school student who was uncertain about the seriousness of her friend's threat to commit suicide but informed authorities anyway. Here's the lesson: if you wait for perfect information, you will never do anything and horrible things might happen.

I have taught dozens of classes on the Kitty Genovese murder. The most impressive statement, one so potent I was physically rocked by its intensity, came from Saiya, a diminutive third grade girl at a private school I visited in 1998. We were talking about the ambiguity concept and the moral implications of the 'diffusion of responsibility' theory.

Saiya slowly raised her hand. Her jaw was set firmly. Her little hands quickly clenched into fists, prepared to fight an invisible foe. Her eyes sparkled as if polishing her thoughts. She leaned forward and slowly moved her right arm in a circle. In a mesmerizing, almost other-worldly voice she spat out these words, "It just goes around and around in a circle, round and round, people just following and nobody does anything."

The moment was extraordinary. Her terse words sent shock waves through the classroom. The teacher looked at me in disbelief, as if seeing this child for the first time. Perhaps she had. Once again I was reminded never to underestimate the depth and seriousness of these little children.

THE PASSIVE TENSE

"Death is not the greatest loss in life.
The greatest loss is what dies inside us while we live."

—NORMAN COUSINS

Every student has said that he or she would have acted to save Kitty Genovese if confronted with the same or similar facts. Yet one hundred percent of the bystanders did not. "Why," I asked, "are you so certain you would have behaved more morally than all those people?"

The typical response is something like, "Well, because . . . hmmm . . . I'm not a bad person."

Here's an issue that, to be candid, plagues me. I'll bet that, if on the day before the killing, you described a hypothetical event to those bystanders that was the same as what occurred the next day, every one of them would have said that they would act aggressively and decisively to save the victim. They would have called the police. They would have formed a militia and marched out there to bring her to safety. They would loathe anyone who failed to save her. And they would have meant it!

But they didn't act that way. None of them. Why?

Morton Hunt, in his inspiring book, *The Compassionate Beast*, uses the term 'self-efficacy' to describe the quality of having mastered strategies that give a sense of control over the events in one's life. Self-efficacy means that, more times than not, you are the driver of the car rather than a tire. Self-efficacy means that you can confidently and competently meet life's challenges. It doesn't mean you will always triumph. It means you will do well by any reasonable measure.

Developing competence of any kind strengthens self-efficacy. The greater one's self-efficacy, the greater the probability that a person will take risks to achieve virtue. The person with self-efficacy will pursue more demanding challenges. These concepts were addressed directly in the Competence, Choices and Consequence chapters.

Self-efficacy is cultivated, in part, by teaching moral reasoning skills, by emphasizing character and by viewing the individual as a free-spirited and free-willed individual. Self-efficacy means understanding there will be moments when you need to protect yourself and others. Todd Beamer and Thomas Burnett understood that.

In the Kitty Genovese situation, ordinary citizens were awakened to and confronted with vile behavior they did not anticipate. They had to make decisions. They needed policies for action, not abstract attitudes. They needed the skills to analyze what was right and they needed the self-efficacy to do it. As Kathy Shaidle astutely observed, "When we say 'I don't know what I would do under the same circumstances,' we make cowardice the default position."

While we must always nurture the goodness of human nature, we must always be vigilant to subdue the evil in human nature. A.M. Rosenthal wrote in his book, *Thirty-Eight Witnesses: The Kitty Genovese Case*, "Every man must fear the witness in himself who whispers to close the window."

I don't get caught up in the undertow of how bad society may be. It is irrelevant. I have little influence over society and I figure the average first grader has even less. It wasn't society's job to protect Kitty Genovese. It was the job of the people that chose to watch her die. Even first graders understood that. Just as with liberty and freedom, public safety needs the protection of power. Kitty's neighbors did not exercise their power to save her. Society didn't fail Kitty. People did.

Sadly, the Kitty Genovese circumstances are not isolated. I'm not saying they occur often, but they are not unique. The common element of this cancerous behavior is passivity, the lack of moral action due to indifference. In some instances, indifference combines with the noxious belief that you don't have to get involved because it is someone else's job or responsibility.

I think of the murder of Swedish Foreign Minister, Anna Lindh. She was stabbed to death in the Nordiska Kompaniet department store in Stockholm on September 10, 2003. Dozens of able-bodied bystanders watched from a few feet away as one man attacked her with a knife. Some bystanders said they were waiting for the police to save her. Such an expectation is as immoral as it is absurd. Other examples, equally or more horrific than this one, can easily be found.

This is the way the world ends
This is the way the world ends
This is the way the world ends
Not with a bang but a whimper.

–T.S.ELIOT'S THE HOLLOW MEN

WAVING GOOD BYE

Thinking of those thousands of folks that have waived to me over the decades on my drives to Nebraska, I have an irrepressible confidence that Kitty Genovese would not have died if she had been attacked in any of the towns and hamlets on the way. The neighbors would not have allowed it. They would have saved her. Those waving folks acknowledged a link, a bridge, a connection among strangers. Waving meant involvement. Waving meant we are each other's business. I choose to believe that these folks understood that passivity can have terrible consequences.

This effervescent exchange from my first Kitty Genovese class shows how quickly, enthusiastically and humorously little children can grasp complex relationships. I asked which other person was supposed to help Kitty. James pointed to Phillip. "He was." Phillip jokingly pointed to Sarah. "She was."

Sarah figured out the game. "I get it," she yelled. "We are all are the other person." She got it indeed. To all but yourself, you are the other. That kind of breakthrough brings joy to the heart.

Lessons from the Kitty Genovese tragedy can elevate our children's moral efficacy and character. Dialogues about the tragedy can nurture attitudes that are likely to produce virtuous outcomes. Conversation by conversation, household by household, parents can change society and influence our culture for the better.

The moral child with self-efficacy can thwart and extinguish the mediocrity of spirit that corrodes individuals and turns them into Roosevelt's 'cold and timid souls' and robotic passive bystanders in life's parade. I've tried to cultivate self-efficacy in my classes and in my home. I do not want my children to surrender their humanity. I do not want my children to be one that shuts the window. I expect you don't either.

CHAPTER 21

THE EGRET
AND THE SCORPION
An Allegory about Evil, Reason and Personal Strength

"There's no art to find the mind's construction in the face.
He was a gentleman on whom I built an absolute trust."

–DUNCAN, KING OF SCOTLAND, TO HIS SON, MALCOLM,
REGARDING EXECUTING THE TRAITOROUS THANE OF CAWDOR
MACBETH, ACT 1, SCENE IV

I 'VE PRESENTED MANY TOPICS based on real events and hypothetical dilemmas. This chapter is about an allegory involving a bird and an insect. An allegory is a symbolic narrative, a fable, a representation of an abstract meaning through concrete or material form. We look for lessons in allegories and it is tempting to search for meaning no matter how attenuated, like finding shapes in clouds if you stare at them long enough. Allegories have their limitations but the limitations do not reduce their value.

The egret story is part of that great body of mythology, the world of fables, where humans create pictures of themselves mirrored through other objects or creatures, real or mythical. Trial lawyers are fond of saying facts are swell but stories sell. The many levels of this allegorical story sell easily understood lessons that can elevate children's moral reasoning.

THE EGRET AND THE SCORPION

Once upon a time a fire burned ferociously on a tropical land and threatened all life. Animals and insects fled to a river to try to escape certain destruction. Birds flew to other lands. A scorpion, which couldn't swim or fly, approached a majestic egret about to take flight and asked, "Would you carry me across the sea?"

"I'm concerned," the egret said. "You're a scorpion."

Acknowledging the egret's wariness, the scorpion said, "I can't escape the fire without you. Why would I harm you? It's not in my interest."

The egret considered the scorpion's words as the flames leaped toward the water's edge. "Okay," the egret said. "Hang on to my leg."

As the egret flew toward the safety of nearby land, excruciating pain surged through one of its legs and into its chest, paralyzing its muscles. The egret dropped like a stone. Just before falling into the water, the egret asked, "Why did you sting me? Now we will both die!"

"That's my nature," the scorpion replied coolly. "I'm a scorpion."

WELL, WHAT DO YOU KNOW?

Ask your child the point of the allegory. Answers will be thrown at you like Frisbees. "Don't trust scorpions." "The bird didn't stand up for itself and died." "You have to be careful who you trust." These insightful answers should prompt us to discuss the allegory to enhance our children's reasoning. But beyond these initial responses are many more dimensions worth examining, as if digging into a mine to explore deeper seams of thought. Hours of enlightening conversations await you.

A flurry of issues appears: the egret's moral dilemma, considerations of trust, dealing with persuasive rhetoric, making a risk assessment, the moral duty to confront and, if appropriate, change one's nature. All these issues intimately relate to our children's lives. The first level is, to continue the mining metaphor, closest to the surface and easiest to identify: should the egret have tried to save the scorpion by allowing it to hang on its leg? A subtle variation of that question is whether the egret was morally *obligated* to save the scorpion? I will treat the wisdom of the action and the morality of the action as interchangeable.

We know about the duty to help others—I will include the bird and the bug as others—and the duty to protect one's self.

Immediately obvious is the egret's ethical dilemma or conflict between Autonomy and Sanctity of Life.

As always, I begin by listing the facts. What was known by each participant when the scorpion's plea for help was made? I don't know how much the average egret knows about the nature of scorpions. Perhaps it logged on to *www.everythingyouneedtoknowaboutscorpions.edu* and got up to speed on the 1400 or so recognized species of these little Arachnida. This egret evidently knew enough to express a concern for its own safety.

The most significant facts listed by my students were:

- The scorpion could not escape the fire without assistance
- The egret could escape the fire on its own
- The egret knew the scorpion was dangerous
- The scorpion knew the egret knew it was dangerous
- The scorpion knew the egret's values
- The scorpion used rational arguments to persuade the egret that it would be safe

All the students thought the egret was foolish. All said that the egret should not have carried the scorpion. All the students thought the egret had no duty to save the scorpion. One student raised a provocatively creative analogy: if a bank robber got a flat tire on his car trying to escape after robbing a bank, would a witness have a moral duty to help him put on a spare tire?

Marvelous! We thought not.

We owe our children the obligation to be practical. To argue that the egret was morally obligated to help the scorpion is to say, putting it bluntly, that it had to risk dying in order to prove it was moral. Such an analysis is morally and intellectually absurd.

The egret didn't have a duty to save the scorpion because the scorpion was a threat to the egret's life. The egret was not morally obligated to accept the scorpion's implied suggestion that it wouldn't hurt the egret. So far, so good, but the topic is not exhausted, although you might feel that way after a spirited discussion.

Many students said initially that the egret was stupid for trusting the scorpion, that is, for being persuaded by the scorpion's argument. "The egret didn't think things through," many said. Sam argued "the egret knew it was dealing with a scorpion, and he knew that scorpions were dangerous, so it was a stupid risk."

Erik thought the students were being unfair to the egret. His argued it was too easy to judge the egret given that we knew what happened at the end. "The scorpion was a smooth talker," Erik said. "It was reasonable for the egret to believe the scorpion. The scorpion made a good case." Erik paused, massaging his words. "Why would the scorpion make up the lie? It made no sense. If the scorpion wanted to die, he could have died in the fire."

That's dazzling reasoning, especially for a third grader.

Note how fifth grader Izzy was able to make distinctions between competing perspectives. "It depends on the point of view. From the scorpion's point of view, the egret was very reasonable." In Aristotelian terms, the scorpion knew its audience and counted on the egret being reasonable and moral and not too analytical.

You can figure out with your child the various outcomes the scorpion could have chosen: perishing in the fire and not harming the egret; causing both to perish in the water; surviving itself and still harming the egret by stinging the egret as it was about to land; or, most happily, having both find safe shelter.

Recall the words 'shrewd and purposeful' used by the social worker to describe James Gipson offering lingerie to women on Denver's Sixteenth Street Mall. Gipson and Melissa Todd were bumblers compared to this savvy scorpion. Note the scorpion's rhetorical skill for deception and manipulation and for ingratiating itself with the egret through clever dishonesty.

The scorpion said it was not in its interest to harm the egret. Well, was it? What was the scorpion's interest? How do we figure out answers to these relevant questions? The scorpion knowingly used the word 'interest' in a way that would not occur to the egret. Each understanding was different. The scorpion knew the difference. The egret didn't.

That's why the scorpion chose the word 'interest' in the first place. That's why it was able to manipulate the bird. It's fun, at least for me, to meticulously analyze words. The exercise with your child will strengthen his or her thinking skills.

In all fairness, it seems the egret could not know this 'interest' analysis at the time it had to decide whether to help the scorpion. Thus, Erik's analysis was persuasive. That didn't mean the egret had to try to save the scorpion. We are just analyzing the wisdom of options. The egret's best strategy was to play the percentages and leave the scorpion. If the egret tried to save it, the egret had a moral duty to itself to be fully been aware of the unhappy consequence if it guessed wrong.

The scorpion's words remind me of the deceitful rhetoric based on un-shared values spewed by Michael Corleone at the end of the first Godfather movie. Michael confronts Carlo for traitorously facilitating the Barzini syndicate's killing his older brother, Santino.

"You have to answer for Santino," Michael tells Carlo. With skillful precision Michael addresses Carlo's well-deserved fears. "Come on, Carlo. Don't be afraid. You think I'd make my sister a widow? I'm Godfather to your son. You're out of the family business. That's your punishment." Carlo was relieved. Five minutes later he was garroted to death.

Michael's is a tough rhetorical act to follow but the scorpion's words merit a high mark. Both understood and addressed and eliminated the fears of their target audience in a rational logical manner. The main difference between the egret and Carlo was, of course, that the egret had a choice. Carlo didn't.

Here's the point worth making: it can be dangerous—in this case, it was fatal to the egret—to project one's own values onto someone else. The egret transposed its morality onto the scorpion. The egret made the reasonable assumption that the scorpion wanted to live. The assumption was false. That's why, in Susan's words, "The scorpion was a careful liar." It had mastered Aristotle's pronouncement about rhetoric: persuade by using the best available argument.

One vital lesson from this allegory, then, is that projecting your values onto another can blind you to the other's values. The egret and the scorpion shared no common values: not for truth or for life or for trust. It is difficult to grasp and uncomfortable to accept that others might reject your values. More difficult yet is to accept that the values you cherish can make you vulnerable.

Harvard professor Ruth Visser created the term *moral solipsism* to describe the state of mind where a person is preoccupied with its own behavior to the exclusion of the others. The failure to see the world through the eyes of the other person—its values and goals and nature—can be both arrogant and fatally self-indulgent.

The values of the egret caused it to self-limit its understanding of the scorpion. Generosity of spirit may be a virtue at times but at other times it may be viewed as a weakness, as a failure of will and resolve and as an invitation for exploitation.

Analyzing the scorpion's use of words, we can reasonably conclude that it understood its victim far better than its victim understood the scorpion. Recall Fred Schuman's words at the beginning of Chapter 6: "Be cynical or you'll never learn anything." This allegory illustrates that if one is not cynical, one might die.

IN US WE TRUST

The trust issue demands exploration in depth. One cannot get through life without trust. We tend to trust our doctors and lawyers and our parents but we also tend to trust a whole bunch of other people, probably without giving the matter too much thought. We trust that the person selling hotdogs and pretzels on the street corner by the baseball field hasn't poisoned them. We trust that the mechanics that fixed our cars didn't fill our gas tanks with mud. We trust that drivers will stop at red lights. If we didn't, we would not move.

Trust involves risk, vulnerability, uncertainty and probability. Children must learn how to evaluate these factors. We trust the hotdog vender because we assume it reached the rational conclusion that poisoning its customers would discourage sales. We trust that other drivers will stop at red lights because it is in their interest to do so.

We can be wrong in each instance, of course, but generally it's a reasonable bet. In other situations, trust becomes a murkier predicament—politicians, credit card hawkers and sub-prime lenders come to mind—where interests do not necessarily coincide with our own or with the interests of many of us.

Trust is a powerful force in your child's life as it is in anyone's life. People anguish over trust—who to trust, when to trust, how much to trust. It is vital, therefore, to discuss trust with children in direct unambiguous terms so they can develop the confidence and strength to judge when to give their trust.

As Lexi said, "Even if you trust someone, you still have to watch out for yourself."

Many students spoke about trust, such as the egret should not have trusted the scorpion or you shouldn't trust strangers or you should get to know someone before you trust that person or an insect.

In ethical terms, Ellie correctly pointed out that Autonomy gave the egret the right to control its life and to protect itself—Autonomy may trump Sanctity of Life. Thus, self preservation may morally limit trust.

The prudent person will acknowledge that trust can be used as an excuse for not pursuing one's own interests. It can be used as cover for weakness, irresponsibility, self-imposed ignorance, naiveté or plain old stupidity.

Countless times I and my divorce lawyer colleagues have experienced situations where one spouse 'trusted' the other to its detriment—finding out too late that credit card bills were out of control; a mortgage had been taken without the knowledge of one spouse; all savings had been depleted. Other examples may be more hurtful and on and on it goes.

Trust is a choice, and as I discussed earlier, prudent and moral choices require information, analysis and strength of character. Parents must teach their children to be judicious with their trust because trust does not exempt them from responsibility.

Nature Is as Nature Does

O most pernicious woman!
O villain, villain, smiling, damn'd villain!
My tables, – meet it is I set it down,
That one may smile, and smile, and be a villain;
At least I'm sure it may be so in Denmark.

–HAMLET ACT 1, SCENE V

I found intriguing and perplexing that a few students said the scorpion was not evil or was not at fault because it was acting according to its nature. I don't know much about a scorpion's nature. Certainly the egret was ignorant of it. This idea deserves careful analysis because it deals with justifying and appeasing evil, two of the greatest injustices.

We have no evidence regarding how much, if at all, a scorpion can influence its nature but it's kind of fun to speculate. We know the scorpion controlled his nature enough to craft a brilliantly persuasive argument to deceive the egret. We know he was in control enough decide when to sting the egret. We know the scorpion was unconcerned about living.

I'll bet, however, that if you discuss this point, your child will quickly discern the moral danger or moral hazard that arises if the scorpion is given a pass on its moral duties based on its so-called nature. Recall Blaise Pascal's statement quoted earlier. "Evil is never done so thoroughly or so well as when it is done with a good conscience." If one is acting according to one's nature, then a good conscience can be justified and the vilest evil may result.

I am pleased to write that my students—even the youngest—did not find persuasive the argument that the scorpion's 'nature' excused it from moral responsibility. The students offered evidence to prove that the scorpion knew its nature—clever argument and when to sting as mentioned above. They judged the morality of the scorpion's nature. Joey got it right when he said, "But if his nature is to kill things, then it's an evil nature!"

The students concluded, significantly, that since it knew its nature to be evil, the scorpion had a moral duty not to act on its nature.

Char picked up on this vital point and ramped it up several notches by making a profound moral judgment. "Well, maybe it's his nature but he should learn to fight his nature." If his nature is evil, she argued, the scorpion has a moral duty to change it.

The duty to fight our nature when it conflicts with virtue is the basis of all morality. Virtuous self-discipline is the foundation for moral behavior.

When discussing this allegory, there is a tendency to think only in terms of what the egret should have done—flown off and left the scorpion or tried to save it—and whether it was foolish or wise or moral or bird-brained. Lest we forget, moral obligation is a two-way street. The scorpion had moral duties also, and it is disingenuous to ignore the scorpion's violation of its moral obligations to the egret.

Brandon hit a metaphoric grand slam homerun when he said ignoring the scorpion's moral duties because of its nature "is letting it out of its responsibility."

When evil is excused or trivialized or appeased because it is attributed to one's nature, the cost of doing evil is reduced. When the cost of evil is diminished, the motivation to reduce evil behavior diminishes. Referring back to the Consequences chapter, when the cost of something is reduced, you get more of it. Accepting evil as a matter of one's nature will lead to more evil.

DRAWING CONCLUSIONS

One of my more creative moments occurred the second or third time I talked about the egret allegory. I confess my creativity was accidental. I was trying to be funny and something insightful happened. It's good to be lucky! I was talking about whether it was possible for the egret to carry the scorpion in a way that could protect itself from a sting. The students offered lots of ideas, some of which raised imaginative points.

Could the egret hold the scorpion in its claw so tightly the scorpion could not get free? Were the feathers on the egret's back thick enough to protect it from a sting? But even if so, could the egret prevent the scorpion from roaming around its body? Some students wondered if there was enough blood flow in the egret's spindly legs to transport venom to its heart or other important organs if the scorpion stung its leg.

In a spontaneous and rare artistic flourish, I advanced to the blackboard, chalk in hand, intent upon inserting visual clarity into my verbal torrent. I drew a rough approximation of a bird with an insect in one of its claws. I stepped away from the board, studied the fruit of my artistry and it hit me...boom!

I had an epiphany, not quite as eureka-like as when Archimedes took that famous bath and soaked his bathroom but it was a new insight that catapulted the conversation to a higher level of analysis.

Maybe you or your child can guess what insight developed from my inelegant drawing. I returned to the blackboard and drew a long slender branch clutched in the egret's claws. Wow! The conversation changed dramatically.

The branch was a new fact, and as I previously wrote, as the facts change, the morality of the circumstances changes. Not only was the branch a new fact. It was a game changer. Think about the implications, factually and morally. The egret could use a branch to transport the scorpion. The branch gave the egret options it previously did not have and those options had moral implications.

Figuring out that it could use a branch to transport the scorpion was a display of moral competence—finding alternatives to resolve a problem. The egret could offer the scorpion a choice: get on the branch and I will risk carrying you to safety. However, if you make any move toward my leg, buddy, I'll drop you like a hot potato and you will fall, probably to your death. If you want to live, it's up to you.

The branch was morally liberating. The egret no longer had to surrender power to the scorpion in order to act virtuously. Now the egret could deal with the scorpion on its terms and not be subjected to the whim and nature of the scorpion. Third grader Maddie eloquently stated, "Maybe that's the way scorpions are, but the egret doesn't have to put up with it." By thinking creatively and competently, more choices developed.

By using the branch, the egret could force the scorpion to be responsible for its own life in a way that would not harm the egret. Well, almost, as many students quickly pointed out. This branch idea is based on the assumption that the egret could maintain visual contact with the scorpion and could drop the branch before the scorpion could inflict any harm.

Whether the egret could or could not do those things may be fine debating points but their significance is dwarfed by the topic's ability to encourage detailed reasoning by the students.

It can be self-destructive to base choices on fantasies and hopes and wishful thinking, such as hoping the scorpion would be moral. The branch gave the egret a tangible tool for moral action while reducing the risk of harm to itself. Did that mean that the egret was morally obligated to carry the scorpion with the branch? I don't know. It's a close call. But the answer doesn't matter. Thinking and analyzing matter. This simple conversation provides a template for handling problems in a way that allows children to be ethical toward others while also protecting their interests.

"I don't know the key to success,
but the key to failure is trying to please everybody."

–BILL COSBY

REASON AND ITS LIMITATIONS

"Talk sense to a fool
and he calls you foolish."

–EURIPIDES

Most of us value reason. Most of us want to be reasonable. Most of us also know—certainly lawyers and politicians know—that a speaker must appear reasonable to its audience no matter how unreasonable or dishonest or bigoted the speaker's presentation.

We may want to persuade our audience through bias, passion and lies, but we generally don't want our audiences to believe they are being influenced by bias, passions and lies. Audiences, at least most of them, want to believe they are being influenced by reason, no matter how delusional they choose to be.

I begin with some immutable truths. You cannot reason with a person whose position is not the product of reason. To be moved by rational argument, a person has to be open to rational discourse. And for rational discourse to exist, a discussion must be based upon shared beliefs and values. It is not enough to speak the same language. There must be shared assumptions and premises.

We saw that the egret and the scorpion did not share the same beliefs and values. We saw that differences could be so microscopic that even the word 'interest' could be interpreted in a diametrically opposite way. We saw, as Lauren pointed out, "The scorpion knew what he was doing. That's why he had to be clever when it spoke to the egret about getting a ride." The cleverness of the scorpion was using the egret's beliefs and values to the detriment of the egret.

Ask your child if she has ever seen anyone use this type of persuasive technique. I'm sure she has. Ben described the time a panhandler approached his mother and pleaded for money as she parked her car. He needed it for transportation to go home to visit his wife and children. Motivated by empathy and compassion, and perhaps guilt, Ben's mother gave him several dollars. They both watched as the panhandler promptly ambled into a liquor store. The panhandler used the mother's values—family, home, compassion—to manipulate her.

Just as did the panhandler, the scorpion spoke in the language of need, of mutual interest, the value of life, the desire to survive, all of which were calculated to appeal to the egret's sense of decency and morality and, perhaps, to its guilt. The result was that the scorpion used the egret's values to kill it.

Allegories may be metaphors about life's issues but they are useful only to the extent that they teach lessons worth learning. This allegory offers several such lessons. A child that learns only "don't trust scorpions" has not learned anything of practical value. With such rudderless rhetoric they will just lope along as if on the prairie without a horse.

More to the point, telling a child not to trust scorpions is quite unhelpful unless the child is also taught to identify scorpions in the first place and then taught how to handle them once they are identified. We do these things by making our children more competent.

Your children will meet scorpions, just as you and your friends have. Think of the clean cut young man with that boy-next-door look that bombed the Alfred P. Murrah Federal Building in downtown Oklahoma City; the charming handsome lawyer that became murderous Ted Bundy; the polite immigrant men that ate hamburgers and spent time at strip clubs and then flew jets into the World Trade Center; the cute high school boys that massacred more than a dozen classmates at Columbine High School and the 'friends' that our children meet on Internet chat rooms that result in damaging and sometimes lethal encounters.

How do we protect those we love? One guiding lesson is teaching children not to confuse kindness with weakness. Acting out of weakness does not make the action kind. The egret may have been motivated by kindness, but another and more persuasive explanation for its behavior was that it was too weak to stand up and say 'no' to the scorpion. Some students said the egret was stupid, but others thought the egret was weak rather than stupid. The argument goes that the egret knew what was right to protect itself but was too weak to do it.

Kindness is an affirmative act of will, freely chosen. Kindness is an act of strength. Weakness comes from intimidation, fear, lack of will and submission. A child confuses one with the other at its peril.

Weakness often is cowardice masquerading as decency. Weakness invites danger. Weakness deters confronting the scorpions because people do not want to confront their weakness. Yet, only vigorous moral strength can reduce a child's susceptibility to the scorpion's whims.

Our young children are capable of appreciating the distinction. "The bird got itself killed," Robert exclaimed, "because it did not have the courage to stand up for itself." The egret risked death—indeed, did die—rather than not be nice. "Being nice," Izzy said, "is kind of a weakness, but it can be a strength. You have to decide when to use your kindness."

We cripple our children if we fail to teach the limits of caring and nice because they will not develop the grit to make tough choices. Imagine if little Lorenzo had given a classmate the pistol because he wanted to be nice. If a friend were shot, I wouldn't be surprised if one of Lorenzo's thoughts would have been, "I should have been stronger."

A concern I have about using allegories as teaching devices is the tendency to reduce complex issues to clichés and platitudes. Decoding allegories can require a lot of effort. I hope my effort in the classrooms reduces your effort to have the discussions this allegory deserves.

Although the nature of scorpions eludes me, I believe *humans* can change their nature. This ability presents a practical limitation to this allegory. None of us *must* be a scorpion. If we are, it is by choice. Then we must fight our nature and strive to perfect it. Becoming morally stronger is the best way I know to accomplish those epic tasks. This little allegory can help children win that fight.

CHAPTER 22

A GIFT AND THE SUPER BOWL

*"More people have talent than discipline.
That's why discipline pays better."*

—MIKE PRICE

YEARS BEFORE JOHN ELWAY, quarterback for the Denver Broncos football team, led his team to the first of two consecutive Super Bowl victories, I read in a local newspaper about a sports writer asking Elway to explain his extraordinary success. Elway replied modestly: "God gave me the gift to play football, and football is something people just happen to find entertaining."

I felt a jolt. Elway had given me a jewel of a discussion topic.

In the previous chapter I showed how a story about a bird and a bug could bloom into conversations drenched in moral significance. In this chapter I show how a throw-away line from a superstar athlete can explode like fireworks into delightful yet meaningful conversations with children.

Ask your child if Elway's success was the consequence of a gift. If you don't know who Elway is or if you don't care to talk about him—you might be a Packers or Falcons fan—just fill in the superstar athlete of your choice and pretend he or she made the statement.

I'll relate some class discussions about what gifts Elway *had*. Remember, we're talking about His Highness of the Huddle, The Sultan of Spiral, The Caliph of Comebacks, The Sovereign of Scramble. Obviously Elway had enormous natural physical talent. Who's kidding whom? I could do sit-ups, lift weights and eat broccoli and soy meat substitutes until the coal in my neighbor's furnace turned into diamonds and I could never be a starting quarterback on even a decent college team.

My students said that Elway was big and strong. He's a great runner for a quarterback, has a powerful arm, is good at reading defenses and is tough. All true, but were these qualities truly the foundation for his greatness? They didn't hurt, of course, but I didn't think they were the true gift. I implored my students to ponder how Elway used his talent. Light bulbs popped on in their minds. They began to identify character traits and mental qualities.

"He works hard," Jason said. "He trains a lot," Shelly yelled. "He studies the films and gets prepared." "He wants to win!" "He's not afraid of getting hurt," a student shouted. "Of course he's afraid," another retorted, "but he plays hard anyway."

Sharon captured the essential requirement for greatness. "He doesn't give up. That's why he's so good in the fourth quarter." Ellie added to the list an extraordinary characteristic I did not expect to be expressed by a young child. "He learns from his mistakes."

"Aha!" as Inspector Clouseau would say. "Now we're getting somewhere!" These qualities—learning from mistakes, discipline, study, playing hard—made Elway into a champion more than muscles and speed and a strong arm. He attained excellence the same ways character and conscience and moral reasoning are developed: through discipline, effort, will and by following Aristotle's principle that excellence is not an act but a habit.

> *"Everyone has the will to win.*
> *What's far more important is having the will to prepare to win."*
>
> –Bobby Knight

THAT WHICH YOU CALL A GIFT BY ANY OTHER NAME

> *"Talent is never enough. With few exceptions,*
> *the best players are the hardest workers."*
>
> –Magic Johnson

"A gift," Jerome said, "is something someone gives to you. You get it for nothing." One receives a gift without regard to work, sacrifice or merit—a birthday gift, some money from grandma, an inheritance. Elway said that his extraordinary achievements were the results of a gift. Ask your child if he was correct. At this point, she will probably say 'no.'

Elway certainly didn't get something for nothing. He worked hard, elevated his strength and knowledge of the game and displayed courage. Lance Armstrong, seven-time winner of the Tour de France said, "The winner of the Tour de France is the one that can best handle pain."

Dealing with pain is not a gift. Being alone in the weight room with cold metal plates, far from the cheering fans and enduring agony and exhaustion are the consequences of will and mental discipline. They are not gifts. Transcending failure is not a gift.

Elway had the discipline to achieve the success he desired. Recall one of the definitions from the Choices chapter: 'It's not what you want. It's what you want more.' "It's always easier to watch television than to practice," Annie, my daughter, said. "But if you want to do well, you have to practice."

In the inspirational book, *Mind Gym: An Athlete's Guide to Inner Excellence*, authors Gary Mack and David Casstevens share this conversation between basketball star Kevin Johnson and the school janitor. As a teenager, Johnson went to the gym every evening to practice. One evening the janitor said to him, "Kevin, it's Saturday night. Why aren't you at parties like everybody else?"

"Parties," Johnson replied, "won't take me where I want to go."

Margot understood Kevin's point. "Going to parties is fun but winning is more fun. You have to do things that aren't fun if you want to win."

One cannot over emphasize the motivation component of Elway's character. Thank back to the Hamilton 'fruit of genius' discussion in the Competence chapter. Crediting great achievement to a gift, just as to genius, implies that there was achievement without great effort. Hamilton would have curled a sneering upper lip at such a suggestion. Those that don't want to work as hard as Elway are pleased to attribute his stunning success to a gift.

Remember ideas have consequences. One consequence of the idea that success is the result of a gift or the fruit of genius is that the motivation to excel will be reduced. Damian, a fifth grader, understood the deficiency in that reasoning. "Only when you work as hard as the natural athlete will be you know if the natural athlete is better."

Attributing success to luck is another variation of the 'gift' and 'fruit of genius' explanations for success. Luck, it is said, is where preparation meets opportunity. One can create an environment that is conducive to luck but generally, luck comes from the whim of fate, not strategic effort. Luck, exists, of course, and as a general rule, it's better to have good luck than to have bad luck.

I share one Olympic gold medal winner's analysis of luck. Several years ago I attended a luncheon at an international sporting goods convention. The guest speaker was Launi Meili, a young woman who looked like one of Raphael's cherubs. Launi had won the gold medal in the 100-meter small bore rifle competition at the 1992 Olympics summer games in Barcelona, Spain.

At the end of her talk, somewhere between the salad and my last bite of cheesecake, she gathered her notes, made the standard farewell statement, "Well, I wish luck to you all" and took a step from the podium. Then she stopped, frozen like the deer in the headlight. She turned to the audience and said, "That's not right. I don't wish you luck. Luck has nothing to do with it. You work at practice every day. Every shot must be a quality shot. Then maybe you will succeed."

My students understood the profound relationship between luck and accountability expressed in Launi's comment. "You don't have responsibility if you believe you're just not lucky," Adam said, brilliantly grasping the psychology of relying on luck. "It's like it's not your fault if you don't win or do well."

I am reminded of basketball superstar Michael Jordan's remark: "Success isn't something you chase. It's something you have to put forth the effort for constantly. Then maybe it'll come when you least expect it. Most people don't understand that."

Launi and Michael J are saying, and they are not alone, that practice does *not* make perfect. Only *perfect* practice makes perfect.

If your practice is sloppy or undisciplined, practice will make you worse.

During Denver's oil boom days in the early 1980's, one of the most popular phrases of the good ole boys in the 'awl biniz' was, "The more I drill, the luckier I get." They had tapped into a fundamental truth. My dentist says the same thing.

"In school they told me 'Practice makes perfect.'
And then they told me 'Nobody's perfect.'
So I stopped practicing."

–STEVEN WRIGHT

A GAME WITHIN A GAME

"When all is said and done, usually more is said than done."

–LOU HOLTZ, NOTRE DAME FOOTBALL COACH

Mark Schlereth is one of the most extraordinary people I've had the pleasure to meet. He was an All-Pro and Super Bowl lineman for the Denver Broncos and is now a successful television and radio sports personality. He is unfairly handsome, witty and modest and obsessed with self-improvement. During two lunches with me and my son, Erik, Mark shared his keen insights into world-class athletes.

"The successful athlete is ruthlessly analytical of his or her performance and training." Mark explained that an athlete cannot improve without self-critiquing his performance. The successful athlete must know how to process information in order to measure performance and be able to measure whether improvement occurred.

"If you keep doing what you've been doing,
you'll keep getting what you've gotten."

–SASHA COHEN, OLYMPIC SILVER MEDAL ICE SKATING CHAMPION,

2006 TORINO, ITALY

Mark has battled dyslexia longer than he has battled defensive linemen. To deal with that handicap, he crafted learning strategies in school—perfect verbatim note taking and memorization—to succeed academically and to deflect the taunting and ridicule hurled at him by classmates and, lamentably, by teachers.

During his football career Mark underwent twenty-four surgeries on his knees. Before many games the pain was so intense he could barely walk. I asked how he transcended pain to perform at Super Bowl levels. As he did with dyslexia, Mark developed success strategies for football, which he called 'creating games within games.'

Mark created small games and then developed strategies to win them. "I wanted to see how much I could put myself through to perform at a high level, even when the suture holes in my knees were oozing blood." His game was seeing if he could ignore the hurt for just one more play and to make one more perfect block. Then he would do it again and again and again, until he retired with several Super Bowl rings.

Another of Mark's games was seeing how well he could self-correct flaws in his skills and weaknesses. Every football movement was broken down into smaller moments and each was evaluated—block a little higher, hold the block another third of a second, lift with the legs rather than with the back. These finesse points allowed Mark to win his games within games.

Self-examination and self-correction are two of Mark's key strategies. "Most athletes are very critical of their own performances," he said. "They are motivated by the fear of not performing at a high level." Super stars are generally the most intensely self-critical athletes. They never stop trying to improve. Winning is oh so yesterday! Today is a blank slate with new challenges.

Mark could have exploited unending excuses to justify not doing well. Why didn't he yield, I asked? His reply drew upon the moral dimension of discipline and effort. "It's all a character issue. I guess you do it for pride, to see if you really can. It's a matter of honor."

MIND CONTROL

"Competitive golf is played on a five inch course;
the space between your ears."

–BOBBY JONES

David Denniston was a nationally ranked swimmer—he holds a 2005 world relay record with Michael Phelps—before snapping his spine in a freak sledding crash a few years ago. Wheelchair bound, he refused to surrender his dreams. He participated as a swimmer in the 2008 summer Paralympic Games in Beijing, China. He is now a coach for the United States Paralympic swim team. Possessing unbounded energy, an unrelenting smile and a gritty will, David continues to be a competitive swimmer, a motivational lecturer and a dedicated worker with disabled veterans.

With riveting forcefulness David spoke to my class at Ebert Polaris in the spring of 2009. His message was as direct as it was poignant. "You must learn to control what you are able to control," he told my fifth graders. "You can't control how much your opponents train. You can't control whether a teammate will get a cramp or mess up a turn. But you can control your training, your preparation and your mind. And that's what you must do."

Control results from self-measurement, introspection, humility and will. His moral framework is based on the duties of an autonomous free-spirited individual. David's illuminating closing statement blazed like a comet across the darkened heavens. "Each of you has the obligation to take ownership and responsibility for your own self-improvement. It's not up to your coach or your parents or your fans. It's up to you!"

My students have been uplifted by the stories of these outstanding athletes. Your children will also. As David wheeled his chair out of the classroom, Armand walked up to me and said softly, "I guess I've been kind of lazy. He makes me want to try harder." That's a successful day at the office!

"Few things are impossible to diligence and skill;
great works are performed not by strength but by perseverance."

–DR. SAMUEL JOHNSON

WINNING THE BATTLE IN THE MIND

"Baseball is 90% mental.
The other half is physical."

–YOGI BERRA

Ask any athlete and most if not all will tell you that the mind quits before the body does. Generally, the body is tougher than the mind. Thus, one of the hallmarks of great athletes is mental toughness. Peter McLaughlin, co-author of *Mentally Tough: The Principles of Winning at Sports Applied to Winning in Business*, explained the components of mental toughness.

"You have to confront yourself. You have to deal with pain. You have to address your weaknesses. You have to do stuff you don't like. You have to do things that are not fun. And you have to keep doing it."

The mentally tough person questions how to become better and then does what needs to be done to become better. Asthma-plagued Amy Van Dyken, the first American woman to win four gold medals in a single Olympics, bluntly defined the performance standard for doing better: "Whatever it takes."

Imagine Elway scrambling out of the pocket. Defenders paid gazillions of dollars to grind him into paté on the turf are rushing him like locomotives. He knows he's going to get slammed. Only one question pounds his brain: "How much do I want to complete that pass?"

"It ain't how hard you can hit," Rocky Balboa said. "It's how hard a hit you can take." Elway got knocked down a lot. He had the will to get up every time. That's no gift!

"Mental toughness is an attitude," Peter McLaughlin told me. "It's confidence derived from knowing that you can succeed. It is the psychology of rising to the occasion." I met Jason Elam at the home of sculptor Steve LeBlanc, a mutual friend. Jason was the All-Pro kicker who played for the Denver Broncos and then the Atlanta Falcons. Jason explained how he develops mental toughness. "You don't practice until you get it right. You practice until you can't get it wrong." Few collections of words have greater relevance to success.

Narrow focus and iron will are the off-spring of mental toughness. During the 2009 American Football Conference championship game against the Tennessee Titans, Ray Lewis, linebacker for the Baltimore Ravens, yelled one command to his teammates: "Beat your man! Beat your man! Beat your man!"

Even the greatest athletes make mistakes, of course. The hallmarks of the great athlete, Peter McLauglin explained, is how the athlete behaves *after* the mistake. The mentally tough athlete blocks out all negative thought. The mentally tough athlete generates an impervious concentration that banishes everything unnecessary to accomplish the successful task.

Marjorie "Missy" Foy had been one of the nation's elite women's marathon runners. By only a few seconds she missed qualifying for a place on the U.S. women's Olympic team. Such an achievement qualifies her as a remarkable athlete. Considerably more remarkable is that she attained such physically demanding excellence as a Type I Juvenile Diabetic.

Missy must deal with blood sugar levels and carbohydrate intake every time she moves. An error could cause her to lapse into a coma right on the course. I asked how she handled all those distracting concerns, some life-threatening. Missy replied without hesitation. "I will not allow any negativity around me. I simply won't tolerate it." In sharp emphatic tones that made my telephone buzz, she added, "I can do anything."

BOXER: Doctor, I broke my nose in two places. Can you help me?
DOCTOR: Don't go back to those places!

MENTAL TOUGHNESS AND OPTIMISM

"They can because they think they can."

–VIRGIL, THE AENEID

The Denver Broncos were heavily favored to win the AFC Divisional playoffs against the Jacksonville Jaguars on January 4, 1997. The game didn't go as the Broncos planned. Their offensive line and their defensive secondary were shredded like mozzarella cheese for a pizza. I watched the game on TV.

After the game an air of stunned devastation permeated the Broncos locker room. Reporters inside asked players such probing questions as, "What went wrong?"

Elway had to endure such silliness. He was seated on a bench, shirt off. The physical brutality of the game showed on his face. His disappointment could not be masked. A reporter asked Elway a question I thought was uniquely moronic, something like "Well, John, what's the future for you?" Keep in mind the sweat on the players hadn't even dried and they had been pummeled like piñatas moments before.

Elway's response transcended the physical realm. It opened a window to his soul. In a monotone impassive voice, Elway answered slowly and respectfully. "I'll start training in the weight room in a few weeks. I feel pretty good. We have a great line, we have great running backs, our defense is solid. We should be competitive next year."

I was stunned! Elway had just been put through a meat grinder, his team had suffered a total failure of expectations and he's infused with optimism! His mind was already in the next season! This game—this devastating loss—was behind him. He's analyzing next season's team. He's focusing on its strengths. He's making positive judgments. He's preparing to work immediately. Elway was physically beaten but he was not mentally beaten.

The next season the Broncos won the Super Bowl. And the year after.

As a matter of full disclosure, by the way, I inform that I don't know John Elway. The only time I spoke with him was when I happened to meet him and his dad in December, 1993 at a shopping mall in south Denver. With stone-faced seriousness I said he looked a lot like the Denver Broncos quarterback.

"I hear that a lot," Elway said with an unguarded smile.

For reasons that escaped me, I asked the older man with him if he were John's father. Chuckling, the man replied that he was Walter Matthau. I took that response as permission to have some fun. "What a coincidence," I exclaimed! "I'm Felix Unger, (from The Odd Couple) and I'm sick and tired of you making a mess of the apartment!" We laughed and I hugged him. He was John's dad. Meeting him was a pleasure. He passed on a few years ago.

By the way, since I'm writing about Super Bowl quarterbacks, I believe that New Orleans Saints quarterback and Super Bowl XLIV MVP Drew Brees broke a Super Bowl record for most kisses given by a player to his child after the game. Drew's display of love for his infant son stirred my soul.

Optimism is a key aspect of mental toughness. Negative emotions, Peter McLaughlin informed, are a survival instinct. They tend to help us flee threatening situations. They don't, however, promote productivity or achievement.

The optimistic athlete believes that his actions will result in success. Of course, this optimistic mindset must have factual support and be based on reality and not delusion. The distinguishing factor of the optimist is that he can 'explain' events in a way that justifies optimism and a positive attitude. Elway redressed negative events— we didn't block well—by changing his mindset to something positive—we are capable of blocking better.

"Pessimists," Peter McLaughlin continued, "see a good event as a matter of chance that is not expected to continue. Optimists have explanations to justify seeing good events as permanent, as something expected as a consequence of their effort and of things they can control. Bad events are just temporary." This optimism is derived from what Peter calls 'positive psychology.' One form of it is that "all else being equal or close to equal, the athlete that believes in his or her skills will out perform the athlete that does not."

Walter Davis had been an All Pro National Basketball Association player for the Phoenix Suns and the Denver Nuggets. He graciously spoke to my students at Ebert Polaris. With a studious air he told my students that when something negative occurs, replace it immediately in your mind with something positive. "You lose the ball, immediately develop a plan for stealing it back."

Walter conceded that other players were quicker, faster, stronger, taller and more talented than he, but, he emphasized, "I had the tougher attitude."

"A man can be as great as he wants to be. If you believe in yourself and have the courage, the determination, the dedication, the competitive drive, and if you are willing to sacrifice the little things in life and pay the price for the things that all worthwhile, it can be done. Once a man has made a commitment, he puts the greatest strength in the world behind him. It's something we call heart power. Once a man has made this commitment, nothing will stop him short of success."

–HALL OF FAME COACH VINCE LOMBARDI

FAILURE AND MENTAL TOUGHNESS

"There is no great champion without great will."

–GUNDE SVAN, OLYMPIC GOLD MEDALIST,
NORDIC SKIING, SWEDEN

The mentally tough athlete deals with failure as a positive learning opportunity rather than as an indictment of inferiority or as an indicator of the inevitability of a failed outcome. Soichiro Honda, founder of Honda Motors, came from a family so poor that malnutrition took the lives of five of his siblings. He dropped out of eighth grade to fix bicycles.

Years later, upon receiving an honorary doctorate from University of Michigan, he said, "Many people dream of success. To me, success can be achieved only through repeated failure and introspection. In fact, success represents the 1 percent of your work that results from the 99 percent that is called failure."

Peter McLaughlin emphasized that failure can be our best teacher. The mentally tough optimist tries to manage failure in a positive way. We saw how Elway dealt with failure after the Jaguars game: it motivated him to succeed. Within weeks after the Jaguars game, Elway began to prepare for the next season. He understood that failing to prepare is preparing to fail.

Great people have written much about failure. Their messages can be easily condensed into a few pithy phrases. Her are some. "Our greatest weakness," Thomas Edison wrote, "lies in giving up. The most certain way to succeed lies in trying just one more time." "The thing that we call 'failure' isn't the falling down; it's the staying down," Mary Pickford said. Winston Churchill defined success as "moving from one failure to another without loss of enthusiasm."

At a writer's conference I attended, Bud Gardner, co-author of *Chicken Soup for the Writer's Soul*, told us to "fail your way to success."

> *"Trying is the first step toward failure."*
>
> –HOMER SIMPSON

The fear of failure is worse than failure itself. Ask your child about failing or losing and they'll likely say what my students always say: "You only fail when you don't try." Recall the discussion about Roosevelt's 'cold and timid souls that taste neither victory nor defeat.' Those timid souls are failures. They make no effort to compete, to learn or to improve.

OUR PERSONAL SUPER BOWLS

> *"Success requires persistence, the ability to not give up in the face of failure. I believe that optimistic explanatory style is the key to persistence."*
>
> –MARTIN SELIGMAN, *LEARNED OPTIMISM*

We all have our personal Super Bowls. We all have to apply the same skills used by highly trained athletes to address our personal challenges. Some people's challenges are, of course, more intense and demanding than others.

The challenge of my personal Super Bowl was comparatively mild, nothing compared to what David Dennison or Mark Schlereth overcame. A little over two years after I got out of the hospital, my dear friend, Nina, persuaded me to run the New York City Marathon with her.

I had never run a marathon. And I had a prosthetic heart valve. Being a cautious and responsible soul, I checked with my doctors. Doctor Kowal advised against it. Doctor Smith said I'd be fine. I took Doctor Smith's advice.

I trained with Nina. We'd run when I was tired. We'd run when I was buried with work. We'd run when I didn't want to run. We'd run early in the morning and late at night. We ran when it was snowing.

Nina is a wisp of a lady, about five foot four, weighing perhaps one hundred ten pounds. When running she seemed to barely touch the ground. She effortlessly trotted by my side until she got bored and then ran circles around me. I trundled along like a pachyderm auditioning for Fantasia. We ran the marathon on November 3, 1992. I couldn't have done it without her. I didn't have the will to train alone. I am indebted to her.

I started the marathon slowly, holding my powerful stride in reserve. Reserve never arrived. My left leg cramped at the eight mile mark. I'd never had a cramp. Bad luck. It tormented me the entire race. I did enjoy a moment of levity running through Williamsburg, Brooklyn, the neighborhood of Hasidic Jews. Many of the spectators handed bagels to the runners. I slowed and asked for one with garlic, preferably toasted. Then I asked, "You got any smoked salmon?"

The man in a heavy black coat sporting a thick beard chortled, "Are you kidding? It's $27.50 a pound! *Meshugenah!*" (crazy person).

Throughout the entire race images of my artificial valve ripping from the aortic heart tissue ran like a movie reel in my mind's eye. I saw myself suffering oxygen deficiency in the brain when the blood stopped flowing, falling to the ground in a coma and then, well, you know. Some optimism! I kept running.

At the twenty-mile mark I began to shake from emotion. I'd never run that far before. Moisture filled my eyes. A passing runner asked if I was okay. "Never felt better," I huffed. Everything hurt but I felt great.

I crossed the finish line at about four and a half hours—nothing to write home about, but I was pleased. Personal victories tend to occur well before the finish line and are rarely acknowledged on the winners' pedestals. Those victories, although rarely dramatic and often unknown, are not to be diminished.

It's inspirational to talk about the Elways and Jordans and Jeeters and Aarons and Federers of the sports worlds, but let's be honest. Carrying an inflated piece of leather over a chalk line or tossing it through a hoop is not particularly useful in the greater scheme of things. Sure, as Elway acknowledged, some folks can make scads of money doing those things. But regarding most of life's challenges, playing with inflated balls and pucks and bats are not helpful skills. They are not inherently moral actions.

Yet, sports are drenched in moral lessons. I teach my students to view sports metaphorically. Sports are about success, and success results from a commitment to excellence. Success is dependent upon developing skills to achieve excellence.

Sports are intimately related to the Greek concept of *arete*, that is, excellence for a specific purpose. *Arete* encompasses moral excellence, physical excellence and excellence for the purpose of a thing, such as a knife that is properly sharpened or the excellence of a well-crafted sculpture. Virtue is realized by pursuing *arete* and requires constant practice.

I love sports because its skills for success are translatable into living a successful life. My friend, Jenny, has been wheelchair bound since she was eight months old. She faces Super Bowl challenges a hundred times each day. She has her games within games and she wins daily—the struggle to get into her re-designed van, to go shopping, to prepare a meal, to get to work, to get dressed. Jenny *never* complains. "You gotta be optimistic," she tells me and I am humbled beyond my ability to convey.

The incredible souls giving their all in the Special Olympics, the Paralympics, the blind skiers and so many others whose physical bodies have been broken and battered by life's whims and calls to duty, face Elwayesque challenges every step and every stroke they take. For war veterans returning with body parts missing, just getting out of bed is likely more challenging than that demanded of any Super Bowl athlete. For some, just feeding their families is equivalent to a Super Bowl.

Life is unfair. It has predominantly a tragic sense. Winning our personal Super Bowls does not lead to lush endorsement contracts for shoes and underwear and drinks. No highlight films trumpet our mundane achievements. No fans throw room keys at us like confetti at a wedding. No one asks for Jenny's autograph because she is able to manipulate the steering wheel of her customized van. Rather than receiving a trophy, many folks simply survive one more day.

> *"I've been a puppet, a pauper, a pirate, a poet, a pawn and a king*
> *I've been up and down and over and out and I know one thing*
> *Each time I find myself layin' flat on my face*
> *I just pick myself up and get back in the race.*
> *That's life."*
>
> —"THAT'S LIFE" SUNG BY FRANK SINATRA

There is a saying among cross-country ski racers that the race is won on the up-hills. It's basically true, although U. S. Olympic Nordic skier Kris Freeman told me that the race is won everywhere. I won't quibble, but the point is that anyone can go fast downhill. That's a useful generalization for dealing with life. Dealing with the up-hills separates the winners from the others.

If our children are not taught to see the lessons of sports as a metaphor for life—mental toughness with an optimistic mindset, never give up, never surrender—they will be more inclined to submit to life's misfortunes and calamities.

"Never stop believing in yourself," I tell my students. Never permit anyone—not even you—to tell you that your goals and dreams are out of reach. Compete until the whistle blows. Then compete again.

I want mentally tough children, possessed of that 'can do' spirit and the confidence to overcome adversity. Not only will they be able to take care of themselves. They'll be able to take care of others. Then they will be winners and they may enjoy their well-earned accomplishments, and even their gifts.

CHAPTER 23

ALL ROADS LEAD TO HOME

"Helping children to develop the moral and intellectual faculties to make responsible choices is what raising kids is all about. Anybody can provide room and board. But developing a child's character is a parent's highest duty."

—AMITAI ETZIONI

IT WAS LATE AT NIGHT, probably close to mid-night, but I wasn't surprised Annie was still sitting at the desk in our small library and working on the computer. She was in middle school and she tended to start her homework late. I was on my way into my tiny home office, a few feet past the desk. I work late also. I leaned over to give her a kiss. Annie was tense and agitated.

"What's the matter?" A friend, she explained, a young man, her age, twelve years old or so, was threatening to commit suicide. He and Annie were typing emails or instant messages or something back and forth. I stopped, looked at the computer monitor and read the dialogue.

Annie had typed something like "Why would you want to die? You have so much to live for? You're scaring me!" In response the boy had written: "I have nothing to live for. I think I'll kill myself soon."

Annie's agitation increased. Her hands trembled. Tears formed.

At my request she scrolled back to earlier text. I reviewed most of the exchange. I was concerned, of course, but there was something about the boy's words that struck me as not believable. I sensed he was enjoying himself and playing with Annie as a cat does with a ball of yarn.

But, why take a chance. I gave it the old "what if I'm wrong" analysis advocated in this book. I dialed a suicide prevention hot line listed in the telephone book. A recording requested I call again during normal business hours or dial 911.

The exchange between Annie and her friend continued to unfold. The black letters materialized on the monitor with ominous foreboding. "Why are you doing this to me?" Annie typed. "Why are you doing this to yourself?"

His words "I have to" menacingly appeared.

Annie's agitation increased. It did not seem this interaction would lead to a favorable outcome. It was time for the adults to take over. "You're not a therapist," I told Annie. "I'll handle it now." The situation was beyond Annie's pay grade, so to speak.

I dictated messages for Annie to type. "Are you home now? I must talk to you. What is your phone number? Who else is in your house?"

His phone number flashed on the screen. He said his parents were in another room. Good. I called his home. His mother answered. I explained why I called. I offered to send her the full transcript of the exchanges. Neither she nor her husband cared to see it. She thanked me. We hung up.

From this point, the friend's situation would be handled by his parents as they saw fit. I unburdened Annie of all responsibility. She was relieved. The boy, by the way was fine. When they next met, he didn't display the slightest hint of a dire condition. He didn't make any gesture of appreciation for Annie's attention and concern. He didn't apologize for causing anguish to Annie.

As I am inclined to do, I thought about the different ways the event could have unfolded. Annie might have objected to my intervention. She might have said it was none of my business and criticized me for invading her privacy.

I've thought a lot about what is appropriate privacy for children in their homes. I've had dozens of class discussions on the topic. The dialogue about the dad and the chemicals implies judgments about a child's privacy. I find a disturbing relationship between the notion of a child's 'privacy' and undercutting the moral authority of parents.

I acknowledge the value of privacy and defer to it generally. Yet, if Annie had accused me of violating her privacy, I would have told her no such right exists in my home. My argument would be based on certain inconvenient truths: her mom and I paid for the computer, the electricity, the Internet fees, the house mortgage and, most significantly, we were responsible for raising her.

We would be accountable for our children's behavior. If my children want to splash around in that enticing pool of rights, they will have to earn those rights. They earn those rights by acting responsibly.

I've been a parent for twenty-five years and only twice did I search a child's room. I've never listened in on a phone call, but I have made it clear I would if I had what we lawyers call a reasonable suspicion that something improper was happening or being discussed. If the Harris and Klebold parents had been more aware of their children's possessions in various rooms in the homes, maybe the Columbine slaughter would have been avoided.

Several years ago a trial judge in some county in the northwest United States dismissed a serious criminal charge against a teenager. The teenager lived at home. As I recall the facts, the teen made or received a telephone call. A parent heard a snippet of the conversation and learned that the son and a friend were discussing a crime they recently committed or were planning to commit. The parent continued to listen to get more details. The parent reported the information to the police. Charges were filed.

The trial judge threw the case out by claiming the parent listening to the telephone conversation violated the child's right to privacy. The phone was in the parent's home, the parent paid for the phone service and the parent incidentally overheard a discussion involving a criminal act and continued to listen to get more information. The judge found no compelling legal significance in those facts.

None but the most biased dogmatic judge could rationally find such a 'privacy right' in the Constitution, state or federal.

Important issues extend beyond the resolution of that particular criminal case. The ruling subverts parental moral authority. The ruling's practical moral consequence is that it is better to have innocent people victimized in the future and/or to have past innocent people suffer injustice than to have a parent listen to its child's telephone call in the parent's home regarding the child's criminal activity.

Not only does this judge's ideology subvert a parent's ability to effect justice—for its child and for innocent victims—but it also destroys families. Such a 'right' turns parents into impotent bystanders unable to enforce their morally-based rules. Perversely, it imbues the child with power over the parents.

Imagine if the dad with the chemicals had been influenced by this judge's ruling. He might reasonably conclude, "Who needs the brain damage? I don't want to be accused of violating my child's rights so I won't get involved. The police and courts won't back me anyway."

People could have died. Ideas have consequences.

Ask your little angel what she thinks about a parent's authority or right to listen in on a child's telephone conversation. You'll probably get answers that will surprise you, just as my students' answers surprised me.

In my classes I contrasted this so-called privacy right with the parents' moral duty to know what their children were doing. "Parents are supposed to know what's going on," Andrew said, his little hands punching the air for emphasis. "How can parents teach us if they don't know anything?" Kacie, said in exasperation.

Third grader Molly, with a voice as pure as a tuning fork, made a forceful case for parental oversight. "Sure we do stuff we shouldn't do. That's why we have parents!"

Not a single child, in any class, ever, thought the parent was wrong for listening in on the conversation. Not a single child denied the parental duty to know what the child is doing. Of course, some boundaries were recommended. The students would not like their parents to constantly listen to or monitor their calls, particularly if they had no reason to believe that improper behavior was occurring.

But, as Julie noted, "that was a matter of trust between the child and the parent, not a matter of rights." Julie's brilliant distinction illustrates how smart your children are.

A variation of this theme was discussed in one class: a parent's authority to determine what kind of music its child should be permitted to hear at home. Alexa told about the time her father listened to one of her Eminem or hip-hop rap CDs. He took it to the back porch of their farm house, threw it in the air and blasted it with a shotgun.

Certainly this is not the preferred method for ridding the home of such products, particularly if one lives in a high rise in Manhattan. But it is worth noting not a single child faulted the father, not even those that liked the—ahem, music. Alexa said she respected her father for getting rid of something he thought was vile and immoral even though she disagreed with his opinion.

"It's his house," she said sparingly.

VACUUM CLEANING AND VACUUMS

Nature, it is said, abhors a vacuum. It will be filled by some substance if given the opportunity. Children abhor a parental vacuum. They will fill it with another force or influence or power.

Children want strong parents. They want parents that stand for virtue. They don't want or respect parental vacuums. Yes, they'll get angry and yell to the point that you will wish they were a new Star Wars character, Obe Quiet. They'll confront and challenge you with the subtlety of a Blues Brothers car crash scene.

It's tough to be a parent. What else is new?

Don't worry whether your children will love or respect you. Parenting is not a popularity contest. We are not craven politicians hustling for votes. Teach them and guide them to be strong, independent and virtuous and they will love and respect you.

Our children hunger for acts of integrity and courage. Parenting demands a gritty in-your-face leadership not for the meek or faint of heart. We must employ insights and policies based on the application of critical faculties, not ones based on emotion or from being intimidated. More than a show of who is in charge, children want to know that their parents deserve to be in charge.

"If you have never been hated by your child,
.   you have never been a parent."

–BETTE DAVIS

THE HOUSE THAT ROARED

"He that troubleth his own home shall inherit the wind."

–SOLOMON, THE BOOK OF PROVERBS

My wonderful neighbor, Paul, told me about the time his son's friend came to his home to spend the night. They were about eleven or twelve. Paul noticed the friend had some VHS tapes, all R rated. The son and the friend knew Paul prohibited such entertainment. Paul took the friend and his tapes back to the boy's home. Paul's son made no objection and the friend never brought such tapes to Paul's home again.

Paul's story brings to mind a topic I've discussed with several parents and in several classes: parents that say they are against certain behavior but allow the behavior in the home based on one or more rationalizations: "The children are going to do it anyway." or "At least they'll be safe here." Other rationalizations exist.

The subject is worth talking about because it raises issues beyond the specific topic and offers insights into the exercise of parental authority.

Let's examine one of the rationalizations in depth. An undesirable behavior—dirty movies, sex, drugs, alcohol, violent video games, whatever—disapproved in theory, will be permitted in the home because the children will do it anyway.

I analyze the issue by discussing three categories of criteria:

• Factual

• Moral

• Parental standards

Perhaps you can think of others.

The first and most obvious question is factual: Is the assumption true? Will a child do those things anyway if a parent expressly prohibits it? Talk to your children and I'll bet you will learn, pleasantly, that it ain't necessarily so.

Your children will likely say that permission and opportunity increase the undesired behavior because the parent has legitimized it and given it protection. Nicole opined, "Since they know they won't get in trouble with the parents they are more likely to do the bad things."

Recall the discussion about economics and incentives and costs in the Choices and Consequences chapters. When the cost of bad behavior is reduced, more bad behavior will result. Allowing children to do at home things disapproved of by the parents reduces the cost of the undesired behavior. Forcing them to find an alternative venue for such behavior increases the cost.

Admittedly, the increase in cost may not be much, but it exists. If some punishment is layered on for disobedience, the increased cost further reduces incentives for such behavior.

But aside from this incentive aspect, such attitudes and behaviors by parents represent the white flag of surrender flapping furiously in the winds of life. Mary's interpretation was in accord with the majority of students. "The parents are giving up."

Children such as Peter found such inconsistent parental beliefs to be morally deficient. "They know it's bad. There's no difference doing it at a friend's house or at your own house." Deficient moral judgment does not generate respect.

James interpreted the matter as an abandonment of parental power. "Why can't they prevent it?" The parent is admitting its authority is neutered. Worse, the neutering is self-inflicted.

This is the parent's message: "I tell you not to do something because it is wrong. I know you will disobey me so I give you permission to disobey me at home." Is disobedience transmuted into obedience? As James said, "It's confusing." Confusion is not a desirable quality for teaching morality to children. Confusion leads to inconsistent behavior and, sometimes, loss of respect.

The parent has voluntarily abandoned the possibility that the child will honor its request. The parent assumes his child will be immune to negative consequences and to parental disapproval. The parent has made meaningless its values and authority. Allowing oneself to be viewed by one's child as helpless and irrelevant is not an indicator of moral leadership.

Permitting undesired behavior because they'll do it anyway is not a morally-based decision. It's the result of factors other than determining right and wrong. It allows expedience to trump parental fortitude.

James saw the contradiction between action and principles. "They're letting you do it. They are not standing up for the parents' values."

Rachel added, "Or what they say are the parents' values. We really don't know what they believe."

Rachel's comment is particularly instructive. The parent is competing against the world for credibility and moral legitimacy. Credibility and moral legitimacy diminish when the parent's values are ambiguous and/or when the parent does not live up to its purported values.

Julie linked parental action to parental accountability. "If they let me do those things, they are not taking full responsibility. It makes no sense at all to have a kid if you let her or him do drugs."

The "they'll do it anyway" philosophy is parental caving in and appeasement, of course, but it also shows that the parent is not willing to take risks or pay a price for its values. If things don't go easily, the parent gives up. The parent shows it is afraid to lose. Only the naïve parent believes that radiating its fear of losing has no consequences.

A parent afraid to lose on one issue motivates a child to challenge it to see if it is afraid to lose on other issues. It's not just a difference in parental style. It's a different belief about integrity.

Parents must pick their battles. They may lose a skirmish here and there, but as we saw in the previous chapter, there are things worse than losing. Losing one battle may make you stronger for the next one. Far worse is not trying.

If the parent enforces behavior rules at the house, as my neighbor, Paul, did, the parent has taken a moral stand. The parent has transmitted its values to its child. If the child violates the rule, the child has failed, not the parent.

Delia Sanchez, an education counselor with Denver Kids, Inc., a program for at-risk students in the Denver Public Schools, shared an anecdote that illustrates unambiguously a child's recognition of the importance of strong parents. In a soft voice, a young student asked Delia, "Could you tell my parents to be stricter with me? I need that." Our children cry out for parents that enforce principled moral stands.

Rather than give our children ambiguous and rudderless guidance, parents should be vigilant in establishing moral standards. Children will respect this, no matter how much they yammer to the contrary. Recall the incident of the dad with the chemicals: all the students supported him. If we are Roosevelt's 'cold and timid souls' with our children, the consequences can be unpleasant.

WE ARE FAMILY

"Example is the school of mankind and they will learn at no other."

–EDMUND BURKE

In the movie *Love Story*, Ryan O'Neal muttered the signature line: "Love means never having to say you're sorry." Few phrases propel the hand to the airline sickness bag more quickly. If ever there exists a class of persons most deserving of apologies it is the people you love. In my world view, my family is at the top of that list. It may not be the case universally, but I think it is the ideal situation.

The family is where, I hope, we would be most comfortable sharing our shortcomings, our fears, our uncertainties and our doubts. The family is the institution where we should take our responsibilities most seriously and perform them most consistently. We can do these things—take risks that might exploit our vulnerabilities—because we are enveloped with love and trust. Thus, those in the family are the ones to whom we *must* say we're sorry.

There is a Jewish concept called Shlom Bayit. Literally, it means peace in the home. Peace, in this context, is not the absence of argument or disagreement. Peace does not mean quietude and ignoring others. Peace does not mean avoiding conflict. Shlom Bayit describes a peace derived from respect and strength and love.

As Rabbi Zwerin explained in one of his elegant sermons, it means respecting one another so much that you can discuss important issues, personal sensitive matters, knowing that no one will betray you or exploit a weakness. Shlom Bayit is the blessing of feeling truly 'at home' when you are at home, that you have a safe harbor; a sanctuary where each person can avoid the world's threats and deviousness.

Often I hear that children don't talk to their parents. Admittedly we live busy lives, but many times our children amble through our doors and self-medicate and self-insulate with iPods, video games, DVD's, YouTube, My Space, Facebook and other formats I haven't bothered to learn.

My attitude is that my home is *my space* and for my family it is *our space*. No space matters more. A home should be more than just a convenient hotel where parents act as concierges dispensing entitlements to hurried youths. Home is where issues get framed and boundaries get set and values are established. The family is not a collection of soloists but is like a small chamber music group. Each player enhances and gives depth and vibrancy to the other rather than pursuing its own cadences and tones.

The concept of Shlom Bayit encourages, in Kate's words, "an exchange of ideas so we can see things differently." With such humble steps we begin the process of bequeathing to our children a sense of human dignity. As captured elegantly in Juliet's immortal words, love is not a zero sum game:

> "My bounty is as boundless as the sea,
> My love as deep; the more I give to thee,
> The more I have, for both are infinite."

–JULIET, ROMEO AND JULIET, ACT 2, SCENE 2, WILLIAM SHAKESPEARE

Parents want to be more than ghosts merely haunting their own homes. Interaction should have more passion than an ATM transaction. We strive mightily to have the respect of people whose respect is worth having and to be justifiably respected. We don't want our children to fear, in the words of Mae West, that we should have kept the stork and let the child fly away.

NOBODY DOES IT BETTER

Good people make the world better. Families are the most efficient and most successful and most motivated institution for creating good people. It doesn't take a village to raise children. It takes parents. Villages can help, but I'm still waiting for my village to pay my children's dental bills and to review their homework.

More than any other person or institution or group, children expect parents to teach them about morality. Recall the children's statements: I learn right and wrong from my parents. I sit at the dinner table and my mom tells me what is right and good.   I hear a lot of talk and read a lot about 'culture.' Interaction with culture is more than eating natural yogurt. Some aspects of culture that relate to the family are worth discussing. Here's a story dealing with culture involving a local high school incident. I found it troubling.

Students were illegally smoking on school grounds. The principal chose not to enforce the law banning smoking. He didn't even inconvenience the students by demanding they leave the school grounds. He embraced the expedient "they're going to do it anyway" philosophy.

The principal justified his indifference by arguing that "the students won't stop smoking until the culture changes." Think about his logic and values for even a moment and their moral debasement becomes evident. He views people as passive organisms without free will, dependent upon the 'culture,' whatever that means, to direct their behavior.

Regrettably, this educator got it exactly backwards. Culture changes when individuals make it change. Individuals make culture as much as the other way around. It is also worth noting that the principal's philosophy provided cover for his cowardice and gelatinous morality.

A slave culture, a sexist culture, a homophobic culture, a pampered culture will change when strong moral individuals make them change. Only the passive and the weak and those benefiting from the defects of a culture will not do what is right. They will advocate waiting until the culture changes. It's always easiest to do nothing. A strong principal would have changed the school's culture rather than use it as an excuse to justify his apathy.

Do what's right and let the culture catch up.

Society cannot be moralized and improved unless and until the individual—at least, many of them—are moralized and improved. The first step toward eliminating society's ills is making one's self into a better person. For young children, no institution can do it better than the family.

As a practical matter, the family is the culture. More than any other institution, the family can change the larger culture. The family should be the first, and it will be the most effective, social organization to teach the "big picture" relationship between individual morality and the morality of the larger world. Even little children intuitively understand this linkage, as we saw in the chapter on being good, where the little folks said being good makes the world better.

> *"Teaching right from wrong has as much bearing on a*
> *culture's survival as teaching reading, writing, or science.*
> *Real education should educate us out of self into something far*
> *finer–selflessness which links us with all humanity."*
> –NANCY WITCHER ASTOR, (1879-1964),
> FIRST WOMAN ELECTED TO THE BRITISH HOUSE OF COMMONS

The core concepts of the big picture are freedom and liberty. Individual morality is the backbone of public morality and liberty, and individual morality is forged on the anvil of the family.

In his best-selling book, *Liberty and Tyranny*, Mark Levin wrote "A people cannot remain free and civilized without moral purposes, constraints and duties." Since individuals enforce moral purposes, constraints and duties, one implication of Levin's words is that a society that values liberty must have strong moral families.

To the depths of my soul I believe that the greatness of this country resides in its families. I believe that great families are the major force that can allow our country to endure and prosper.

UNLOCKING THE ANGEL IN THE MARBLE

One Hundred Years from now
It will not matter
what kind of car I drove,
What kind of house I lived in,
how much money was in my bank account
nor what my clothes looked like.
But the world may be a better place because
I was important in the life of a child.

–ONE HUNDRED YEARS FROM NOW
(EXCERPT FROM *"WITHIN MY POWER"* BY FOREST WITCRAFT)

In the last class of the 2008 year at Ebert Polaris Elementary School, Mrs. Abeyta asked what they had learned in my classes. Ari answered, "They made me a better person."

Delighted yet curious, I asked, "How did my classes do that?"

"You taught me to ask, 'How can I do good?' and you taught me how to do it."

Once again the eyes became moist. But, after a moment's thought I realized that all I had done was talk to his class for perhaps twenty-five hours during the entire school year.

Compared with a parent's interaction, mine was trivial. This realization unambiguously demonstrates why we parents must never underestimate our power and value. As Jeanne Kirkpatrick, former U S Ambassador to the United Nations, said in another context, "We have to admit the truth about ourselves, no matter how good it is."

I work hard to have conversations that effervesce like bubbles in fine champagne and that borrow patches of color from a rainbow, as someone more poetic than I wrote somewhere. I put my soul into these talks, knowing that if I don't, I am no longer a teacher or a parent but just a manual.

"The happiness of life is made up of minute fractions,
the little soon forgotten charities of a kiss or smile, a kind look,
a heartfelt compliment, and the countless infinitesimals of
pleasurable and genial feeling."
–SAMUEL TAYLOR COLERIDGE, 1772-1834

Some parents, perhaps many, think their verbal abilities lie somewhere between the Rain Man and a silent movie. Don't worry. Your child does not want eloquence. Your child doesn't want slick presentations. Your child wants *you*. Your children are bursting with potential waiting to be decanted by *you*.

Rebecca Hagelin wrote, "How does a child spell 'love'? Answer: T-I-M-E!" Peter McLaughlin referred to talking with one's children this way: "What's the downside? Even if it's not perfect, at least you're spending time with your kids."

Elise was already in high when I asked her a question that had been on my mind—not plaguing me—but on my mind: "What will be one of the things you will remember about me after I'm gone?"

Without hesitation she said, "You talked to us. You tried to help us grow up better." I hope my chapters help parents with the first part so they can accomplish the second.

WHERE THE BATTLE WILL BE WON

The initial skirmishes in the unending battle for a just and moral world will be won or lost in the home—at the dinner tables, riding in the car, when helping wash the dishes, helping with homework and during all those unplanned moments when we converse with our children. Yet we must be ever mindful that if we want moral children, we must fight for it, just as those who want freedom have to fight for it. Nothing is free and no situation is static. Things change.

Much of this book is about conversations. But words and dialogue are not ends in themselves, of course. One is not converted by arguments alone and those that trade in words predominantly are frauds. But words and dialogues matter. They are vehicles to action and action is needed unceasingly.

Andrew McCarthy, lead prosecutor in the first World Trade Center bombing trial, wrote, "Civilization is not an evolution of mankind but the imposition of human good on human evil. It is not an historical inevitability. It is a battle that has to be fought every day, because evil doesn't recede willingly before the wheels of progress."

Parents have tough battles. The morally degrading currents running deep in our pop culture, our entertainment industry, our justice system, our education system and the pervasive immorality and corruption of our political class pose epic challenges to even the most informed, dedicated and astute parents.

Yet we must battle on. We must resist the all-too-human tendency to yield to cynicism and resignation and worst of all, to yield to accommodation. If we fight valiantly and consistently for virtuous ethical standards in our homes, I believe parents will win more battles than they will lose. They certainly will win more battles than they expected.

Children expect action from their parents. They want our protection. Thus, parents must be leaders. Leaders shape the times through events. Parents can shape events through dialogues. We can unlock our angels from the rough marble. Our little ones haven't yet accomplished great things but they offer infinite promise.

Ethics can be taught only imperfectly in a classroom and by argument. Ethics can be taught best by nurturing, example and incentives. Parents can be the most effective source of an unwavering standard of dignified behavior. Parents know their influence is transient and their magnetic field quickly disperses. But we also know that our words will resonate in the souls and minds of our children throughout the decades long after we have left the stage.

Writing this book has been a journey of continuously examining how to capture in words the principles for teaching young children—and me—to live a just and honorable life.

I have shared the rewarding joy of hearing a child exclaim, "Oh, I get it now!" "This is how I can be better." "This is how I can be proud of myself." You can hear those words also. If I can do it, so can you. It's just a matter of practice. The process begins with a topic and a few words.

I hope that the principles and examples in this modest book, born in a hospital room after a medical triumph, will serve as the hammers and chisels to sculpt your little angels. May all your conversations overflow with laughter, joy and love.